VOLUME ONE HUNDRED AND FOUR

Advances in

COMPUTERS

Creativity in Computing and DataFlow SuperComputing

VOLUME ONE HUNDRED AND FOUR

ADVANCES IN
COMPUTERS
Creativity in Computing and DataFlow
SuperComputing

Edited by

ALI R. HURSON
*Missouri University of Science and Technology,
Rolla, MO, United States*

VELJKO MILUTINOVIĆ
*University of Belgrade,
Belgrade, Serbia*

ACADEMIC PRESS

An imprint of Elsevier
elsevier.com

Academic Press is an imprint of Elsevier
50 Hampshire Street, 5th Floor, Cambridge, MA 02139, United States
525 B Street, Suite 1800, San Diego, CA 92101-4495, United States
The Boulevard, Langford Lane, Kidlington, Oxford OX5 1GB, United Kingdom
125 London Wall, London, EC2Y 5AS, United Kingdom

First edition 2017

ISBN: 978-0-12-811955-6
ISSN: 0065-2458

For information on all Academic Press publications
visit our website at https://www.elsevier.com/

**Working together
to grow libraries in
developing countries**

www.elsevier.com • www.bookaid.org

Publisher: Zoe Kruze
Acquisition Editor: Zoe Kruze
Editorial Project Manager: Shellie Bryant
Production Project Manager: Surya Narayanan Jayachandran
Cover Designer: Greg Harris

Typeset by SPi Global, India

CONTENTS

Preface   *vii*

1. **A Systematic Approach to Generation of New Ideas for PhD
   Research in Computing**   **1**
   V. Blagojević, D. Bojić, M. Bojović, M. Cvetanović, J. Đorđević, Đ. Đurđević,
   B. Furlan, S. Gajin, Z. Jovanović, D. Milićev, V. Milutinović, B. Nikolić, J. Protić,
   M. Punt, Z. Radivojević, Ž. Stanisavljević, S. Stojanović, I. Tartalja,
   M. Tomašević, and P. Vuletić

   1. Introduction   2
   2. Classification of Innovation Methods   4
   3. Representative Examples From the Authors' PhD Theses   11
   4. Conclusions   20
   Acknowledgments   21
   References   21
   About the Authors   25

2. **Exploring Future Many-Core Architectures:
   The TERAFLUX Evaluation Framework**   **33**
   R. Giorgi

   1. Introduction   35
   2. Terminology and Related Work   37
   3. COTSon Framework Organization   45
   4. Targeting a 1000-Core Simulation   46
   5. How to Simulate 1000 Cores   49
   6. The Search for "Efficient Benchmarks"   60
   7. Simulation Experiments   61
   8. Conclusions   66
   Acknowledgments   66
   References   66
   About the Author   72

3. **Dataflow-Based Parallelization of Control-Flow Algorithms**   **73**
   N. Korolija, J. Popović, M. Cvetanović, and M. Bojović

   1. Introduction   74
   2. Problem Statement   78

3. Dataflow Approaches and the Feynman Paradigm   80
4. Existing Solutions and Their Criticism   88
5. Exploring Dataflow Potentials   103
6. Performance Evaluation   113
7. Conclusions   118
Acknowledgments   119
Appendix   119
References   120
About the Authors   123

4. Data Flow Computing in Geoscience Applications   125

L. Gan, H. Fu, O. Mencer, W. Luk, and G. Yang

1. Introduction   126
2. Data Flow Computing in HPC   128
3. Geoscience Applications in HPC   131
4. Case Study 1: Global Shallow Water Equations   133
5. Case Study 2: Euler Atmospheric Equations   140
6. Case Study 3: Reverse Time Migration   147
7. Summary and Concluding Remarks   153
Acknowledgments   153
Appendix   154
References   155
About the Authors   156

5. A Streaming Dataflow Implementation of Parallel Cocke–Younger–Kasami Parser   159

D. Bojić and M. Bojović

1. Introduction   160
2. Problem Statement   161
3. Existing Solutions and Their Criticism   170
4. A Dataflow Implementation of a CYK Parser   180
5. Performance Analysis   184
6. Conclusion   190
Acknowledgment   191
Appendix   191
References   197
About the Authors   199

Author Index   201
Subject Index   209
Contents of Volumes in this Series   215

PREFACE

Traditionally, *Advances in Computers*, the oldest series to chronicle the rapid evolution of computing, annually publishes several volumes, each typically comprised of four to eight chapters, describing new developments in the theory and applications of computing. The 104th volume entitled "Creativity in Computing and DataFlow SuperComputing" is a thematic volume inspired by the advances in computer architecture in general and more specifically on dataflow processing. In addition, this volume includes a chapter summarizing the collective experiences of the faculty of the Department of Computer Engineering and Informatics, University of Belgrade in developing PhD research. This volume is a collection of five chapters that were solicited from authorities in the field, each of whom brings to bear a unique perspective on the topic.

In Chapter 1, "A Systematic Approach to Generation of New Ideas for PhD Research in Computing," Blagojević *et al.* articulate a 10-step process in formulating a potentially successful PhD research topic. The aforementioned 10 steps are Mendeleyevization, Generalization, Specialization, Revitalization, Crossdisciplinarization, Implantation, Adaptation, Hybridization, Transgranularization, and Extraparameterization. Authors attempted to justify each step by at least one historical example. Finally, this chapter presents several recent PhD theses that have been inspired through these steps.

In Chapter 2, "Exploring Future Many-Core Architectures: The TERAFLUX Evaluation Framework," Giorgi introduces TERAFLUX aiming at a high-performance computing using 3-D stacked chip consisting of 10^{12} transistors on a single chip by 2020. Such an enormous density could result in massive number of general-purpose cores on a single chip. TERAFLUX handles execution of threads based on dataflow execution model. This chapter enumerates different options for simulating a 1000 general-purpose-core system and addresses the setup that successfully allows to evaluate 1000 core target while running a full-system Linux operating system.

Chapter 3, "Dataflow Based Parallelization of Control-Flow Algorithms," by Korolija *et al.* argues that advantages of dataflow processing such as inherited parallelism, lower power consumption, and run-time adaptability relative to its control-flow counterpart are not enough to switch the computational paradigm. Transformation of the application programs written within the framework of the control-flow computational paradigm to dataflow paradigm is the main obstacle to overcome. Consequently, this chapter is intended to articulate transformation of control-flow application programs to dataflow computation model. It overviews methods from systolic arrays, dataflow analysis, and compilers that could be used for such a transformation. Available tools for compiling source codes to dataflow hardware are addressed, and results of an implemented application in the dataflow and control-flow computational models are compared and contrasted.

In Chapter 4, "Data Flow Computing in Geoscience Applications," Gan *et al.* emphasize the needs for higher performance and finer resolutions in geoscience research. With such a need in mind, they are using a data flow computing engines based on reconfigurability of FPGAs for geoscience applications. This chapter summarizes their initial efforts and experiences of using Maxeler dataflow Engines targeting at eliminating the main bottlenecks and in three computing kernels from two popular geoscience application domains, i.e., climate modeling and exploration of geophysics. A set of customization and optimization techniques based on the reconfigurable hardware platforms are addressed showing their superiority in performance and power consumption over traditional multi-core and many-core architectures.

Finally, in Chapter 5, "A Streaming Dataflow Implementation of Parallel Cocke–Younger–Kasami Parser," Bojić and Bojović emphasize on efficient parsing techniques in application such as natural language processing, bioinformatics, and pattern recognition. The Cocke–Younger–Kasami (CYK) algorithm as a well-known parsing algorithm operating on context-free grammars in Chomsky normal form is used for execution on parallel machines. A novel and efficient streaming dataflow implementation of the CYK algorithm on Maxeler dataflow engine is addressed. This study shows an $18 \times$ to $76 \times$ speedup over optimized sequential implementation of real-life grammars for natural language processing.

We hope that you find these chapters of interest, and useful in your teaching, research, and other professional activities. We welcome feedback on this volume, and suggestions for topics for future volumes.

ALI R. HURSON
Missouri University of Science and Technology,
Rolla, MO, United States
and
VELJKO MILUTINOVIĆ
University of Belgrade,
Belgrade, Serbia

CHAPTER ONE

A Systematic Approach to Generation of New Ideas for PhD Research in Computing

V. Blagojević[✠], D. Bojić, M. Bojović, M. Cvetanović, J. Đorđević,
Đ. Đurđević, B. Furlan, S. Gajin, Z. Jovanović, D. Milićev, V. Milutinović,
B. Nikolić, J. Protić, M. Punt, Z. Radivojević, Ž. Stanisavljević,
S. Stojanović, I. Tartalja, M. Tomašević, P. Vuletić
School of Electrical Engineering, University of Belgrade, Belgrade, Serbia

Contents

1. Introduction   2
2. Classification of Innovation Methods   4
    2.1 Mendeleyevization (M)   5
    2.2 Generalization (G)   6
    2.3 Specialization (S)   7
    2.4 Revitalization (R)   7
    2.5 Crossdisciplinarization (C)   8
    2.6 Implantation (I)   8
    2.7 Adaptation (A)   9
    2.8 Hybridization (H)   9
    2.9 Transgranularization (T)   10
    2.10 Extraparameterization (E)   10
3. Representative Examples From the Authors' PhD Theses   11
4. Conclusions   20
Acknowledgments   21
References   21
About the Authors   25

Abstract

This article represents an effort to help PhD students in computer science and engineering to generate good original ideas for their PhD research. Our effort is motivated by the fact that most PhD programs nowadays include several courses, as well as the research component, that should result in journal publications and the PhD thesis, all in a timeframe of 3–6 years. In order to help PhD students in computing disciplines to get

---

[✠] Deceased 22 January 2015.

Advances in Computers, Volume 104
ISSN 0065-2458
http://dx.doi.org/10.1016/bs.adcom.2016.09.001

focused on generating ideas and finding appropriate subject for their PhD research, we have analyzed some state-of-the-art inventions in the area of computing, as well as the PhD thesis research of faculty members of our department, and came up with a proposal of 10 methods that could be implemented to derive new ideas, based on the existing body of knowledge in the research field. This systematic approach provides guidance for PhD students, in order to improve their efficiency and reduce the dropout rate, especially in the area of computing.

1. INTRODUCTION

During the past decade, in many European countries, the process of restructuring higher education system according to the Bologna process brought transition to three-level (bachelor, master, PhD) degrees. This restructuring imposes serious changes in the practice of doctoral studies: instead of awarding the PhD degree based exclusively on academic research, with practically unlimited duration, the new doctoral programs additionally require successful completion of a regimen of coursework. The workload of PhD students is evaluated by at least 180 *European Credit Transfer and Accumulation System* credits beyond the master's level, and should be finished in 3–6 years, according to higher education regulations.

In the previous higher education system, nominal duration of the first-level engineering studies was 5 years, which is equivalent to the current total duration of bachelor-plus master-level studies. Our calculation of time period between finishing first-level studies and achieving doctoral degree, for faculty members of our department in the area of computing, shows that the average duration of this period was 10.75 years, including six master courses, master thesis, and the PhD thesis (the average period for PhD, after obtaining the master degree, was 5.79 years). This calculation applies to 18 faculty members, who graduated according to the previous higher education rules, based on the research-only PhD (without the coursework). The goal to get to the same point in 3–6 years for present doctoral students, with the requirement to take nine courses, publish at least an article in a journal from the Thomson Reuters Journal Citation Reports (JCR) list, and write the PhD thesis, has proved to be extremely demanding. At our school, the first generation of PhD students were enrolled in the new PhD program in computing in 2007, and since then, 60 new students were enrolled each year. However, only about 50 candidates have graduated so far, including only two members of our department. Although the program nominally lasts 3 years only, most of the candidates finish it in 6 years, since they are employed in the industry on the regular basis. In addition to economic and logistic reasons, one of the main obstacles in achieving this goal in a pre-determined timeframe may be found in the high latency of inventing sufficiently profound research topics and generating results of scientific value. Therefore, most of PhD students express their eager desire to be guided by an appropriate methodology, which makes the motivation for this work.

The area of computing worldwide has some specific characteristics, which may result in longer actual duration of PhD studies. The opportunities to get employed with master degree are currently better in computing than in similar technical disciplines. On the other hand, the nature of PhD research, which is based not only on theoretical mathematical models or measurements but also on system implementation and programming, often takes more time and efforts to be done. Finally, publication habits are different in computing compared to other scientific and technical disciplines, while the formal requirements for PhD regarding published articles are typically the same. For example, analysis presented in Ref. [1] shows that for each citation that an article receives in the area of computing, an article in general engineering receives 4.64 citations, an article in physics receives 11.9 citations, while an article in molecular biology receives 32.89 citations, according to the analysis applied to all papers indexed by the ISI Thomson Reuters, 1996–2006. These results show the focus of publishing in archive journals in other disciplines, while the focus in computing, caused by rapid changes, is on conferences, project reports, and other less formal publishing forms on the Internet. For this reason, Google Scholar as a less formal source than Web of Science (WoS) shows significantly higher indicators' scores than WoS for computer scientists, roughly five times for article-based indicators and eight times for citation-based indicators [2]. Having in mind our goal to bring more efficiency in generating ideas for PhD, publishing the research results, and thus reducing the number of PhD students who drop out in this process, we have started this work as a follow-up of four previous articles on different aspects of research conducting methodology [3–5] and research presentation methodology [6,7].

There are numerous studies related to systematic creativity methods in engineering design. Ogot and Okudan explored three dominant learning styles in the engineering education literature [8]. Yoram *et al.* conducted analysis of Advanced Systematic Inventive Thinking (ASIT) using the C–K theory, a design theory that offers a formal model of creative thinking [9]. Horowitz was dealing with a set of sufficient conditions that characterize creative engineering solutions and their empirical and psychological validation [10]. Several learning and teaching styles in engineering education were explored in Ref. [11]. Similarly, many studies tackle methodologies for research innovation in science and engineering [12–14], as well as the process of authoring a PhD thesis [15,16]. Finally, understanding and explanation of creativity from different perspectives is an important issue [17,18].

This article builds on the top of these representative studies, especially Ref. [5], and tries to systemize existing methods of innovation into a set of 10 different methodological approaches to innovation in computer science and engineering. Our aim is to identify and classify various methods of innovation that led to well-known research contributions in computer science and engineering in the past, in order to provide PhD students with some potentially useful methodological guidelines and encouragement for their research. As a case study, we will show how the PhD thesis research of the members of our department (and authors of the article) fits into the proposed classification.

2. CLASSIFICATION OF INNOVATION METHODS

Generally speaking, scientific innovations may be classified into two basic categories: (1) Revolutionary, for paradigm-shifting breakthroughs, and (2) Evolutionary, for nonparadigm-shifting improvements of existing solutions.

In the category of Revolutionary innovations, all ideas, in their essence, have only one basic characteristic: Creation of a genius inspired by an undeterminable cause and realized through a thinking process that is extremely difficult to define and classify. In the category of Evolutionary innovations, however, ideas may belong to various patterns, and this article observes 10 different classes of ideas (methods for generating ideas), leading to important evolutionary innovations in the past.

In a research process that should lead to a PhD thesis research, the following phases may be observed: (1) precise problem specification, (2) studying of related work and existing approaches, (3) generating an idea for a new solution, (4) formulating an essence of the approach, (5) qualitative analysis, order of complexity estimation, and comparison with the state-of-the-art approaches, (6) analysis of valid assumptions and conditions for the solution, (7) formulating details of the solution, (8) quantitative analysis in spatial and temporal domain and comparison with state-of-the-art solutions, (9) implementation analysis, and (10) determining drawbacks of the solution and proposal for future research avenues. Definitely, this scenario is typical for a PhD thesis research which is based on a hardware or software engineering innovation, which overcomes existing solutions in quality and/or performance.

For theses based on comprehensive surveys and comparison of existing solutions or theses that focus on theoretical contributions, this scenario would not be appropriate. Generally, we have no intention here to give a prescription for complete PhD thesis research development process. We just want to point to the step in the typical process for the targeted thesis research type, where our methodology may help both the candidate and the supervisor. Obviously, the point in this process where our classes of methods for generating ideas for innovations could serve as a road sign for PhD candidate is phase 3.

The 10 classes presented in this article should be considered only as idea generation guidelines, not as orthogonal classes such that each and every idea belongs to only one of them. In other words, an idea may belong to a number of classes, i.e., it may be characterized with properties of several classes presented here. Also, we do not consider that our classification is closed, meaning that it does not cover all possible ways of generating new ideas for PhD research. Referring to the UML 2 terminology [19], specifically to the *generalization set* notation, our classification may be described as *Overlapping* and *Incomplete*. Each class name in the classification has a unique initial, so single-letter class description is unambiguous.

The rest of this section respects the following template for each particular idea generation class: (a) description of the idea generation method, (b) a figure that illustrates the method, and (c) one or more examples that illustrate the method. All used examples consider well-known innovations, because our criterion to include an example was that it (i.e., the innovation based on the related idea generation class) or its crucial elements are taught in the curriculum of computer engineering, software engineering, information systems, information technologies, and computer science and well described both in formal literature and informal sources such as the Wikipedia website.[a]

2.1 Mendeleyevization (*M*)

Description. If one of the categories in an existing taxonomy of a problem domain includes no examples, it first has to be checked why is that so. If it is so because it makes no sense, an appropriate explanation is in place. If it is so because the technology or the applications are not yet ready for such an approach, one could act in the same way as the famous chemists Mendeleyev: Empty positions in any classification are potential avenues leading to new

---

[a] http://www.wikipedia.org/.

inventions. We refer to such an approach as Mendeleyevization (M). Precisely, any real innovation inherently fits to an empty place in some classification. However, a researcher is sometimes unaware of the classification, or the classification does not exist at the moment when the new approach is being invented. We consider Mendeleyevization as a method of generating a research idea only in the case when a researcher is explicitly aware of the classification and the empty places in the classification, which influences an idea for the innovation. This class represents a top-down approach of idea generation (Fig. 1).

Examples. The famous taxonomy of computer systems by Mike Flynn (SISD, SIMD, MISD, MIMD) [20] initially included no examples of the MISD (Many Instructions Single Data) type. Systolic arrays [21], which may be classified as MISD computers, as well as the space shuttle flight computer, which works on this principle to achieve fault tolerance [22], appeared years later. We could assume that Flynn's taxonomy influenced the inventions.

2.2 Generalization (G)

Description. Frequently, there are many versatile concrete solutions to a problem, but there is no common model that could encompass all of the existing solutions. Somebody may catch the important common properties of the existing solutions and could make an abstraction that presents a common model or a language (notation and semantics) for describing each particular solution. Such an abstraction may help in producing a number of new solutions of the problem. We refer to such an approach as Generalization (G). Contrary to Mendeleyevization, this class represents a bottom-up approach to idea generation, based on inductive reasoning (Fig. 2).

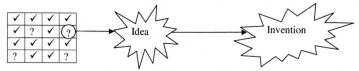

Fig. 1 The existing classification is represented with the table where some cells contain existing solutions (✓), while the others are empty (?); empty-cell analysis may lead to an idea for innovation.

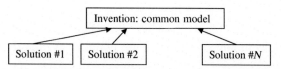

Fig. 2 Generalization of particular concrete solutions to a common model.

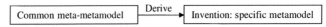

Fig. 3 Deriving specific metamodel from common meta-metamodel.

Examples. The Harel's statecharts [23] that represent an abstraction of finite-state automata, and Petri nets [24] that represent an abstraction of concurrent flows. Also UML [19] that combines specific properties of a number of previously invented modeling languages.

2.3 Specialization (*S*)

Description. Starting from a well-established general approach, someone could derive a specific knowledge/technology for a specific domain. We refer to such approach as Specialization (*S*). Similarly to Mendeleyevization, and contrary to Generalization, this class represents a top-down approach to idea generation, based on deductive way of thinking (Fig. 3).

Examples. Starting from a common meta–metamodel, someone could derive a specific metamodel (e.g., language) for specific domain. Examples are development of the domain-specific metamodel BPMN (Business Process Model and Notation) [25] based on the common meta–metamodel MOF (Meta-Object Facility) [26]. Another example of specialization is partial evaluation, which is used as a technique for different types of program optimization [27]. The main goal of optimization is to produce new programs which run faster than the originals while being guaranteed to behave in the same way.

2.4 Revitalization (*R*)

Description. Sometimes, there is some theoretical invention that is practically dead, since the technology is not ready to support it, and the invention becomes forgotten. In the meantime, the technology upgrades, but nobody is aware that the existing theoretical invention may revive, until a new idea is born to apply the new technology on the old invention. We refer to such approach as Revitalization (*R*) (Fig. 4).

Example. Computational model of artificial neural networks had been invented in early 1940s [28], but it was revitalized and research in the field exploded in early 1980s [29], when the technology of parallel processing matured.

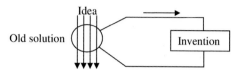

Fig. 4 A dead theoretical invention (resistor) becomes alive when a new idea (variable magnetic field) uses a new technology (inductor).

Fig. 5 An existing solution to a problem in the field A inspires the idea on invention in the field B. Modification is possible but not necessary.

2.5 Crossdisciplinarization (C)

Description. Many times, good new ideas appear if some solutions (models, algorithms, mechanisms—not only in computer science) are ported from one field to another field, along the lines of crossdisciplinary research methodologies and applied analogies (Crossdisciplinarization). The degree of the solution modification during crossdisciplinarization may vary. On the first end of the scale, the solution may be ported directly, and only the interpretation of related variables is different. On the other end of the scale, just an analogy is used to generate a new idea from some existing solution in a different field, so the new solution has almost nothing to do with the initial solution (Fig. 5).

Examples. Popular examples include introduction of mathematical neural networks inspired by biological neural networks [29], or introduction of genetic algorithms based on the principles of evolution of live organisms [30].

2.6 Implantation (I)

Description. A new solution is invented by implanting a resource into an existing solution. The characteristics of the new solution overcome the mere sum of the characteristics of the old solution and implanted resources; it brings a new quality or a significant performance gain (Fig. 6).

Example. Translation lookaside buffer (TLB) [31,32] is a specific cache memory that represents an implant in the virtual memory mechanism. Virtual memory may work without TLB, but TLB considerably improves the mechanism.

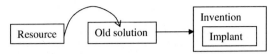

Fig. 6 A resource implanted into an existing solution creates a new solution.

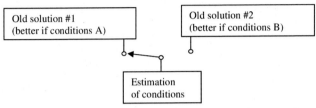

Fig. 7 Selecting among existing solutions to adapt a new solution to the conditions.

2.7 Adaptation (*A*)

Description. The assumption here is that one solution is better under one set of conditions, and the other solution is better under another set of conditions. The idea is a dynamic combination of different solutions, thus adapting a new solution to work the best way in different conditions. Consequently, the complexity of a new solution method is always higher than the complexity of each existing solution used to generate the solution (Fig. 7).

Example. Adaptive switching mechanism in computer networking [33] changes port-running mode from cut-through switching mode, which is normal switching mode that achieves better performance in the case of moderate error rate, via fragment-free mode, to store-and-forward mode when error rate becomes too high.

2.8 Hybridization (*H*)

Description. Sometimes elements of two or more existing solutions, or two or more complete solutions, could be combined, in order to obtain a hybrid solution. Although the Adaptation method already presents a kind of dynamically combining existing solutions, we will use the term hybridization only for referring to the method of static combination of resources from existing solutions in the new solution. The aim is to select elements from a set of existing solutions in a way to outperform each one of the existing solutions (Fig. 8).

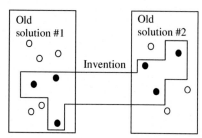

Fig. 8 A new hybrid solution combines parts of the existing solutions.

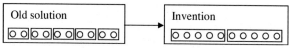

Fig. 9 Elements of an old solution are fine grained, and invention is achieved by changing granulation of the solution elements.

Example. Combination of the back-face culling algorithm with the z-buffer algorithm [34] improves performance of the hidden surface detection and removal algorithm, since back-face culling is much more efficient than z-buffer, but not as general as z-buffer.

2.9 Transgranularization (*T*)

Description. Sometimes a similar algorithm or mechanism may be applied with a different level of granularity, solving a problem never solved before. The direction of transformation may be to a coarser or to a finer granularity from the existing solution. Such an approach we will call Trans-granularization (Fig. 9).

Examples. One example is applying the well-known virtual memory [35] principles to the lower level of memory hierarchy—processor cache [36]. Similar principles may be applied to a web browser, proxy, or server caches. The essence of innovation is in changed granularity of data that the mechanism manipulates with: a data block is a cache-line of a few words in processor caches, a page in a virtual memory system, or data file (and possible folder) in webcaching.

2.10 Extraparameterization (*E*)

Description. An existing solution is based on a simpler model that depends on a relatively small set of parameters. By adding new parameters to the model,

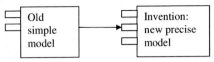

Fig. 10 Adding an extra parameter transforms an existing simple model to a more complex, but more precise or more efficient, one.

it becomes more complex and leads to a new, more precise, efficient, and sophisticated solution to the problem. Of course, it is possible to start from a more complex model and to downgrade it to a simpler model by ignoring some of the negligible (under some conditions) parameters, but introducing extra parameters to the model is a more frequent requirement for new model inventions (Fig. 10).

Examples. Introduction of extra parameters could lead to a refined model. Contrary to intuitive expectations, new parameters and variables could make it easier for programming implementation, which enables experiments with a broader range of basic parameters. The experiments could result in an optimal solution for reconfiguration of the system. An example could be found in the performance analysis of multiprogrammed systems represented by closed queuing networks, based on state probabilities. The computation of state probabilities has been made easier by introduction of the Buzen's algorithm [37], based on the Gordon–Newell theorem [38]. This algorithm introduces a new parameter called the normalization constant $G(K)$ and implements its computation in a simple nested-loops programming structure. Once G is computed, the probability distributions for the network could be found. On the other hand, introduction of new parameters on the conceptual level could result in new solutions in all areas of computer science. For example, introduction of compression techniques that do not decompress data back to 100% of the original, known as lossy methods, provides high degrees of compression suitable for images that have to be transferred over the Internet. JPEG file format is one of such solutions, which parameterizes image quality, contrary to its optional lossless mode.

3. REPRESENTATIVE EXAMPLES FROM THE AUTHORS' PhD THESES

This section presents the essence of past innovations of the authors of this article and classifies them into the 10 idea generation methods introduced in this article.

The PhD thesis research of Vladimir Blagojević entitled "Analysis of anharmonicity of ZnSFe monocrystal reflectivity spectra" was an interdisciplinary one, covering both material science and software science. The field of research is either "Computational materials science" or "Computational physics." The essence of the material science part of the thesis research is in developing a new physical model for monocrystal reflectivity spectra fitting in two variants—classical (additive) and semiquantum (factorized), as well as introducing a generalized hybrid physical model. Within the software science part of the thesis research, a general high performance and extensible software system was formally specified, designed, and implemented. Finally, the software system developed was successfully applied for analyzing the monocrystal reflectivity spectra of ZnSFe that could not be treated by using previously existing physical models, and the results were published in Ref. [39]. This thesis research introduces an innovation predominantly along the lines of two methods: M and G.

The PhD thesis research of Dragan Bojić was in the domain of reverse engineering behavioral elements of the UML software model, and introduced an innovation predominantly along the lines of the method T. Previous approaches to feature interaction problem in mapping features to code considered either a single feature or a pair of them. By using a novel representation, the concept lattice, a full set of features is considered at once. Results were published in Refs. [40,41].

The PhD research of Miroslav Bojović covered the field of synchronization and communication mechanisms in fault tolerant multiprocessor systems, and introduced an approach which minimizes the latency and the number of messages used in order to accomplish secure and consistent data exchange, along the method M. All approaches existing in the open literature till that moment utilized some form of strict consistency maintenance, so the classification developed by the author included no examples based on loose consistency. In order to be able to generate a novel solution which is based on loose consistency, the author introduced three different mechanisms that acted as implants according to method I: the event mechanism, the resource usage synchronization mechanism, and the mutual exclusion mechanism. As indicated in Ref. [42], the approach introduced by this PhD thesis research enabled that the worst case latency be $N+1$ (rather than $(N(N+1)/2) - 1$, which was the best of the open literature till the moment when the thesis was published) and that the worst case message count be $N-1$ (rather than $2(N-1)$).

The PhD research of Miloš Cvetanović explored the automated comparison of relational database models and led to the development of an educational system that helps students to bridge the gap between database management system theory and practice. The system permits active tutoring of students by providing interactive feedback by comparing the answer given by a student with the correct solution. This research introduced an innovation predominantly along the lines of the method M in the case of conceptual database models, and the method C in the case of logical database models. Results were published in Ref. [43].

In name-space architectures, which are the subject of the PhD thesis research by Jovan Đorđević, the mapping of names onto fast registers is a hardware, rather than a software, function. The MU5 computer is an example of such an architecture, having a single-address instruction format. Two-store-address and three-store-address architectures developed from MU5 concepts are proposed, using the method S. ISPS descriptions of all three architectures have been written, verified, and used in a series of experiments [44], conducted at Carnegie-Mellon University, Pittsburgh, from Manchester University, England, using the ARPA Network. Results for a number of benchmark programs run on the ISPS simulation model of MU5 are first related to actual results obtained by hardware monitoring of the MU5 processor, and some comment is included on the validity of this type of architectural evaluation. Results of measurements of static and dynamic code usage for the same benchmark programs run on the ISPS simulation models of these systems are then presented, and comparisons between the three architectures are made on the basis of these results.

The PhD research of Đorđe Đurđević was in the domain of parallel compression of regular height fields (matrices of elevations of 3D points), along the method M, with elements of method R. Previous methods were mostly sequential, parallel only on coarse granularity (batches of points). On the other hand, the proposed method is per-point parallel, suitable for implementation on modern highly parallel GPUs (Graphics Processing Unit), which became widely available in the recent years. The essential innovation is that the previous methods predominantly compress data by predicting the elevation of a point from elevations of previously compressed points, while the proposed method approximates elevations of a set of points by a mathematical function. Only a few previous methods, dating from the pre-GPU or pre-multicore CPU era, considered approximation, but did not consider parallelization. The proposed method was published in Ref. [45].

The PhD thesis research of Bojan Furlan described a methodology for Intelligent Question Routing Systems (IQRS) design. IQRS aims to provide a good quality answer for question sent by a user. The answer is provided by selecting a certain number of competent users and forwarding the question to them. The thesis research first surveys existing solutions and introduces an original presentation paradigm that generalizes the essence of these solutions (method G). Existing solutions were then analyzed and the outcome was a proposal for a new approach that tackles identified problems (method M). The rest of the thesis research describes an IQRS prototype that implements the proposed ideas. The ideas relate to the three major problems of system implementation: question analysis, question forwarding, and users' knowledge profiling. The question analysis module enables question visualization and combines a fully automatic text processing with manual correction of the results, giving a user ability to increase the accuracy of the output (method E). For the question forwarding phase a new algorithm—LInSTSS—was proposed. It calculates the semantic similarity between two short texts, by including, among other parameters, the specificity of words that these texts contain (method E). The specialized version of this algorithm—P2Q—was designed to compare questions with available user profiles (method S). Finally, the text processing module, used both for question and answer analysis, combines two complementary approaches for information extraction from text (method E). Results were published in Refs. [46,47].

The PhD of Slavko Gajin focused on analytical modeling for performance evaluation of routing in multicomputer systems, along the method G, with elements of the method H. Solutions existing at the time of the PhD research of Gajin were using different models for different interconnection network topologies. The research of Gajin created a look from above and introduced a performance model that applies to all possible interconnection network topologies. The first ideas were published in Ref. [48], and detailed research results in Ref. [49].

The PhD thesis research of Zoran Jovanović was in the area of simulation and development of a VLIW (Very Large Instruction Wordmachine) used for digital signal processing. The simulator developed with a high-level language was used both for the machine design and testing of highly parallel programs developed by using a machine-specific parallel assembler. At the time the machine was developed, the name of such machines was Peripheral Array Processors and when compiler technology became mature for aggressive instruction-level parallelization, the name was changed to VLIW. In the available literature, there was only limited information about the leading processors of that type produced by Floating Point Systems (AP-120). The new design developed through simulation was done by using the first integrated floating point ALU pipelines that had a specific 22-bit floating point format. The developed machine was faster and logically more complex than the existing machines known in the open literature, but due to the reduced floating point precision and range, it was applicable only in digital signal processing. This approach could be classified as *Specialization (S)*.

The PhD thesis research of Dragan Milićev [50] was in the field of model transformations in modeling tools. It was a pioneering work in what was later shaped into the Model-Driven Architecture (MDA). Its idea emerged from analyzing the problem of generating ultimate output forms (e.g., code) in specific semantic domains (e.g., textual programming languages) from highly abstract models (e.g., UML or domain-specific modeling languages). For such conceptually distant domains, defining transformations is tedious and error prone, and the thesis research proposed introducing one or more intermediate modeling domains (defined in terms of metamodels in MOF) and defining multiple successive transformations between the source, intermediate, and target models. Because the intermediate domains are semantically closer, the transformations are easier to define and implement. In that sense, the proposed method could be classified as *implantation (I)*. Second, the thesis research also proposed a novel modeling technique for defining transformations by using UML object models with a specific, object creational semantics. The core UML object diagrams were extended with additional constructs for conditional, iterative, recursive, and polymorphic creation. By this, the method had reused some well-established concepts and notations from other software engineering disciplines in a new context, but with a different interpretation and semantics, and thus could be classified as *crossdisciplinarization (C)*.

The PhD research of Veljko Milutinović covered the field of suboptimal detection of data signals, and introduced a method that eliminates both the A/D converter in the input stage and the sample memory (SM) at the processing stage of the system, for a minimal performance degradation, along the methods $M + I$. Existing approaches eliminated either only the A/D converter or only the sample memory, but not both. Consequently, when all four possibilities were combined, a classification was obtained in which one class (neither A/D, nor SM) was not covered by examples from the open literature. Results were published in Ref. [51].

The PhD research of Boško Nikolić covered the field of Web-based visual simulation, designed to help teaching and learning computer architecture and organization courses. Simulation offers a unique environment that exposes students to both the programmer and the designer's perspective of the computer system. The Web-based simulator features an interactive animation of program execution and allows students to navigate through different levels of the educational computer system's hierarchy—starting from the top level with block representation down to the implementation level with standard sequential and combinational logic blocks. This work introduces an innovation predominantly along the lines of the method T. Results were published in Ref. [52].

The PhD thesis research of Jelica Protić explored the consistency maintenance of shared data in a distributed shared memory systems, and examined the potential for performance improvements of the protocol based on entry consistency, using different techniques, some of which were inspired by the lazy release consistency implementation, predominantly along the lines of the method H. At the time this research was conducted, the two most sophisticated relaxed consistency models were entry consistency (EC) implemented in Midway and lazy release consistency (LRC) implemented in TreadMarks. The main goal of this research was to combine the advantages of LRC and EC, taking into account communication and computation costs of the memory consistency protocol, as well as synchronization costs, which makes it a representative example of H research method, with the elements of E introduced by including new parameters in the analytical modeling. The first ideas were published in Ref. [53], and detailed analysis in Ref. [54].

The PhD research of Marija Punt was in the field of human–computer interaction (HCI), exploring user interaction scenarios in an integrated environment of digital TV, mobile devices, and the Internet. In the beginning of the research, existing HCI systems targeting a living room environment were explored. Using methods M and H, a list of HCI scenarios that applications, developed for an integrated environment, could offer were identified: sharing content on multiple screens (private content showing on the mobile device screen and public content showing on the central screen), using the mobile device to control actions on the central screen, motion detection using sensors, supplemental sensory feedback (haptic feedback, background lighting), combining passive viewing of television with parallel interaction, enriching the user experience with access to various information services (such as DVB, social media, and metadata databases), and combining interaction between colocated and non-colocated people. The research spanned multiple fields as in method C. After identifying the scenarios, the SHARP development framework was designed and implemented providing the building blocks to quickly construct distributed applications offering different combinations of the aforementioned HCI scenarios. A series of different games was developed using the SHARP framework, showing its flexibility and demonstrating novel applications that offer new combinations of scenarios to the users. Results were published in Ref. [55].

The PhD research of Zaharije Radivojević involved defining methodological approach that should help students connect theory and practice in the domain of computer architecture and organization simulator design, and to design simulators capable to work in a concurrent and distributed environment. In this manner, knowledge from two domains was interchanged as in method C. The approach is based on a multilayer design, where each layer is responsible for different type of processing and communication, which is done in accordance with method M. A referent simulator implementation created according to the methodology was demonstrated. Results were published in Ref. [56].

The PhD research of Žarko Stanisavljević was in the field of cryptographic algorithms visual representation, intended for use in an e-learning tool for teaching data security course. The result is COALA (CryptOgraphic Algorithms visuaL simulAtion) system that supports five different types of cryptographic algorithms and enables detailed analysis of their execution. Methods C and G were used to acquire knowledge from e-learning tools design principles in various areas of use. Then systems for visual representation of algorithms were analyzed and method G was used to define important characteristics of these systems. Finally, systems for visual representation of cryptographic algorithms were analyzed and using methods S and M the new approach was developed. Results were published in Ref. [57].

The PhD research of Saša Stojanović is related to the process of revealing whether a software library available in source code is used in a binary code. The essence of the proposed approach is to speedup searching for procedures originating from a software library, by comparing procedures resulting in an estimated measure of similarity between the searched procedure originating from a software library and each one of the procedures in binary code; all that is done in order to rank procedures from binary code according to decreased similarity with the searched procedure. Procedure comparison is a technique that could be used in many different domains, and there is a significant possibility to apply it in the domain of software violations that have elements of methods M and C. Moreover, new software metrics are proposed, meaning that the approach also includes elements of method E. Along with the proposed approach, five techniques are proposed based on an analysis of the points where information is lost; this corresponds to method M. Some of the proposed techniques are inspired by existing approaches where comparison of code is used, leading to the conclusion that the research includes elements of method C. Results are published in Refs. [58,59].

The PhD research of Igor Tartalja covered the field of software methods for cache coherence maintenance, where the author proposed a dynamic method for conditional invalidation of shared data segments, along the methods $M + H + C$. Existing approach suffered from unnecessary invalidations, resulting in performance degradation. Eager consistency model of the existing dynamic (run-time) software method mutated to the lazy consistency model, by applying a version control mechanism similar to the one proposed in a static (compile-time) cache coherence scheme. First results were published in Ref. [60] and later in Ref. [61].

The PhD research of Milo Tomašević was focused on the hardware methods for preserving the cache coherence in shared memory multiprocessors and proposed the principle of partial block invalidation, being alike both to the H and A methods. The contemporary solutions at that time followed the principle of full block invalidation which could incur a significant overhead in conditions of increased false sharing. The proposed WIP protocol starts with partial, word-based invalidations trying to preserve the valid block contents and switches to full block invalidation when a threshold that signals its excessive pollution is reached. The proposed protocol and its evaluation analysis were published in Ref. [62].

The PhD research of Pavle Vuletić described in Ref. [63] presents the analysis of the statistical nature of the cross-traffic on paths in computer networks as a foundation for choosing among active available bandwidth measurement strategies. Due to the highly variable statistical nature of network traffic, common bandwidth estimation tools and methods are not enough accurate and robust to function in different networking environments. Therefore, this work analyzed theoretical foundations for active available bandwidth measurement strategy through the self-similar process sampling analysis. The results obtained show a relationship between the main parameters in the measurement procedure, such as the number of samples, sample length, and sample distance and their impact on the measurement accuracy.

The facts that previous research work in this field did not analyze at all these parameters, or used very simplified models, classify this work as E. Through the analysis of several existing Internet packet traces, it was recommended that the minimum single sample probe stream length must be longer than the average cross-traffic interarrival. Following these findings, a new method for available bandwidth estimation, along the lines of the method A, was proposed that has shown significant accuracy under different network setups.

Table 1 summarizes the proposed classification and illustrates classes with examples from above cited PhD research studies.

As the experiences are gained during the work with PhD students, a follow-up research (maybe a decade from now) could summarize new findings related to the advisory work with young researchers, using the idea generation methodologies advocated in this article. Some of the PhD students at our Department of Computer Engineering and Informatics have recently published the papers or articles in Thomson Reuters JCR publications [64–67]. Their younger colleagues currently explore some challenging research areas and they have presented their work in progress at national and international conferences [68–71]. Finally, the youngest generation of associates is continuing their research efforts toward master degree, after

Table 1 The 10 Approaches to Evolutionary Innovations With Examples

	Class Name	Authors of Example PhD Thesis Research
1	Mendeleyevization	Blagojević, Bojović, Cvetanović, Đurđević, Furlan, Milutinović, Punt, Radivojević, Stanisavljević, Stojanović, Tartalja
2	Generalization	Blagojević, Furlan, Gajin, Stanisavljević
3	Specialization	Đorđević, Furlan, Jovanović, Stanisavljević
4	Revitalization	Đurđević
5	Crossdisciplinarization	Cvetanović, Milićev, Radivojević, Punt, Stanisavljević, Stojanović, Tartalja
6	Implantation	Bojović, Milićev, Milutinović
7	Adaptation	Tomašević, Vuletić
8	Hybridization	Gajin, Protić, Punt, Tartalja, Tomašević
9	Transgranularization	Bojić, Nikolić
10	Extraparameterization	Furlan, Protić, Stojanović, Vuletić

successful completion of their diploma thesis [72,73]. Some of the PhD candidates have already recognized the methodological classes of their ideas. Marko Mišić is intensifying his research on plagiarism detection in programming assignments [66], by exploring the social network analysis along the methods $I + R + C$. Sofija Purić and Živojin Šuštran demonstrated the method S by using a standard parser in the process of automatic generation of exam questions about syntax analysis for programming courses [71]. We assume that the other young researchers will also recognize the benefits of introducing methodological classes to their research, in order to speed up the process of shaping their PhD research.

4. CONCLUSIONS

This article introduces and explains 10 different methods that one could use to generate ideas for PhD research in the area of computing. It also provides a case study based on the examples of the PhD research of the authors of this article, and shows how they fit into the proposed classification.

The presented methodology implies that a PhD student is first asked to create a survey of existing solutions to the problem attacked by his/her PhD research, and to classify them. The classification may include classes without existing examples, which opens doors for *Mendeleyevization*. In this process, one could also catch the important common properties of the existing solutions and make an abstraction, which leads to *Generalization*. On the other hand, if a well-established common meta-metamodel is identified, it could be used for development of a metamodel for the specific domain, following the method of *Specialization*. During the survey process, some theoretical inventions that are practically dead could be revisited and applied using the technology upgrades, which results in the approach that we refer to as *Revitalization*. *Crossdisciplinarization* occurs when one finds the way to port some good ideas from one field to another. If a new solution is invented by implanting a (relatively small) resource into an existing solution, we follow the path of *Implantation*. Algorithms/approaches inherent to various solutions could be combined based on conditions in which one of them performs better, which opens doors for a method that we named *Adaptation*. On the other hand, by recombining parts of existing solutions, we sometimes could create a good new solution along the lines of *Hybridization*. Further on, taking the direction of transformation to coarser or to finer granularity from the existing solution, with less or more modifications, leads to *Transgranularization*. Finally, by adding new parameters to the model, it becomes more complex and may lead to a new, more precise solution to the problem, so one could perform *Extraparameterization*. Although the set of the proposed methods is not closed (playing with anagrams made of first letters of the proposed methods—*M, G, S, R, C, I, A, H, T*, and *E*), this set of methods may be considered as *CHARMInGEST*, but PhD candidates have to keep open their minds and take care not to be caught in the *TRAGIC MESH*.

Future work on this subject should examine more well-known examples of innovations in computer science and engineering, as well as the on-going research of our PhD students. Since we have qualified the proposed classification as *Incomplete*, some new categories may be added in the future.

ACKNOWLEDGMENTS

This research was partially supported by the projects TR32039, TR32047, III44006, and III44009 of the Ministry of Science and Technological Development of the Republic of Serbia.

REFERENCES

Methodology-Related References

[1] S. Filipi-Matutinovic, Scientific information in Serbia, University Library Svetozar Markovic, Belgrade, 2011(in Serbian).

[2] M. Franceshet, A comparison of bibliometric indicators for computer science scholars and journals on Web of Science and Google Scholar, Scientometrics 83 (1) (2010) 243–258.

[3] V. Milutinovic, The best method for presentation of research results, IEEE TCCA Newsl. 214 (1996) 1–6.

[4] V. Milutinovic, S. Tomazic, How to ruin the career of a PhD student in computer science and engineering: precise guidelines, IPSI BgD Trans. Internet Res. 4 (2) (2008) 24–26.

[5] V. Milutinovic, A structured approach to research for PHD students in computer science and engineering: how to create ideas, conduct research, and write papers, IPSI Trans. Internet Res. 11 (2) (2015) 47–54.

[6] V. Milutinovic, A good method to prepare and use transparencies for research presentations, IEEE TCCA Newsl. (1997) 1–8.

[7] S. Omerovic, S. Tomazic, M. Milutinovic, V. Milutinovic, Methodology for written and oral presentation of research results, J. Prof. Issues Eng. Educ. Pract. 136 (2) (2010) 112–117.

[8] M. Ogot, G. Okudan, Systematic creativity methods in engineering education: a learning styles perspective, Int. J. Eng. Educ. 22 (3) (2006) 566–576.

[9] R. Yoram, A. Hatchnel, O. Shai, E. Subrahmanian, A theoretical analysis of creativity methods in engineering design: casting and improving ASIT within C-K theory, J. Eng. Des. 23 (2) (2012) 137–158.

[10] R. Horowitz, Creative problem solving in engineering design, PhD thesis, Tel Aviv University, Israel, 1999.

[11] R. Felder, L. Silverman, Learning and teaching styles in engineering education, Eng. Educ. 78 (7) (2002) 674–681.

[12] W. Faulkner, Conceptualizing knowledge used in innovation: a second look at the science-technology distinction and industrial innovation, Sci. Technol. Hum. Values 19 (4) (1994) 425–458.

[13] M.C. Linn, Establishing a research base for science education: challenges, trends, and recommendations, J. Res. Sci. Teach. 24 (3) (1987) 191–216.

[14] D. Prost O'Leary, Graduate study in the computer and mathematical sciences: a survival manual, http://www.cs.umd.edu/~oleary/gradstudy/gradstudy.html. Accessed 25 June 2014.

[15] P. Dunleavy, Authoring a PhD: How to Plan, Draft, Write and Finish a Doctoral Thesis or Dissertation, Palgrave Macmillan, Basingstoke, 2003.

[16] H. Kearns, M. Gardiner, K. Marshall, Innovation in PhD completion: the hardy shall succeed (and be happy!), High. Educ. Res. Dev. 27 (1) (2007) 77–89.

[17] M. Stierand, V. Dorfler, Methods against methods, in: A. Mesquita (Ed.), Technology for Creativity and Innovation: Tools, Techniques and Applications, IGI Global, Hershey, PA, 2011, pp. 121–134.

[18] V. Dorfler, Z. Baracskai, J. Velencei, Understanding creativity, Trans. Adv. Res. 6 (2) (2010) 17–25.

[19] OMG Unified Modeling Language™ (OMG UML), Superstructure, Object Management Group. http://www.omg.org/spec/UML/2.4.1/Superstructure/PDF/, 2011 (accessed 25.06.14).

Common Examples

[20] M. Flynn, Very high-speed computing systems, Proc. IEEE 54 (12) (1966) 1901–1909.

[21] H.T. Kung, C.E. Leiserson, Algorithms for VLSI processor arrays, in: C. Mead, L. Conway (Eds.), Introduction to VLSI Systems, Addison-Wesley, Reading, MA, 1979.

[22] A. Spector, D. Gifford, The space shuttle primary computer system, Commun. ACM 27 (9) (1984) 872–900.

[23] D. Harel, Statecharts: a visual formalism for complex systems, Sci. Comput. Program. 8 (3) (1987) 231–274.

[24] C.A. Petri, Communication with automata, New York: Griffiss Air Force Base: Technical Report, RADC TR-65-377-vol-1-suppl-1 Applied Data Research, Princeton, NJ, Contract AF 30(602)-3324, 1966).

[25] Business Process Model and Notation (BPMN), Object Management Group. http://www.omg.org/spec/BPMN/2.0/PDF/, 2011 (accessed 25.06.14).

[26] OMG Meta Object Facility (MOF) Core Specification, Object Management Group. http://www.omg.org/spec/MOF/2.4.1/PDF/, 2011 (accessed 25.06.14).

[27] N.D. Jones, C.K. Gomard, P. Sestoft, Partial Evaluation and Automatic Program Generation (with chapters by L.O. Andersen and T. Mogensen), Prentice Hall International, New Jersey, 1993.

[28] W.S. McCulloch, W. Pitts, A logical calculus of ideas immanent in nervous activity, Bull. Math. Biol. 5 (4) (1943) 115–133.

[29] J.J. Hopfield, Neural networks and physical systems with emergent collective computational abilities, Proc. Natl. Acad. Sci. U.S.A. 79 (8) (1982) 2554–2558.

[30] J.H. Holland, Adaptation in Natural and Artificial Systems, University of Michigan Press, Ann Arbor, MI, 1975.

[31] F. John, J.F. Couleur, E.L. Glaser, Shared-access data processing system, 1968). Patent 3412382, November 1968.

[32] R.P. Case, A. Padegs, The architecture of the IBM system/370, Commun. ACM 21 (1) (1978) 73–96.

[33] Intel Corporation, Intel adaptive technology optimizing network performance, 1997.
[34] E. Catmull, A subdivision algorithm for computer display of curved surfaces, PhD thesis, Report UTEC-CSc-74-133, Computer Science Department, University of Utah, Salt Lake City, UT, 1974.
[35] J. Fotheringham, Dynamic storage allocation in the Atlas computer, including an automatic use of a backing store, Commun. ACM 4 (10) (1961) 435–436.
[36] M.V. Wilkes, Slave memories and dynamic storage allocation, IEEE Trans. Electron. Comput. EC-14 (2) (1965) 270–271.
[37] J. Buzen, Computational algorithms for closed queueing networks with exponential servers, Commun. ACM 16 (9) (1973) 527–531.
[38] W.J. Gordon, G.F. Newell, Closed queueing systems with exponential servers, Oper. Res. 15 (2) (1967) 254–265.

Author's PhD-Related References

[39] V. Blagojevic, G.A. Gledhil, A. Hamilton, S.B. Upadhuay, P.M. Nikolic, M.B. Pavlovic, D.I. Rakovic, Far infrared optical properties of ZnS highly doped with Fe, Infrared Phys. 31 (4) (1991) 387–393.
[40] D. Bojic, D. Velasevic, Reverse engineering of use case realizations in UML, ACM SIGSOFT Softw. Eng. Notes 25 (4) (2000) 56–61.
[41] D. Bojic, T. Eisenbart, R. Koschke, D. Simon, D. Velasevic, Addendum to locating features in source code, IEEE Trans. Softw. Eng. 30 (2) (2004) 140–141.
[42] M. Bojovic, Z. Konstantinovic, Synchronization and communication mechanism for a highly reliable multiprocessor system, in: The 15th IFIP Conference on Real Time Programming, May 1988, Valencia, Spain, 1988.
[43] M. Cvetanovic, Z. Radivojevic, V. Blagojevic, M. Bojovic, ADVICE—educational system for teaching database courses, IEEE Trans. Educ. 54 (3) (2011) 398–409.
[44] J. Djordjevic, R.N. Ibbett, F.H. Sumner, Evaluation of some proposed name-space architectures using ISPS, IEE Proc. E (Comput. Digit. Tech.) 127 (4) (1980) 120–125.
[45] Đ. Đurđević, I. Tartalja, HFPaC: GPU friendly height field parallel compression, GeoInformatica 17 (1) (2013) 207–233.
[46] B. Furlan, B. Nikolic, V. Milutinovic, A survey and evaluation of state-of-the-art intelligent question routing systems, Int. J. Intell. Syst. 28 (7) (2013) 686–708.
[47] B. Furlan, V. Batanović, B. Nikolić, Semantic similarity of short texts in languages with a deficient natural language processing support, Decis. Support Syst. 55 (3) (2013) 710–719.
[48] S. Gajin, Z. Jovanović, Explanation of performance degradation in the turn model, J. Supercomput. 37 (3) (2006) 271–295.
[49] S. Gajin, Z. Jovanovic, An accurate performance model for network-on-chip and multicomputer interconnection networks, J. Parallel Distrib. Comput. 72 (10) (2012) 1280–1294.
[50] D. Milićev, Automatic model transformations using extended UML object diagrams in modeling environments, IEEE Trans. Softw. Eng. 28 (4) (2002) 413–431.
[51] V. Milutinovic, A comparison of suboptimal detection algorithms applied to the additive mix of orthogonal sinusoidal signals, IEEE Trans. Commun. 36 (5) (1988) 538–543.
[52] J. Djordjevic, B. Nikolic, A. Milenkovic, Flexible web-based educational system for teaching computer architecture and organization, IEEE Trans. Educ. 48 (2) (2005) 264–273.
[53] J. Protic, M. Tomasevic, V. Milutinovic, Distributed shared memory: concepts and systems, IEEE Parallel Distrib. Technol. Syst. Appl. 4 (2) (1996) 63–79.

[54] J. Protic, V. Milutinovic, A comparison of three protocols for entry consistency maintenance based on MVA algorithm, in: Proceedings of the 8th International Symposium on MASCOTS 2000, San Francisco, USA, August 2000, 2000, pp. 517–523.

[55] M. Punt, M.Z. Bjelica, V. Zdravkovic, N. Teslic, An integrated environment and development framework for social gaming using mobile devices, digital TV and Internet, Multimedia Tools Appl. 74 (18) (2015) 8137–8169.

[56] Z. Radivojevic, M. Cvetanovic, Z. Jovanovic, Reengineering the SLEEP simulator in a concurrent and distributed programming course, Comput. Appl. Eng. Educ. 19 (2011) 1–13.

[57] Z. Stanisavljevic, J. Stanisavljevic, P. Vuletic, Z. Jovanovic, COALA—system for visual representation of cryptography algorithms, IEEE Trans. Learn. Technol. 7 (2) (2014) 178–190.

[58] S. Stojanović, Z. Radivojević, M. Cvetanović, Approach for estimating similarity between procedures in differently compiled binaries, Inf. Softw. Technol. 58 (1) (2015) 259–271.

[59] Z. Radivojević, M. Cvetanović, S. Stojanović, Comparison of binary procedures: a set of techniques for evading compiler transformations, Comput. J. 59 (1) (2016) 106–118.

[60] I. Tartalja, V. Milutinovic, An approach to dynamic software cache consistency maintenance based on conditional invalidation, in: Proceedings of the 25th HICSS, USA, vol. 1, January 1992, 1992, pp. 457–466.

[61] I. Tartalja, V. Milutinovic, Classifying software-based cache coherence solutions, IEEE Softw. 14 (3) (1997) 90–101.

[62] M. Tomasevic, V. Milutinovic, The word-invalidate cache coherence protocol, Microprocess. Microsyst. 20 (1) (1996) 3–16.

[63] P. Vuletic, J. Protic, Self-similar cross-traffic analysis as a foundation for choosing among active available bandwidth measurement strategies, Comput. Commun. 34 (10) (2011) 1145–1158.

Selected References of Young Researchers on the Faculty of the Department of Computer Engineering and Informatics, School of Electrical Engineering, University of Belgrade

[64] S. Vujicic Stankovic, N. Kojic, G. Rakocevic, D.M. Vitas, V.M. Milutinovic, A classification of data mining algorithms for wireless sensor networks, and classification extension to concept modeling in system of wireless sensor networks based on natural language processing, Adv. Comput. 90 (2012) 223–283.

[65] Z. Sustran, G. Rakocevic, V.M. Milutinovic, Dual data cache systems: architecture and analysis, Adv. Comput. 96 (2015) 187–233.

[66] M. Mišić, Ž. Šuštran, J. Protić, A comparison of software tools for plagiarism detection in programming assignments, Int. J. Eng. Educ. 32 (2) (2016) 738–748.

[67] D. Drašković, M. Mišić, Ž. Stanisavljevic, Transition from traditional to LMS supported examining: a case study in computer engineering, Comput. Appl. Eng. Educ. 24 (5) (2016) 775–786.

[68] K. Milenkovic, D. Draskovic, B. Nikolic, Educational software system for reasoning and decision making using Bayesian networks, in: IEEE Global Engineering Education Conference (EDUCON) 2014, Istanbul, Turkey, April 2014, 2014, pp. 1189–1194.

[69] S. Tubic, D. Draskovic, Realization of A* search algorithm in a computer game (in Serbian), in: Proceedings of the 59th ETRAN Conference, Srebrno jezero, Serbia, June 2015, 2015.

[70] M. Prodanov, D. Drašković, Software simulation of intelligent system based on search algorithms (in Serbian), in: YU INFO 2016, Kopaonik, Serbia, February 2016, 2016, pp. 379–383.

[71] S. Purić, Ž. Šuštran, J. Protić, Software tool SinGen for generating questions and answers about syntax analysis in programming courses (in Serbian), in: YU INFO 2016, Kopaonik, Serbia, February 2016, 2016, pp. 351–356.

[72] S. Delcev, Simulator of the superscalar processors with the reservation stations, Diploma thesis (in Serbian), University of Belgrade, School of Electrical Engineering, 2015, October 2015.

[73] F. Hadzic, An implementation of superscalar processor on the FPGA chip, Diploma thesis (in Serbian), University of Belgrade, School of Electrical Engineering, 2015, October 2015.

ABOUT THE AUTHORS

Vladimir Blagojević was on the faculty of the Department of Computer Engineering in the School of Electrical Engineering, University of Belgrade, Serbia. His PhD thesis, defended in the year 1996, was related to Physics. He taught courses on Databases and Information Systems. His research was in the fields of Data Modeling and High Performance Computing.

Dragan Bojić is on the faculty of the Department of Computer Engineering in the School of Electrical Engineering, University of Belgrade, Serbia. His PhD thesis, defended in the year 2001, was related to software engineering. He teaches courses on Compiler Construction and Software Engineering. His current research is in the fields of Formal Language and Parsing, Software Engineering Techniques and Tools, and eLearning.

Miroslav Bojović is on the faculty of the Department of Computer Engineering in the School of Electrical Engineering, University of Belgrade, Serbia. His PhD thesis, defended in the year 1988, was related to computer engineering. He teaches courses on Database Systems. His current research is in the fields of Database Systems, Fault Tolerance and Big Data.

Miloš Cvetanović is on the faculty of the Department of Computer Engineering in the School of Electrical Engineering, University of Belgrade, Serbia. His PhD thesis, defended in the year 2012, was related to database management systems. He teaches courses on Information Systems and Computing Infrastructure. His current research is in the fields of Reverse Engineering and Natural Language Processing.

Jovan Đorđević is on the faculty of the Department of Computer Engineering in the School of Electrical Engineering, University of Belgrade, Serbia. His PhD thesis, defended in the year 1979, was related to computer architecture. He teaches courses on Digital Logic and Computer Architecture. His current research is in the fields of Digital Systems Simulation and Parallel Computer Systems.

Đorđe Đurđević is on the faculty of the Department of Computer Engineering in the School of Electrical Engineering, University of Belgrade, Serbia. His PhD thesis, defended in the year 2013, was related to data compression on graphics processors. He teaches courses on Computer Graphics, Functional Programming, and Object Oriented Programming. His current research is in the field of Computer Graphics.

Bojan Furlan is on the faculty of the Department of Computer Engineering in the School of Electrical Engineering, University of Belgrade, Serbia. His PhD thesis, defended in the year 2013, was related to intelligent question routing systems. He teaches course on Machine Learning. His current research is in the fields of Knowledge Extraction and Machine Learning.

Slavko Gajin is on the faculty of the Department of Computer Engineering in the School of Electrical Engineering, University of Belgrade, Serbia. His PhD thesis, defended in the year 2007, was related to interconnection network in multicomputer and system on chip. He teaches courses on Computer Networks. His current research is in the fields of Network Management and Network Behavior Analysis.

Zoran Jovanović is on the faculty of the Department of Computer Engineering in the School of Electrical Engineering, University of Belgrade, Serbia. His PhD thesis, defended in the year 1988, was related to vector processors. He teaches courses on Parallel Processing and Concurrent and Distributed Programming. His current research is in the fields of Parallel Computers, Distributed Systems, and Data Security.

Dragan Milićev is on the faculty of the Department of Computer Engineering in the School of Electrical Engineering, University of Belgrade, Serbia. His PhD thesis, defended in the year 2001, was related to model transformations. He teaches courses on Operating Systems and Software Engineering. His current research is in the fields of Model-Based Software Engineering and Information Systems.

Veljko Milutinović is on the faculty of the Department of Computer Engineering in the School of Electrical Engineering, University of Belgrade, Serbia. His PhD thesis, defended in the year 1982, was related to data communications. He teaches courses on Data Flow and Processor Design. His current research is in the fields of Data Analytics and Spatial Computing.

Boško Nikolić is on the faculty of the Department of Computer Engineering in the School of Electrical Engineering, University of Belgrade, Serbia. His PhD thesis, defended in the year 2005, was related to education software systems. He teaches courses on Artificial Intelligence and Expert Systems, Internet Programming, and Web Design. His current research is in the fields of Artificial Intelligence and Web Applications.

Jelica Protić is on the faculty of the Department of Computer Engineering in the School of Electrical Engineering, University of Belgrade, Serbia. Her PhD thesis, defended in the year 1999, was related to distributed shared memory. She teaches courses on Programming and Computer Systems Performance Analysis. Her current research is in the fields of Computer Supported Education and Network Analysis.

Marija Punt is on the faculty of the Department of Computer Engineering in the School of Electrical Engineering, University of Belgrade, Serbia. Her PhD thesis, defended in the year 2015, was related to human–computer interaction. She teaches courses on Computer Architecture, Web Design and User Interface Programming. Her current research is in the fields of Digital Systems Simulation, Human–Computer Interaction and Consumer Electronics.

Zaharije Radivojević is on the faculty of the Department of Computer Engineering in the School of Electrical Engineering, University of Belgrade, Serbia. His PhD thesis, defended in the year 2012, was related to Computer Simulator Design. He teaches courses on Computer Architecture and Organization and Concurrent and Distributed Programming. His current research is in the fields of Computer Simulations, Reverse Engineering and Computer Architecture.

Žarko Stanisavljević is on the faculty of the Department of Computer Engineering in the School of Electrical Engineering, University of Belgrade, Serbia. His PhD thesis, defended in the year 2015, was related to visual representation of cryptographic algorithms. He teaches courses on Computer Architecture and Organization and Information Security. His current research is in the fields of Information Security Visual Simulators and eLearning Tools.

Saša Stojanović is on the faculty of the Department of Computer Engineering in the School of Electrical Engineering, University of Belgrade, Serbia. His PhD thesis, defended in the year 2015, was related to software similarity. He teaches courses on Embedded Systems and Mobile Devices Programming. His current research is in the fields of Software Similarity and Reverse Engineering.

Igor Tartalja is on the faculty of the Department of Computer Engineering in the School of Electrical Engineering, University of Belgrade, Serbia. His PhD thesis, defended in the year 1997, was related to software cache coherence. He teaches courses on Object-Oriented Programming, Software Analysis and Design, and Computer Graphics. His current research is in the fields of Automatic Test Assembly, Edutainment tools, and Terrain Modeling, Compression and Presentation.

Milo Tomašević is on the faculty of the Department of Computer Engineering in the School of Electrical Engineering, University of Belgrade, Serbia. His PhD thesis, defended in the year 1992, was related to cache coherence protocols. He teaches courses on Algorithms and Data Structures, Programming and Multiprocessors. His current research is in the fields of Parallel Processing and Cryptanalysis.

Pavle Vuletić is on the Department of Computer Engineering in the School of Electrical Engineering, University of Belgrade, Serbia. His PhD thesis, defended in the year 2011, was related to traffic characterization and network performance verification. He teaches courses on Computer Networks and Software Defined Networking. His current research is in the fields of Network Management and SDN

CHAPTER TWO

Exploring Future Many-Core Architectures: The TERAFLUX Evaluation Framework

R. Giorgi
University of Siena, Siena Italy

Contents

1. Introduction   35
2. Terminology and Related Work   37
    2.1 The Trade-off Between Simulation Accuracy and Speed   37
    2.2 Simulation vs Emulation   37
    2.3 The "Functional-Directed" Simulation Technique   38
    2.4 Using Sampling and FPGAs to Accelerate Simulation of Large Systems   39
    2.5 Other Relevant Simulator Features   40
3. COTSon Framework Organization   45
4. Targeting a 1000-Core Simulation   46
    4.1 Comparison Among Approaches to Evaluate Novel 1000-Core Architectures   47
    4.2 Notes on the Evaluations Based on Physical Machines   47
5. How to Simulate 1000 Cores   49
    5.1 Setup #1: Physical Machines, MPI Programming Model   51
    5.2 Setup #2: Virtual Machines Running on Several Physical Machines, MPI Programming Model   52
    5.3 Setup #3: Virtual Machines Running on a Single Physical Computer, MPI Programming Model   53
    5.4 Setup #4: Virtual Machines Running on a Single Physical Computer, Flexible Programming Model on Top of a Distributed Machine Guest   55
    5.5 Setup #5: Virtual Machines Running on a Single Physical Computer, Flexible Programming Model on Top of a Shared-Memory Guest   56
    5.6 Setup #6: Single Virtual Machine Running on a Single Physical Computer, Flexible Programming Model on Top of a Shared-Memory Guest   58
6. The Search for "Efficient Benchmarks"   60
7. Simulation Experiments   61
    7.1 TERAFLUX Basic Node With up to 32 Cores   62
    7.2 TERAFLUX Basic Communication Case With Two Nodes   62
    7.3 TERAFLUX 1024-Core Machine (32 Nodes by 32 Cores)   63
8. Conclusions   66

Advances in Computers, Volume 104
ISSN 0065-2458
http://dx.doi.org/10.1016/bs.adcom.2016.09.002

Acknowledgments   66
References   66
About the Author   72

Abstract

The design of new computer systems always requires a strong simulation effort in order to evaluate different design options. This is especially true if the system is to be produced at a date far in the future, such as in the case of TERAFLUX, a system aimed at containing something like 10^{12} (1 TERA) transistors in a single package or a (multi-layer) chip by 2020.

At the basis of a TERAFLUX system, a dataflow execution model supports the execution of threads. In order to explore the design space, TERAFLUX provides an appropriate evaluation framework, at the scale of at least 1000 general purpose cores on a single chip.

Predicting the performance of such a next-generation platform is not a trivial task. Today, no software-based tool exists that can provide cycle-level full-system simulation and faithfully predict the behavior of 1000 general-purpose cores, in an acceptable amount of time and with reasonable accuracy, while providing the flexibility of changing the execution model at the architectural level. A solid evaluation framework represents an important base for exploring future many cores.

In this chapter, different options for simulating a 1000 general-purpose-core system are explored. Finally, we show the setup that successfully allowed us to evaluate our 1000 core target while running a full-system Linux operating system.

ABBREVIATIONS

AC auxiliary core
CAS cycle accurate simulator
CPU central processing unit
DRAM dynamic random access memory
FDU fault detection unit
Fm functional model
FPGA field programmable gate array
ILP instruction–level parallelism
I/O input/output
ISS instruction set simulator
KIPS kilo instruction per second
L1$ level–1 cache
L2$ level–2 cache
NIC network interface controller
NoC network on chip
OS operating system
PCI peripheral component interconnect—a standard for interconnection of peripherals
PCIbar a set of peripheral registers (base address register set) on a PCI bus
RTL register transfer level

RVI rapid virtualization indexing
SC service core
SMP symmetric multiprocessor
SSI single system image
Tm timing model
TSU thread scheduling unit
VT-x virtualization extension in Intel CPUs

1. INTRODUCTION

TERAFLUX aims at modeling a future architecture possibly composed of a 3D stacked chip/package consisting of 10^{12} transistors [1]. In the first instance TERAFLUX aimed at modeling a machine with 1000 or more cores—possibly general purpose cores—a network on chip (NoC), a memory subsystem, without neglecting the necessity of running a full operating system to govern the I/O, runtime libraries, legacy software, and other system processes (Fig. 1).

In the general vision of TERAFLUX, as indicated in Fig. 1, a future computing system is likely to be based on a multidie package including one layer consisting of both several smaller cores (auxiliary cores or ACs) and bigger cores (service cores or SCs) [2–4]. Other layers may include the NoC and several other dies of memory subsystem (e.g., DRAM). Some of the SCs may be even dedicated to some special purpose I/O or provide

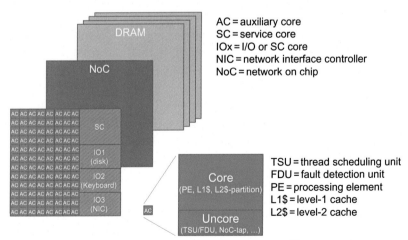

AC = auxiliary core
SC = service core
IOx = I/O or SC core
NIC = network interface controller
NoC = network on chip

TSU = thread scheduling unit
FDU = fault detection unit
PE = processing element
L1$ = level-1 cache
L2$ = level-2 cache

Fig. 1 Thinking at the simulation of a Future Teradevice (10^{12} transistors) System.

full range operating system services [5], and they may rely on aggressive out-of-order superscalar cores. The smaller cores can be general-purpose cores too (e.g., in-order superscalar cores) as well as customized ones. Essential and novel parts of the TERAFLUX system are the thread scheduling unit (TSU) [6] and the fault detection unit (FDU) [7,8].

Assuming this kind of architecture, the next challenge is to program efficiently and easily such machine. In order to overcome the classical issues of large-scale computing system, TERAFLUX relies on a dataflow-based execution model and a novel Memory Model. In particular the TER-AFLUX TSU allows for an execution model and a Memory Model of threads that highly exploits dataflow concepts [9–17] and transactional memory [18–20]. Each core has an associated TSU, and the TSUs are organized to enable scalable and lightweight communication of the thread distribution across the cores.

After analyzing the many available options for evaluating this kind of architecture, we decided to rely on and extend the COTSon simulator [21]. The main reasons for starting from this simulator are: (i) its capability of modeling a situation with a very high number of cores, compared to what we have nowadays, e.g., 1000 general purpose cores at an acceptable simulation speed; (ii) the ability of providing cycle-level measurements of the behavior of the system, not only an approximate high-level or user-code-only evaluation; (iii) the ability to model the cores, extending the instruction set of an x86-64 system, modeling new architectural blocks such as the TSU and the FDU; and (iv) the public availability of the source code (except for SimNow [22], the virtualizer). Moreover, the extended version of COTSon that was developed in TERAFLUX allowed us to explore the global organization of the cores and the execution model (including where to run the operating system, for instance). This is the main topic of this chapter, i.e., trying to answer the question: *How should a future many-core computing system (including 1 TERA transistors in a package) be organized?*

The innovation presented in this chapter can be viewed as a combination of the creativity methods classified as revitalization (R), implantation (I), adaptation (A), transgranularization (T), and extraparametrization (E) of the chapter by Blagojevic *et al.* [23]. In the following, we recall and briefly explain the terminology that we use and we contrast the benefits of COTSon in comparison to other simulators (Section 2). We briefly recall the COTSon simulator structure in Section 3. We compare several options for simulating a target of 1000 cores in Section 4. Section 5 details advantages and disadvantages of choosing different models for the 1000-core simulation based on COTSon. In Section 6, the role of the benchmarks is briefly discussed. Finally, we describe some of the initial tests that permitted the evaluation of the 1000-core system in Section 7.

2. TERMINOLOGY AND RELATED WORK

In this section, we motivate our choice in TERAFLUX of relying on the COTSon simulator [21] compared to the large number of available simulators. We also recall and briefly explain the terminology that we use, and we contrast the benefits of COTSon in comparison with other simulators.

2.1 The Trade-off Between Simulation Accuracy and Speed

Future architectures will expose a massive number of parallel simple processors (besides some bigger instruction-level-parallelism-, or ILP-, focused processors) with on-chip memories connected through a network-on-chip, whose speed is more than 100 times faster than their off-chip speed [24]. The number of general-purpose cores in a single die is increasing and postulated to reach 1000 and beyond. In order to evaluate such a future design, we set up an appropriate evaluation framework.

In the computer architect's and researcher's toolbox, a cycle-accurate software simulator (CAS) is one of the most important tools [25]. In fact, a CAS allows us to simulate microarchitectures on a cycle-by-cycle basis, without the need of building a physical chip. More in general, simulators allow us to carry out platform exploration and evaluation of the different architectural options under several types of requirements (e.g., performance, reliability, power consumption, temperature). However, a CAS is extremely slow. Chiou reports that the simulators for single-core processors used at Intel and AMD often operate at 1 KIPS (kilo instruction per second) to 10 KIPS, implying 1–10 years to simulate a 3 GHz target for 2 min [26]. Even worse, simulators are getting slower and more complicated under multicore or many-core scenarios.

2.2 Simulation vs Emulation

It is worthwhile to recall some terminologies about architecture and microarchitecture simulation. In this section, we will review the concept, classification, and detail challenges of simulators.

When we talk about *simulation*, another concept, *emulation*, is often mentioned. Sometimes, *emulation* and *simulation* are used interchangeably in the computing system literature. To make it easy for discussion, we illustrate the difference between these two concepts. Emulation means that the function of a platform is repeated on another platform. The main concern of emulation is the correctness of the function. Simulation is an extension of emulation. Besides ensuring the functional correctness, simulation must provide accurate time information, which is related to performance. In this document, if there is no explicit specification, an emulator is related to the bare functional behavior, while a simulator is related to performance. Other two widely used concepts are *functional simulator* and *performance simulator*. In this context, the term "simulator" means "timing simulator (cycle-accurate)," and the term "emulator" means "functional simulator" (in case of an emulated processor we also use instruction set simulator or ISS) [27]. Finally, we use the term "power simulator" when we have a power model or "power–timing simulator" when we use both a power model and a timing model [28].

2.3 The "Functional-Directed" Simulation Technique

A (timing) simulator can also use different approaches depending on the relationship between the "functional model" (*Fm*) and the "timing model" (*Tm*) [29] (Table 1).

We distinguish: (i) "*functional-first*" or "*trace-driven*," the *Fm* is run first and separately and the *Tm* is run later on in a completely decoupled fashion (the whole *Fm* is run before the *Tm* is run); (ii) "*timing directed*" or "execution driven," the *Fm* and *Tm* are closely coupled (no decoupling);

Table 1 Relationship Between Timing and Functional Simulation in Different Simulation Techniques

Name of the Simulation Technique	Functional and Timing Combination	Decoupling Between *Fm* and *Tm*	Feedback Between *Fm* and *Tm*
Functional first (trace driven)	*Fm* then *Tm*	Yes	No
Timing directed (execution driven)	*Tm* then *Fm*	No	Yes
Timing first	*Tm* then *Fm*	Yes	Yes
Functional directed	*Fm* then *Tm*	Yes	Yes

(iii) *"timing-first,"* the *Tm* drives the *Fm*, both are completely decoupled, but the functional execution has to be checked later on and eventually undone; and (iv) *"functional directed,"* the *Fm* drives the *Tm*, both are completely decoupled, the functional model is always the right one but a timing feedback from *Tm* is needed to correct the timing behavior so that it becomes visible to the applications being simulated [21].

For functional simulators or emulators, there are also several existing systems. One of the most popular ones is QEMU (quick emulator) [30]. QEMU is open source software for creating Virtual Machine (VM) environments, developed by Fabrice Bellard. As an emulator, it is used to run operating systems and applications written for another hardware platform, for example, running ARM software on an x86-based PC. For virtualization, QEMU is used to emulate devices and certain privileged instructions and requires the KQEMU/KVM kernel module and the host operating system to provide a virtual machine environment. An extension of QEMU for emulating multi-/many cores is COREMU [31]. SimNow [22] and SIMICS are other examples of functional simulators when used as virtualizers.

COTSon is a full-system simulator that uses the "functional-directed" approach; it can take advantage of sampling techniques; it uses AMD SimNow as an emulator engine to functionally process the workload; it can run several emulator instances in parallel. In the rest of this section, we describe some multicore simulators and contrast them with COTSon.

2.4 Using Sampling and FPGAs to Accelerate Simulation of Large Systems

Since the cycle-accurate simulation takes an extremely long time, there is a large body of literature on how to accelerate the cycle-accurate simulation. The most popular simulation acceleration technique is *sampling*. This technique selects some instructions for cycle-accurate simulation, while other instructions are simulated in a functional mode called fast-forwarding. According to the different sampling strategies, a lot of simulation sampling techniques are developed. Conte *et al.* [32] employed simple random sampling strategy to speed up simulation. Wunderlich *et al.* [33] and Wenisch *et al.* [34] used systematic sampling in acceleration of microarchitecture simulation. They also tried to use a stratified sampling scheme for acceleration [35]. Perelman *et al.* [36] applied representative sampling to speed up microarchitecture simulation. Yu *et al.* [37] employed a more flexible sampling scheme, two-stage sampling, to accelerate micro-architecture simulations.

Although sampling can accelerate simulation significantly with relatively high accuracy, it is complicated to prepare the sampling parameters before the real simulation. Therefore, simplifying the acceleration of microarchitectures is becoming important. A few researchers have tried to simplify this procedure. UNISIM is one example because it provides transparent techniques to speed up the simulation time [38]. Another example is the CantorSim approach, which employs fractals to simplify the parameter preparation for simulation acceleration [39]. COTSon supports more than seven different sampling techniques.

When sampling techniques are used, the simulation rate is limited by the speed of the functional simulator. Although the speed of the functional simulator is much faster than the speed of a performance simulator, it is still too slow for computer architects. Researchers have tried to accelerate performance simulators by using FPGAs. Penry *et al.* [40] provide a much more detailed, low-level simulation and are targeting hardware designs with FPGA support. Their simulator, while fast for a cycle-accurate hardware model, does not provide the performance necessary for rapid exploration of different ideas or software development. Other examples are Proto-Flex [41], FAST [42], and HASim [43]. These simulators use FPGAs to accelerate the timing models. However, FPGA-based simulation is less flexible than software-based simulation. For instance, implementing a new model in an FPGA such as in the RAMP project is more difficult than in software (typically requiring an RTL-level description), making it harder to quickly experiment with different designs [44,45]. Although FPGA-based simulators are faster, one of the main advantages of software-based techniques, such as COTSon, is their easier modeling and higher flexibility to model architectural components.

2.5 Other Relevant Simulator Features

Since simulation is so important, many different kinds of simulators or simulation methodologies have been developed over the years. In order to classify a simulator, there are different features of simulators and with some overlapping (Table 2).

According to whether the modeled processor is a single core or a multicore, we have *single-core simulators* and *multicore simulators*. SlackSim [57] and SimpleScalar [54] are examples of single-core simulators, while COTSon is a typical multicore simulator [21].

Table 2 A List of Features Present in Simulators That May Be Relevant for Simulating a Large System (The List of Features and Simulators Is Nonexhaustive)

Simulator Name and Reference	Simulated Features				Simulator Features						
	Single-Core Only	User-Level Multicore Only	Full-System	Power Modeling	Sequential Simulation	Parallel Simulation	Sampling Support	Software Based	FPGA Based	Virtual Machine Based	Fast Forwarding
BigSim [46]		x									
CantorSim [39]		x					x	x			
Chidester [47]		x				x					
COTSon [21]		x	x	McPAT [28]		x	x	x		x	x
FAST [42]		x							x		
FastMP [48]		x									
GEMS [49]		x	x	McPAT [28]						x	
Graphite [50,51]		x		McPAT [28]							
HASim [43]		x							x		
LIBERTY [40]		x									
MPTLsim [52]		x								x	
ProtoFlex [41]		x	x						x		

Continued

Table 2 A List of Features Present in Simulators That May Be Relevant for Simulating a Large System (The List of Features and Simulators Is Nonexhaustive)—cont'd

Simulator Name and Reference	Simulated Features							Simulator Features					
	Single-Core Only	Multicore	User-Level Only	Full-System	Power Modeling	Sequential Simulation	Parallel Simulation	Sampling Support	Software Based	FPGA Based	Virtual Machine Based	Fast Forwarding
RAMP [44]		x		x								
SESC [53]		x	x									
SimFlex [34]		x		x				x			x	
SimpleScalar [54]	x		x			x			x			
SimNow [22]		x		x								
Simics [55]		x		x							x	
SimOS [56]		x		x								
SlackSim [57]	x					x			x			
Trace Factory [58]		x		x								
UNISIM [38]		x	x						x			
WWT [59]		x										

Based on whether the OS behavior is included or not, there are *user-level simulators* and *full-system simulators*. SimpleScalar is also an example of a user-level simulator. SimOS [56], Simics [55], GEMS [49], SimNow [22], and COTSon [21] are examples of full-system simulators.

According to whether the simulator can execute in parallel or not, we have *parallel simulators* and *sequential simulators*. Sequential simulators are quite accurate [53,60] but as the complexity of the simulated platform increases, the simulation time becomes unreasonably long. Parallel simulation [21,59,61–63] requires multiple processing cores to increase the simulation rate. Nowadays, power consumption, vulnerability, and thermal dissipation of processors are becoming more and more important. Therefore, besides focusing on performance, attempts were made to develop simulators capable of modeling these latter characteristics as well. Some simulators combine several of the above aspects. For example, McPAT is a power simulator for multicore processors developed at HP Labs. It can also be used to model both power and performance [28]. In TERAFLUX, we use the McPAT tool to estimate power consumption.

There are many multicore simulators developed over the past few decades. The typical examples are: BigSim [46], the simulator developed by Chidester and George [47], COTSon [21], FastMP [48], GEMS [49], Graphite [50,51], LIBERTY [40], MPTLsim [52], SimFlex [34], SlackSim [57], Trace Factory [58], and Wisconsin wind tunnel (WWT) [59,64].

SimFlex and GEMS both use an off-the-shelf sequential emulator (Intel's Simics) for functional modeling plus their own models for memory systems and core interactions. GEMS uses the timing-first simulation approach: their timing model drives Simics one instruction at a time which results in much lower performance than COTSon. SimFlex uses statistical sampling of the application to speed up the simulation but therefore does not observe its entire behavior.

MPTLsim is a cycle-accurate, full-system x86 and x86-64 multicore simulator. MPTLsim uses the hardware abstraction provided by the Xen hypervisor [65] to fast-forward execution and reach a given point in time where simulation can start. MPTLsim provides a significant faster simulation rate compared to GEMS. MPTLsim makes use of a cycle-accurate out-of-order core design implementing the x86-64 ISA, but the fast-forwarding using Xen is completely opaque to the simulator, and during the Xen execution nothing can be inferred about memory, instructions, or I/O.

However, among the aforementioned multicore simulators, only COTSon and Graphite are targeting 1000 cores. Graphite is a simulator under development at MIT and is based on the PIN binary instrumentation package, i.e., a functional-first (trace-driven) simulator (cf. Table 1). We evaluated its initial version and found it lacking several usability features for the TERAFLUX context. On the contrary, COTSon is relatively mature and allows simulating complete systems ranging from multicore nodes up to full clusters of multicores with complete network simulation. It is composed of a pluggable architecture, in which most features can be substituted for proprietary development, thus allowing researchers to use it as their simulation platform. For example, COTSon has been used for modeling a 1000-core shared-memory multiprocessor [66] or for the CORONA studies [67].

COTSon [21,66] is a node-level parallel simulator (i.e., several SimNow instances can run in parallel, while each SimNow execution is sequential). COTSon uses AMD's SimNow for functional modeling. The sequential instruction stream coming out of each SimNow functional core is interleaved to account for correct time ordering before timing simulation. Previous to TERAFLUX, COTSon performed multi-(guest-) machine simulations like in a cluster system, e.g., by using applications that are written assuming a distributed memory machine (e.g., using a messaging library like MPI). Moreover, COTSon experiments were used with a slightly different methodology—a hybrid between trace-driven and feedback-driven simulation (a similar technique has been used in Refs. [58,68]). This kind of model did not address specifically an "evolving machine" like TERAFLUX and the full-system functional-directed approach was limited to specific scenarios (e.g., datacenters) rather than a tightly coupled system like TERAFLUX. Therefore the COTSon simulator has been extended in the context of TERAFLUX as explained in the next sections.

Another possibility that we considered is to take advantage of the large parallelism of GPGPUs to emulate a guest core on the host GPU core [69]. Compared to COTSon, this is not yet fully developed (only part of the x86 ISA is emulated), and it is not a full-system simulator (it is only an emulator).

COTSon permits to integrate the architectural elements to enable a dataflow-based execution model on the top of control-flow elements, as explained in Section 1. Further recent research on dataflow-based system can be found in the literature [70–75].

In summary, exploring a future many-core architecture like TER-AFLUX requires the flexibility, simulation speed, and scalability of COTSon.

3. COTSon FRAMEWORK ORGANIZATION

In this section, we provide more detailed information about the COTSon framework. HP Labs' COTSon [21] simulator is a full-system simulation infrastructure, based on AMD's SimNow. It can simulate complete systems ranging from multicore nodes up to full clusters of multicores with complete network simulation. It is composed of a pluggable architecture, in which most features can be substituted by your own developments, thus allowing researchers to use it as their simulation platform.

COTSon uses SimNow [22] to model the functional behavior of one node containing multiple cores (tested up to 32 cores as of version 4.6.2 used in 2015). SimNow is based on dynamic binary translation principles along the lines of what is used in some virtual machine hypervisors (e.g., Oracle's VirtualBox [76], VMware [77], Microsoft Virtual-PC [78]) with additional capabilities for timing simulation, as well as possibilities for external extensions.

More specifically, SimNow is a configurable x86-64 dynamically translating instruction-level platform simulator. However, in COTSon, SimNow is essentially used as a full-system emulator.

In order to flexibly model a variety of architectural features, in the "timing models" (see Fig. 2) we can provide the necessary timing behavior. For example, if we want to test different L1 cache sizes, we can provide a timing model for L1 caches and change cache size in such models. As explained in this example, we disregard the internal timing information of the SimNow. The SimNow then acts as an emulator or ISS (cf. Section 2). A very similar situation happens for other architectural components where we introduced our custom timing models, such as the TSU [9] and the FDU [8].

The interconnection network among the nodes (see Fig. 2) is provided by the "Mediator." HP provided a reference implementation of the network Mediator (also known as "Q Mediator" [79]) that essentially models an Ethernet Switch.

The Mediator provides (simulated) Ethernet functional connectivity among simulators and works with simulations distributed across multiple hosts. It manages the timing models (not shown in Fig. 2, for the sake of

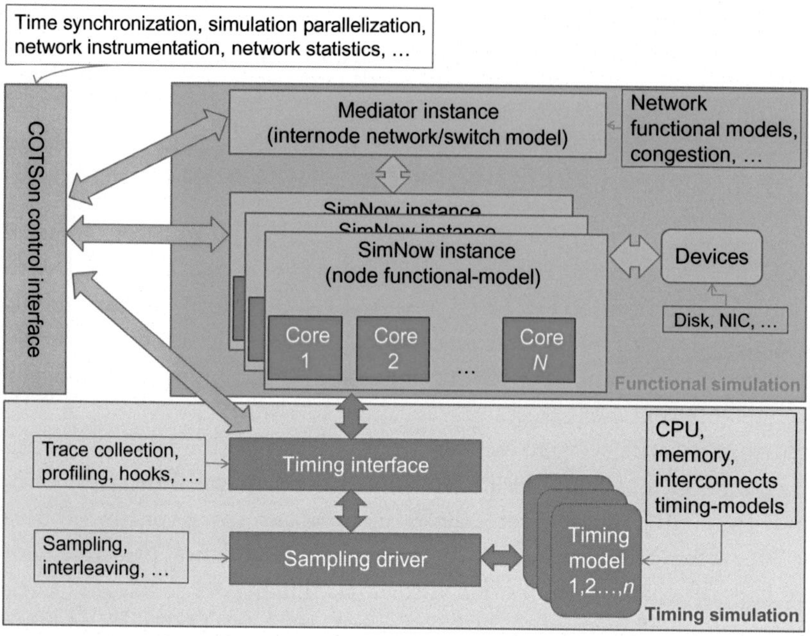

Fig. 2 COTSon overview.

clarity) for a networked group of nodes and is responsible for network modeling (topologies, switches, cards, etc.), queuing up pending network packets and computing the delays due to network congestion.

4. TARGETING A 1000-CORE SIMULATION

Several approaches have been proposed in order to study and research a computing system of the size of 1000 cores [80,81]. There are also chips that currently work with 48–72 cores (Intel SCC [82], Intel Xeon Phi), which could eventually scale to a 1000-core processor [83]. In the market, there are also 1000-core CC-NUMA machines (like the SGI Altix UV). Of course, many supercomputers reach that size: one could "just build" the machine.

The ambition of TERAFLUX is however to be able to *change* such machines in a flexible way, while tackling research challenges on programmability, architectural design, and reliability. Other relevant feature (discussed in Section 2), such as the ability of running full-system, sampled simulation, is also essential. Moreover, in the TERAFLUX evaluation framework, we needed to properly design the basic simulation infrastructure, in order to be able to simulate 1000 cores (cf. Section 5).

In Section 4.1, we extend a comparison initially proposed in the RAMP project [44,45], comparing approaches like using a physical SMP, a physical Cluster, FPGA, Emulator, and Simulator approaches toward 1000-core platforms. In Section 4.2, we briefly discuss evaluations based on physical (not simulated) machines.

4.1 Comparison Among Approaches to Evaluate Novel 1000-Core Architectures

Table 3 reports a comparison between different approaches that allow us to evaluate and experiment with 1000 cores. One additional constraint in TERAFLUX was the ability to target a complex instruction set like the x86-64: we added that feature too in this comparison.

The main drawback of SMP is the high cost of 1000-core machines and the fact that it is not possible to modify the architecture. Another problem is the difficulty of observing results and the inability to reconfigure the hardware to extend the ISA. Building a cluster of computers to get 1 K cores is feasible, but it has similar disadvantages to SMP. A major FPGA disadvantage is the complexity of building these kinds of systems since hardware and software must be set up. Available soft processors such as NIOS II for Altera and microblaze for Xilinx do not support x86-64 ISA. The available platforms are currently restricted to 32 bits.

An emulator (see previous section) has the main problem that it does not provide timing, which draws us to the use of simulators.

The main problem of simulators is their credibility but, as the simulators evolve, their credibility also increases. The simulator performance (i.e., its "speed") is a key point in the success of a given simulator: we currently obtain a 1/10 to 1/1000 slowdown, that we consider very competitive for obtaining the same level of accuracy, same scalability, and same simulation speed; more importantly is that COTSon made feasible the type of design exploration that we needed for a future many-core, dataflow execution-based computing system.

4.2 Notes on the Evaluations Based on Physical Machines

The use of real platforms has several limitations, as it is not always possible to get the "perfect" setup. There are several reasons for that. Sometimes, the programming model cannot be changed, sometimes the machine cannot

Table 3 Comparison Among Different Approaches for Doing Research Related to 1000-Core Computing System

	SMP	Cluster	FPGA	Emulator	Simulator
Scalability (1 K cores)	C	A	A	A	A
Cost (1 K cores)	F(€40 M)	C	B(€0.1–0.2 M)	A+ (€0.01 M)	A+ (€0.01 M)
Power/space (kw, racks)	D (120 kw, 12 racks)	D (120 kw, 12 racks)	A (1.5 kw, 0.3 racks)	A+ (0.1 kw, 0.1 racks)	A+ (0.1 kw, 0.1 racks)
Observability	D	C	A+	A+	A+
Reproducibility	B	D	A+	A+	A+
Reconfigurability	D	C	A+	A+	A+
Credibility	A+	A+	B+/A−	F/D	C
Development time	B	B	C	A+	A+
Performance (clock)	A (2 GHz)	A (3 GHz)	C (0.1 GHz)	B (≈0.9 of original)	C (1/10–1/1000 SMP)
x86-64 ISA	A+	A+	F	A+	A+
Modifiable	F	F	B	A	A
GPA	D	D	B+/A−	B	A

GPA (grade point average: $A = 5$ points, $B = 4$ points, $C = 3$ points, $D = 2$ points, $E = 1$ points, $F = 0$ points).
Information Revised From Data of the RAMP Project.

be changed, and sometimes we do not have all the necessary flexibility. Here we consider some of the options: BSC's MareNostrum-2 as representative of message passing machines and the SGI Altix UV as representative of shared-memory machines. Smaller scale experiments have been also performed on an in-house 48-cores shared-memory system.

MareNostrum-2 is based on the 2560 Blade JS21, each with two dual-core IBM 64 bits PowerPC 970MP, 2.3 GHz with 10,240 Cores, $R_{max} = 63.83$ (number identifying the maximum LINPACK performance), $R_{peak} = 94.21$ TeraFLOPS (peak performance) [84].

The Altix UV has more than 1 K cores and 16 TB of memory. Altix UV scales up to 2048 cores (256 sockets). It supports up to 16 TB of global shared memory through a single system image OS (cf. Section 5.4), i.e., relies on a Distributed Operating System.

A smaller shared-memory machine that we used is a 48-cores (AMD x86-64) on a single board and 256 GB of shared memory (NUMA single Board Symmetric Multiprocessor) named here "TFX2." This machine has four processors (sockets) and each processor has 12 cores (Opteron 6168 1.9 GHz with 512 KB L2 cache). It also has 32 quad-channel slots supporting up to 512 GB of DDR3-1333 registered ECC.

5. HOW TO SIMULATE 1000 CORES

In order to address the challenges of a 1000-core system, we should be able to simulate a platform encompassing:

1. A full-system (including OS and devices);
2. The use of "efficient applications" able to load the system and stress its limits;
3. State-of-the-art scaling (about 1000 cores or 1 K cores) as many work are addressing (see, for example, Refs. [44,45,50,66,69,80,81]).

In order to explain the motivations for the choices we are currently exploring, we briefly analyze here the options that permit a 1000-core simulation, highlighting their advantages and disadvantages. We actually set up and tested them when it was necessary or useful for advancing the mainline experiments on the COTSon framework. We think it is useful also to recall them in order to underline the reasoning behind our choices on the COTSon framework.

In the following, it is important to note that our aim is to be able to choose the Programming Model and the Architecture flexibly. Of course, for reference reasons, the initial setup takes the existing available Programming Models and Architectures, but we note this exploration allows us to evolve this machine toward the TERAFLUX dataflow models [85]. Therefore the simulation environment must also reflect this flexibility. In Table 4, we summarize the main features of six testbeds that are analyzed and discussed in detail in the next sections.

Table 4 Summary of the Desired Features for a Flexible 1000-Core Modeling That Have Been Considered in Six Different Testbeds (Setup#1, ..., Setup #6 in the Following)

Desired Features for a Flexible 1000-Core Modeling	SETUP ID and Availability of the Features					
	1	2	3	4	5	6
Runs both on a real machine and on COTSon	Yes	Yes	Yes	Yes	Yes	Yes
Rapid test for parallel applications	Yes	Yes	Yes	Yes	Yes	Yes
Provides reference results	Yes	Yes	Yes	Yes	Yes	Yes
Simulation parallelization	n/a	Yes	Yes	Yes	Yes	Yes
Avoiding to copy buffers across nodes during simulation	No	No	Yes	Yes	Yes	Yes
Uses the RVI/VT-x virtualization extensions across nodes	No	No	Yes	Yes	Yes	Yes
Avoids to mix simulated and simulation traffic on the interconnection network	n/a	No	Yes	Yes	Yes	Yes
Runtime not necessary for scheduling tasks	No	No	No	Yes	Yes	Yes
Good performance when scaling the cores and changing the programming model	No	No	No	No	No	Yes
Possibility to modify the machine architecture or microarchitecture	No	Some	Some	Some	Yes	Yes
Possibility for using nondistributed programming models across nodes	No	No	No	Partially	Yes	No
Avoiding to be not bound to the specific machine	No	No	No	No	Yes	No
Avoiding a custom OS	Yes	Yes	Yes	No	Yes	Yes
Customization via OS drivers	No	No	No	No	Yes	No
Timing modeling	No	Yes	Yes	Yes	Yes	No
Can reach the simulation of 1000 cores	Yes	Yes	Yes	Yes	Yes	No

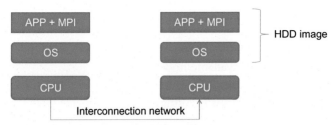

Fig. 3 Two Physical Machines running MPI applications.

5.1 Setup #1: Physical Machines, MPI Programming Model

This setup is mainly useful for reference. The ith Physical Machine is a node including C_i cores. For the sake of simplicity, we can assume a fixed number of cores per node, say C_N.

The simplest solution to scale to 1 K cores is to connect N nodes with C_N cores so that $N \times C_N$ equals 1000. We represent this situation in Fig. 3 (for simplicity we represent the case of just two nodes). The simplest off-the-shelf network can be Ethernet based.

Each computer runs a lightweight Operating System (e.g., Linux with MPI libraries).

On top of each OS runs a set of applications compatible with MPI libraries. These applications with MPI allow load balancing of computations among the different CPUs, at the expense of software overhead.

In this setup, we can also extract "HDD images" (hard-disk drive images) and then run those images as a virtual disk of a virtual machine (see next sections):

Advantages

- This setup can run both on real machines (at least on a small scale for tests) and on the COTSon simulator.
- It is a rapid configuration to test parallel applications in a first instance.
- It provides some reference number for execution times of the running applications or other characterizations of the applications.

Disadvantages

- It is not possible to modify the architecture of the machine.
- Taking into account that we aim to flexibly change the programming model and architecture toward a dataflow-based execution model and architecture, this setup may end up in poor performance when N (number of nodes) increases.
- It binds the application to the machine, which is exactly the opposite of what we want, as we aim to decouple the applications from the machine

with appropriate Programming Models, Compilation Tools, and Execution Models.

- The runtime is constantly involved to appropriately schedule the ready tasks/threads on the available nodes.
- The physical architecture that is more natural to model is a Distributed Machine, which may not fit a single-chip design.

5.2 Setup #2: Virtual Machines Running on Several Physical Machines, MPI Programming Model

This setup is also provided for reference. For simplicity, we assume that each Physical Machine is running exactly one virtual machine (each Physical Machine could run several virtual machines in a general case).

Here, instead of running the set of applications on top of a Physical Machine, we use virtual machines such as the one provided by SimNow. In particular, one important advantage is that we can use most of the off-the-shelf behavior of the VM, while we can add the additional instructions (ISA extensions) that we identified [6].

In Fig. 4, we show an example of this setup. We also highlight that, instead of having a single (host) OS, in this case the virtual machine runs its own (guest) OS with a separate address space. The VM on a given host runs on top of the Host OS that manages this host.

In particular, in this case there are two levels of address spaces (the guest one and the host one). More recent x86-based computers have ways to map more efficiently guest to host address spaces (AMD RVI, Intel VT-x [86–88]). To simulate 1 K cores we can use, e.g., N Physical Hosts, each one with C_N cores, such that $N \times C_N = 1000$.

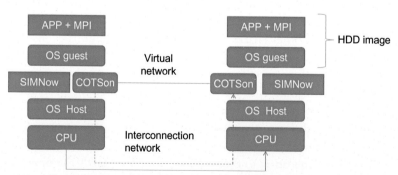

Fig. 4 Two Physical Machines each one running a virtual machine.

Advantages

- This setup can run both on real machines (at least on a small scale for tests) and on the COTSon simulator.
- It allows us to modify system parameters like the number of cores in each simulated instance.
- It allows for a parallelization of the simulation (the several instances are running in parallel on completely independent hosts).

Disadvantages

- Taking into account that we aim to flexibly change the programming model and architecture (e.g., the dataflow-based execution model and architecture proposed in Ref. [85]), this setup may end up in poor performance when N (number of nodes) increases.
- It binds the application to the machine, which is exactly the opposite of what we want, as we aim to decouple the applications from the machine with appropriate Programming Models, Compilation Tools, and Execution Models.
- The MPI runtime is constantly involved to appropriately schedule the ready tasks/threads on the available nodes.
- The communication and synchronization among the simulation instances adds up to the Application traffic on the Physical Interconnection Network, thus slowing down the simulation.
- The guest address space in one node can only pass information to the guest address space on another node through the Physical Interconnection Network (operations for the support of the Memory Model may considerably slow down the simulation due to the copying of data buffers).
- We cannot take advantage of RVI/VT-x virtualization mechanisms across different Physical Machines.

5.3 Setup #3: Virtual Machines Running on a Single Physical Computer, MPI Programming Model

This setup has been used during the first year of experiments in order to develop a framework for baseline comparisons.

In this setup, we use just one host machine. The machine essentially provides shared memory and a number of cores (e.g., a CC-NUMA with 48 cores and 256 GB of memory as explained in Section 4.2 and in the experiment of next sections). The interconnection network is completely provided by the COTSon Mediator. This is shown in Fig. 5.

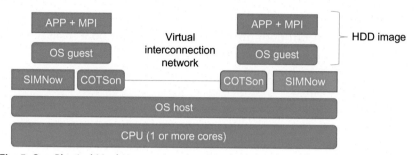

Fig. 5 One Physical Machine running two virtual machine instances that communicate through the virtual network (mediator).

To simulate 1 K cores, we can use, e.g., N COTSon (or better SimNow) instances, each one with C_N cores, such that $N \times C_N = 1000$.

Advantages

- This setup can run both on real machines (at least on a small scale for tests) and on the COTSon simulator.
- It allows us to modify system parameters like the number of cores in each simulated instance.
- It allows for a parallelization of the simulation (the several instances are running in parallel on the available cores—load balancing automatically provided by the Host OS scheduler).
- It is possible to avoid copying buffers among instances because they reside in the Host Shared Memory Network (operations for the support of the Memory Model may take advantage of this).
- It is possible to take advantage of RVI/VT-x virtualization mechanisms across different Physical Machines (under development).
- The communication and synchronization among the simulation instances adds up to the Application traffic, but could bypass TCP/IP and avoid using the Physical Interconnection Network.
- No need to use the Physical Network.

Disadvantages

- Taking into account that we aim to flexibly change the programming model and architecture (e.g., a dataflow-based execution model and architecture), this setup may end up in poor performance when N (number of nodes) increases.
- Tightens the applications to the Machine, which is exactly the opposite of what we want as we aim to decouple the applications from the

machine with appropriate Programming Models, Compilation Tools, and Execution Models.

- The MPI runtime is constantly involved to appropriately schedule the ready tasks/threads on the available nodes.
- The physical architecture that is more natural to model is a Distributed Machine not like the general one we aim in TERAFLUX.

5.4 Setup #4: Virtual Machines Running on a Single Physical Computer, Flexible Programming Model on Top of a Distributed Machine Guest

In this setup, we use a Single System Image OS to achieve the illusion of a shared-memory system on top of the simulated cluster as provided by COTSon. The situation is shown in Fig. 6.

Advantages

- It allows us to run shared memory applications like OpenMP ones (can still run MPI as if it was a single big node).
- It can run both on real machines (at least on a small scale for tests) and on the COTSon simulator.
- It allows us to modify system parameters like the number of cores in each simulated instance.
- It allows for a parallelization of the simulation (the several instances are running in parallel on the available cores—load balancing automatically provided by the Host OS scheduler).
- It is possible to avoid copying buffers among instances because they reside in the Host Shared Memory Network.
- It is possible to take advantage of RVI/VT-x virtualization mechanisms across different Physical Machines (under development).

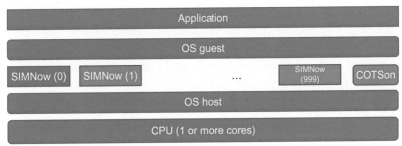

Fig. 6 VM instances governed by a single source image (SSI) OS.

- The communication and synchronization among the simulation instances adds up to the Application traffic, but could bypass TCP/IP and avoid using the Physical Interconnection Network.
- Load balancing for the Application is managed by the Guest OS.
- No need to use the Physical Network.

Disadvantages

- This setup requires the use of a Distributed OS as Guest OS (e.g., Kerrighed [89], which offers the view of a unique SMP machine on top of a cluster) or in general an SSI (single system image) OS.
- Has relatively poor performance when N (number of nodes) increases.
- Partially tightens the Application to the Machine, which is in the opposite of what we want as we aim to decouple the applications from the machine with appropriate Programming Models, Compilation Tools, and Execution Models.
- The underlying Guest Architecture is a "cluster," which is then more naturally mapped to a physical Distributed Machine not a generic one like we aim for in TERAFLUX.

5.5 Setup #5: Virtual Machines Running on a Single Physical Computer, Flexible Programming Model on Top of a Shared-Memory Guest

This setup resembles the previous one but now we use a "standard" OS (like Linux). However, we need to perform a trick in the OS so that this main OS, which acts as "Master Node," is aware of all N of the VM instances (i.e., of the all SimNow instances). The Guest therefore appears like a single node with as many cores as $N \times C_N$ (C_N is the number of cores provided by each VM). The "Slave" nodes just provide the cores in the same fashion as the Master Cores provides its ones. It is the Guest OS that provides the illusion of a large shared memory guest machine to the Applications. The master core (0) is aware of the precise memory map (Fig. 7).

We add a special module to the SimNow environment that maps a shared-memory block allocated on the host. This module presents itself to the guest OS as a physical device (e.g., PCIbar), and the shared block is seen by the guest OS as memory inside that device. This memory can then be *mapped* into the virtual address space of guest processes using a special device driver in the guest OS (Fig. 8).

Advantages

- It allows us to run shared memory applications like OpenMP ones (can still run MPI as if it was a single big node).

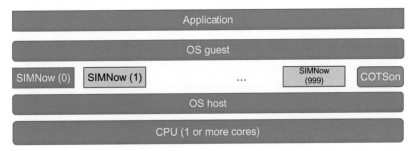

Fig. 7 One core aware of all the other cores.

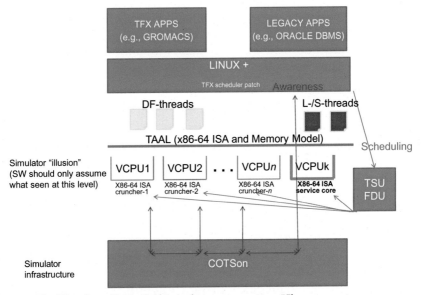

Fig. 8 The "Simulator Illusion" (this is the same as setup #5).

- It can run both on real machines (at least on a small scale for tests) *and* on the COTSon simulator.
- It allows us to modify system parameters like the number of cores in each simulated instance.
- It allows for a parallelization of the simulation (the several instances are running in parallel on the available cores—load balancing automatically provided by the Host OS scheduler).
- It is possible to avoid copying buffers among instances because they reside in the Host Shared Memory Network.
- It is possible to take advantage of RVI/VT-x virtualization mechanisms across different Physical Machines (under development).

- The communication and synchronization among the simulation instances adds up to the Application traffic, but could bypass TCP/IP and avoid using the Physical Interconnection Network.
- Load balancing for the Application is managed by the Guest OS.
- No need to use the Physical Network.
- No need to use a very different OS like an SSI OS.
- The underlying Guest Architecture is a shared memory machine; however thanks to the availability of a global address space, there is now the full possibility of evolving the machine into a more "general one" as we aim to for TERAFLUX. The TERAFLUX Execution Model can completely decouple the architecture of the machine.

Disadvantages

- Has relatively poor performance when N (number of nodes) increases.
- Requires some patches to the Linux OS; however, we shall need to patch the Memory Manager and the Scheduler anyway in order to properly support the TERAFLUX DF-threads (DF + L + S) [90].

5.6 Setup #6: Single Virtual Machine Running on a Single Physical Computer, Flexible Programming Model on Top of a Shared-Memory Guest

As clearly shown in Fig. 9, in this setup we substitute the many instances of several virtual machines (SimNow or QEMU ones) with a single instance of a virtual machine (COREMU [31]).

COREMU [31] is a scalable and portable full-system emulator built on QEMU. Currently, COREMU supports x86-64 and ARM (Cortex A9) target on an x64_86 Linux host system. COREMU is able to boot 255

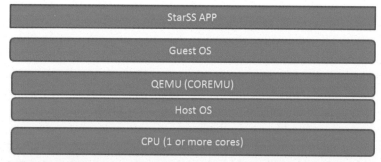

Fig. 9 One host CPU runs a VM with, e.g., 255 cores (COREMU), emulating shared memory communication.

emulated cores running Linux on one testing machine which has only, e.g., four physical cores with 2 GB of physical memory.

Similar to the use of QEMU, in order to provide the timing models we need to patch this software in order to provide an interface to the COTSon. COTSon will provide the "timing feedback" as explained in Section 1.

Currently, there is a limitation of 255 QEMU instances. There are some approximations that allow connecting several QEMU instances via PCI [91].

Advantages

- It allows us to run shared memory applications like Open MP ones (can still run MPI as if it was a single big node).
- Parallelization is performed by several tricks inside the COREMU (they are in the form of patched to QEMU).
- It has relatively acceptable performance when C_N (number of nodes) increases.
- It allows us to modify system parameters like number of cores in each simulated instance.
- It is possible to avoid copying buffers among instances because they reside in the Host Shared Memory Network.
- It is possible to take advantage of RVI/VT-x virtualization mechanisms across different Physical Machines (under development).
- The communication and synchronization among the simulation instances adds up to the Application traffic, but could bypass TCP/IP and avoid using the Physical Interconnection Network.
- Load balancing for the Application is managed by the Guest OS.
- No need to use the Physical Network.
- No need to use a very different OS like an SSI OS.
- The underlying Guest Architecture is a shared memory machine; however thanks to the availability of a global address space, there is now the full possibility of evolving the machine into a more "general one" as we aim to for TERAFLUX. The TERAFLUX Dataflow Execution Model [90] can completely decouple the architecture of the machine.

Disadvantages

- Requires modification of the COTSon in order to interface it with the COREMU (this work however is quite similar to the one necessary to interface with QEMU).
- We do not know if we are able to overcome the current limit of 255 cores that are emulated by COREMU.

• We are completely missing the timing interface as provided by COTSon (unless the modifications pointed out above are implemented).

6. THE SEARCH FOR "EFFICIENT BENCHMARKS"

Another core problem in order to evaluate correctly the performance of a large system like TERAFLUX is to be able to properly load all the cores of the machine. In order to do that also an appropriate choice of benchmarks is crucial.

In this section, we briefly explain through an example the methodology to choose applications/benchmarks at the scale of 1000 cores: we call this "efficient benchmarks" since they should have the following requirements: (i) do not present "algorithmic bottlenecks" when scaling to 1000 or more cores; (ii) reasonably load interconnects and memory (without an "exponential explosion" of their data set). This is very important to adequately avoid leaving idle most of the 1000 cores. In other terms, one of the concerns was to properly select benchmarks and input sets that effectively need the computational power of 1000 cores.

One more important observation is that the TERAFLUX evaluation framework is aimed at supporting any programming model, not a specific one. However, in order to avoid purely sequential benchmarks, we mainly supported the OmpSs programming model [85,92,93]. OmpSs has the good potential for the TERAFLUX architecture also because it allows at runtime a "Superscalar-like" execution, which favors dataflow among threads.

A first step in order to detect if there are "algorithmic bottlenecks" is to analyze an application using tools like "cilkscreen" and "cilkview" to detect the *parallelism* of the application [94,95]. While we are not necessarily interested in supporting Cilk, it is important to observe that Cilk permits the identification of the parallelism available in a given algorithm by analyzing fundamental quantities like the *work* and the *span*. Frigo *et al.* defined the *parallelism* as the ratio between "work" and "span." The "work" is the total time needed to execute sequentially all threads in the Control-Data Flow Graph that represents the application. The span is the execution time of the computation on an infinite number of processors [96]. This gives us an upper bound on the available Thread Parallelism in the application: if there is not enough parallelism in the application, it is not worth adding more cores to the machine.

As an example, we consider here the dense matrix multiplication benchmark: in Fig. 10 we show the parallelism of this benchmark. This

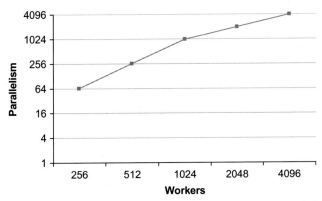

Fig. 10 The parallelism detected in a simple matrix multiply benchmark for different matrix sizes.

information tells us that in order to have an efficient benchmark for 1000 cores, we must also consider an input data set consisting in matrices of a size above 1024. Smaller sizes cannot reach the desired scalability level of 1024 as their parallelism is limited.

The same methodology can be repeated on other benchmarks. This methodology was used successfully in our more recent experiments [9,90].

7. SIMULATION EXPERIMENTS

The COTSon simulator accuracy and its limited slowdown compared to other simulator have been already discussed in the previous work [21,66,79,97,98]. In the TERAFLUX evaluation framework, COTSon has been extended to support the simulation of future many-core systems based on dataflow execution [6,90].

In this section, we illustrate the capabilities of the TERAFLUX evaluation framework to properly simulate a future many-core system based on the setup #5 (see Section 5.5 for multiple virtual machine running on a single host; the master guest has the illusion of a single shared-memory address space), which provide more advantages compared to the other five simulation setups that we considered.

The selected host is the "TFX2" machine described in Section 4.2. This machine has 48 cores and 256 GB of memory: the availability of a large amount of memory is very important to scale up the core count of the simulated machine, i.e., to reach the 1000-core target as the simulation framework is approximately using 6–10 GB per simulated node (depending on the installed main memory per node and the number of cores per node).

In the following, three basic experiments to verify the functionality of the TERAFLUX simulation framework are presented: (i) a single full-system node with up to 32 cores; (ii) two nodes that can communicate through the simulated switch via standard Ethernet; and (iii) the 1024 setup that is the basis for the 1024-core evaluation (32 nodes with 32 cores each).

7.1 TERAFLUX Basic Node With up to 32 Cores

In the TERAFLUX project, we were experimenting nodes with up to 32 cores. This is not a limitation of a general TERAFLUX system, not a limitation of the AMD SimNow virtualizer, and not a limitation of the COTSon simulator: this limit is essentially due to the availability of an appropriate firmware to boot the machine. Currently available general-purpose CPUs (as of September 2015) like the Intel Xeon E7-8890v3 have 18 cores: the availability of 32 cores in a full-system virtual machine is currently above the state of the art.

In Fig. 11, we show the SimNow overview of a system with 32 cores.

The guest screen appears as shown in Fig. 12; in this case we show the Linux console and we issued the command "cat /proc/cpuinfo | grep processor | tail -22" in order to verify that all the 32 cores are visible to the operating system. In this case, we used one of the available SimNow CPU models called "AweSim processor," which models an x86_64 processor. However, the methodology already illustrated in the previous sections disregards the SimNow timing characteristics of this processor: the timing model is totally rebuilt in the COTSon environment (functional-directed approach [21]).

7.2 TERAFLUX Basic Communication Case With Two Nodes

The second experiment that we show is related to making sure that two nodes as described in Section 7.1 can communicate across a simulated Ethernet connection. The simplest program that we can run is a ping–pong test from the guest consoles: this is shown in Fig. 13. In this figure, we show the host machine in the background, while two SimNow guests are launched under the COTSon control: each guest gets its own graphical connection and the Linux console launches can launch a given script (in this case the classical "ping" utility). This setup corresponds to what described in the setup #3 in Section 5.3. This setup can be used for diagnostic purposes.

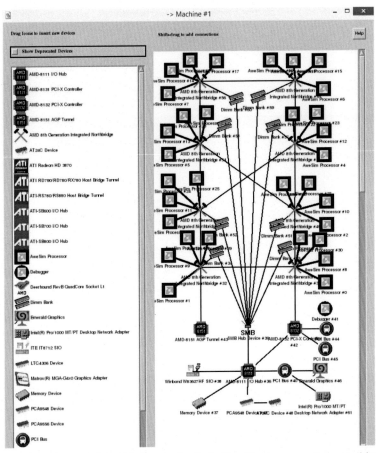

Fig. 11 Construction of the 32-core node. Each "AweSim processor" square block in the figure represents a core. The user can plug-in any appropriate component like in a real PC.

7.3 TERAFLUX 1024-Core Machine (32 Nodes by 32 Cores)

This experiment shows the possibility of effectively simulating the 1024-core system envisioned in the TERAFLUX project. The researcher starts from this basis to change anything in the machine, like the dataflow execution support [6,85,99] or double execution to provide core or node redundancy [7,8]. Each node is running a full-system Linux operating system.

There are other combinations that could have been feasible, e.g., 16-cores by 64 nodes; however, we selected this case for the reduced virtual machine footprint. In Fig. 14 we show the process statistics of the simulation

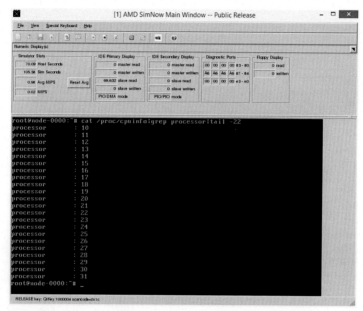

Fig. 12 Construction of the 32-core node. Each "AweSim processor" *square block* in the figure represents a core. The user can plug-in any appropriate component like in a real PC.

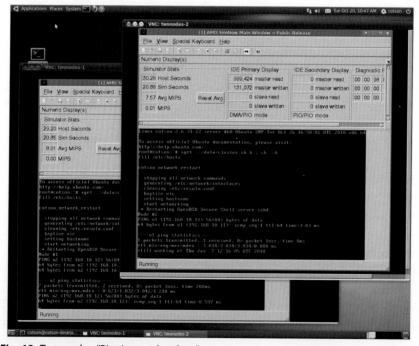

Fig. 13 Two nodes "Pinging each other."

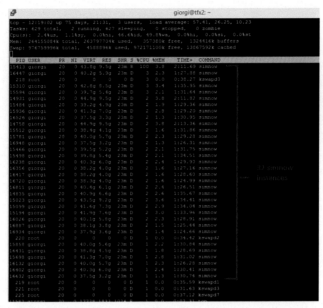

Fig. 14 Snapshot of the simulation running 1024 cores: the output of the "top" command shows the statistics of most active process. As we can see, 32 instances of the AMD SimNow virtualizer are active on the machine and the used memory exceeds 256 GB (third line of the screen) including the swapped memory (fourth line of the screen).

host "TFX2," while it is running the 32 nodes by 32-core simulation. As we can see, that machine is fully loaded and all physical host memory is used by the simulation (256 GB). This demonstrates that the simulation setup #5 can run on the host machine. The simulation slowdown that we observed is about 10 times: in fact, the guests are simulating instructions at about 100 k instruction per second. Also note, from Fig. 14 the ability of COTSon to parallelize the simulation at node level.

In later experiments, we installed a more powerful host in order to be able to manage more easily a simulation with so many cores. The selected machine is a HP Proliant G7 565 with 1024 GB of main memory and 64 Opteron cores organized as a CC-NUMA system (each socket has a CPU with 16 cores). In such case, the largest configuration that we were able to simulate was exceeding 220 nodes for a total of more than 7000 cores. Each node contained 32 cores and it was running an off-the-shelf Linux operating system.

8. CONCLUSIONS

We successfully demonstrated the feasibility of performing cycle-level full-system simulations of a 1024-core future many-core system that supports a dataflow execution model.

The current TERAFLUX evaluation framework allows us to perform the design space exploration considering for example interesting research directions toward a 3D stacked chip/package consisting of, e.g., 1024 cores.

In particular, this environment makes it possible to explore a different execution model based on dataflow at thread level by providing TSUs that are integrated with existing processors.

ACKNOWLEDGMENTS

The author would like to thank Jem Macy and Nenad Koroljia for their useful discussions and Paolo Faraboschi and Zhibin Yu for their insightful comments. This work is partly funded by the European Commission under the projects TERAFLUX (ID 249059), HiPEAC (ID 687698), and AXIOM (ID 645496).

REFERENCES

[1] S. Wesner, L. Schubert, R.M. Badia, A. Rubio, P. Paolucci, R. Giorgi, Special section on terascale computing, Future Gener. Comput. Syst. 53 (C) (2015) 88–89.

[2] M.D. Hill, M.R. Marty, Amdahl's law in the multicore era, Computer 41 (7) (2008) 33–38.

[3] M. Suleman, et al., ACMP: balancing hardware efficiency and programmer efficiency: Technical report, HPS, 2007.

[4] M.A. Suleman, O. Mutlu, M.K. Qureshi, Y.N. Patt, Accelerating critical section execution with asymmetric multi-core architectures, in: Proceedings of the 14th International Conference on Architectural Support for Programming Languages and Operating Systems (ASPLOS XIV), ACM, New York, USA, 2009, pp. 253–264.

[5] B.D. de Dinechin, R. Ayrignac, P.-E. Beaucamps, P. Couvert, B. Ganne, P.G. de Massas, F. Jacquet, S. Jones, N.M. Chaisemartin, F. Riss, T. Strudel, A clustered many-core processor architecture for embedded and accelerated applications, in: High Performance Extreme Computing Conference (HPEC), 2013, 10–12 September, IEEE, Waltham, MA, 2013, pp. 1–6.

[6] R. Giorgi, TERAFLUX: exploiting dataflow parallelism in teradevices, in: ACM Computing Frontiers, 2012, pp. 303–304.

[7] S. Weis, A. Garbade, J. Wolf, B. Fechner, A. Mendelson, R. Giorgi, T. Ungerer, A fault detection and recovery architecture for a Teradevice dataflow system, in: Proceedings of the IEEE International Workshop on Data-Flow Execution Models for Extreme Scale Computing (DFM), 2011, pp. 38–44.

[8] S. Weis, A. Garbade, B. Fechner, A. Mendelson, R. Giorgi, T. Ungerer, Architectural support for fault tolerance in a teradevice dataflow system, Int. J. Parallel Prog. 44 (2) (2016) 208–232.

[9] R. Giorgi, A. Scionti, A scalable thread scheduling co-processor based on data-flow principles, Future Gener. Comput. Syst. 53 (2015) 100–108.

[10] N. Ho, A. Portero, M. Solinas, A. Scionti, A. Mondelli, P. Faraboschi, R. Giorgi, Simulating a multi-core x86 64 architecture with hardware ISA extension supporting a dataflow execution model, in: IEEE Proceedings of the AIMS-2014, Madrid, Spain, 2014, pp. 264–269.

[11] K.M. Kavi, B. Lee, A.R. Hurson, Multithreaded systems, in: M.V. Zelkowitz (Ed.), Advances in Computers, vol. 46, Academic Press, 1998, pp. 287–328.

[12] K. Kavi, R. Giorgi, J. Arul, Scheduled dataflow: execution paradigm, architecture, and performance evaluation, IEEE Trans. Comput. 50 (8) (2001) 834–846.

[13] A. Mondelli, N. Ho, A. Scionti, M. Solinas, A. Portero, R. Giorgi, Dataflow support in x86 64 multicore architectures through small hardware extensions, in: IEEE Proceedings of DSD, 2015, pp. 526–529.

[14] B. Fechner, G. Gao, A. Garbade, S. Girbal, D. Goodman, B. Khan, S. Kolia, F. Li, M. Lujan, A. Mendelson, L. Morin, N. Navarro, A. Pop, P. Trancoso, T. Ungerer, M. Valero, S. Weis, S. Zuckerman, R. Giorgi, The TERAFLUX project: exploiting the dataflow paradigm in next generation teradevices, in: IEEE Proceedings of the 16th EUROMICRO-DSD, Santander, Spain, 2013, pp. 272–279.

[15] Kyriacou, et al., Data-driven multithreading using conventional microprocessors, IEEE Trans. Parallel Distrib. Syst. 1045-9219, 17 (10) (2006) 1176–1188.

[16] L. Verdoscia, R. Vaccaro, R. Giorgi, A clockless computing system based on the static dataflow paradigm, in: Proceedings of the IEEE International Workshop on Data-Flow Execution Models for Extreme Scale Computing (DFM-2014), Edmonton, Canada, 2014, pp. 30–37.

[17] L. Verdoscia, R. Vaccaro, R. Giorgi, A matrix multiplier case study for an evaluation of a configurable dataflow-machine, in: ACM CF'15—LP-EMS, 2015, pp. 1–6.

[18] R. Giorgi, Accelerating haskell on a dataflow architecture: a case study including transactional memory, in: Proceedings of the International Conference on Computer Engineering and Applications (CEA), Dubai, UAE, February, 2015, pp. 91–100.

[19] R. Giorgi, Transactional memory on a dataflow architecture for accelerating haskell, WSEAS Trans. Comput. 14 (2015) 794–805.

[20] M. Herlihy, J.E.B. Moss, Transactional memory: architectural support for lock-free data structures, in: Proceedings of the 20th Annual International Symposium on Computer Architecture, ser. ISCA'93, ACM, New York, NY, 1993, pp. 289–300.

[21] E. Argollo, et al., COTSon infrastructure for full system simulation, Oper. Syst. Rev. 43 (2009) 52–61.

[22] AMD SimNow™ Simulator 4.6.1 User's Manual. Revision 2.13 November 2009. http://developer.amd.com/wordpress/media/2013/02/SimNowUsersManual4.6.2.pdf.

[23] V. Blagojević, et al., A systematic approach to generation of new ideas for PhD research in computing, Adv. Comput. 104 (2017) 1–31.

[24] K. Asanovic, et al., A view of the parallel computing landscape, Commun. ACM 52 (10) (2009) 56–67.

[25] T. Janjusic, K. Kavi, Hardware and application profiling tools—a survey, Adv. Comput. 12 (1) (2014) 105–160. published by Academic Press.

[26] D. Chiou, H. Angepat, N.A. Patil, D. Sunwoo, Accurate functional-first multicore simulators, IEEE Comput. Archit. Lett. 8 (2) (2009) 64–67.

[27] D.E. Knuth, The Art of Computer Programming, third ed., vol. 1, Fundamental Algorithms, Addison Wesley Longman Publishing Co., Inc., Redwood City, CA, USA, 1997, p. 202.

[28] S. Li, J. Ho Ahn, R.D. Strong, J.B. Brockman, D.M. Tullsen, N.P. Jouppi, McPAT: an integrated power, area, and timing modeling framework for multicore and manycore architectures, in: ACM MICRO 41, 2009.

[29] C.J. Mauer, M.D. Hill, D.A. Wood, Full-system timing-first simulation, in: SIGMETRICS'02: Proceedings of the 2002 ACM SIGMETRICS International Conference on Measurement and Modeling of Computer Systems, New York, NY, 2002, pp. 108–116.

[30] F. Bellard, QEMU, a fast and portable dynamic translator, in: ATEC'05: Proceedings of the USENIX Annual Technical Conference 2005 on USENIX Annual Technical Conference, Berkeley, CA, USA, 2005.

[31] Z. Wang, R. Liu, Y. Chen, X. Wu Fudan, H. Chen, W. Zhang, B. Zang, COREMU: a scalable and portable parallel full-system emulator, in: PPoPP'11 Proceedings of the 16th ACM symposium on Principles and Practice of Parallel Programming, 2011.

[32] T.M. Conte, M.A. Hirsch, K.N. Menezes, Reducing state loss for effective trace sampling of superscalar processors, in: Proceedings of International Conference on Computer Design, IEEE Computer Society, Austin, TX, 1996, pp. 468–477.

[33] R.E. Wunderlich, T.F. Wenisch, B. Falsafi, J.C. Hoe, SAMRTS: accelerating microarchitecture simulation via rigorous statistical sampling, in: Proceedings of the 30th Annual International Symposium on Computer Architecture (ISCA'03), IEEE Computer Society, June 9–11, 2003, San Diego, USA, 2003, pp. 84–95.

[34] T.F. Wenisch, R.E. Wunderlich, M. Ferdman, A. Ailamaki, B. Falsafi, J.C. Hoe, SimFlex: statistical sampling of computer system simulation, IEEE Micro 26 (4) (2006) 18–31.

[35] R.E. Wunderlich, T.F. Wenisch, B. Falsafi, J.C. Hoe, An evaluation of stratified sampling of microarchitecture simulations, in: Proceedings of the Third Annual Workshop on Duplicating, Deconstructing, and Debunking, IEEE Computer Society, June 19–23, 2004, München, Germany, 2004, pp. 13–18.

[36] E. Perelman, G. Hamerly, M. Van Biesbrouck, T. Sherwood, B. Calder, Using SimPoint for accurate and efficient simulation, in: Proceedings of the 2003 ACM SIGMETRICS International Conference on Measurement and Modeling of Computer Systems (SIGMETRICS '03), ACM, New York, NY, USA, 2003, pp. 318–319.

[37] Z. Yu, H. Jin, J. Chen, L.K. John, TSS: applying two-stage sampling in microarchitecture simulations, in: Proceedings of IEEE International Symposium on Modeling, Analysis & Simulation of Computer and Telecommunication Systems, 2009 (MASCOTS2009), 2009, pp. 1–9.

[38] http://unisim.org, December 2010.

[39] Z. Yu, H. Jin, J. Chen, L.K. John, CantorSim: simplifying acceleration of microarchitecture simulations, in: Proceedings of the IEEE International Symposium on Modeling, Analysis & Simulation of Computer and Telecommunication Systems, 2010 (MASCOTS2010), 2010, pp. 370–377.

[40] D.A. Penry, D. Fay, D. Hodgdon, R. Wells, G. Schelle, D.I. August, D. Connors, Exploiting parallelism and structure to accelerate the simulation of chip multiprocessors, in: HPCA'06: The Twelfth International Symposium on High-Performance Computer Architecture, 2006, pp. 29–40.

[41] E.S. Chung, M.K. Papamichael, E. Nurvitadhi, J.C. Hoe, K. Mai, B. Falsafi, ProtoFlex: towards scalable, full-system multiprocessor simulations using FPGAs, ACM Trans. Reconfig. Technol. Syst. 2 (2) (2009) 1–32.

[42] D. Chiou, D. Sunwoo, J. Kim, N.A. Patil, W. Reinhart, D.E. Johnson, J. Keefe, H. Angepat, FPGA-accelerated simulation technologies (FAST): fast, full-system, cycle-accurate simulators, in: MICRO'07: Proceedings of the 40th Annual IEEE/ACM International Symposium on Microarchitecture, 2007, pp. 249–261.

[43] N. Dave, M. Pellauer, J. Emer, Implementing a functional/timing partitioned microprocessor simulator with an FPGA, in: 2nd Workshop on Architecture Research Using FPGA Platforms (WARFP 2006), 2006.

[44] G. Gibeling, A. Schultz, K. Asanovic, The RAMP Architecture & Description Language, WARFP, Austin, TX, 2006.

[45] A. Krasnov, A. Schultz, J. Wawrzynek, G. Gibeling, P.-Y. Droz, RAMP blue: a message-passing manycore system in FPGAs, in: Proceedings of the International Conference on Field Programmable Logic and Applications, Amsterdam, The Netherlands, 2007.

[46] G. Zheng, G. Kakulapati, L.V. Kal´e, BigSim: a parallel simulator for performance prediction of extremely large parallel machines, in: 18th International Parallel and Distributed Processing Symposium (IPDPS), 2004, p. 78.

[47] M. Chidester, A. George, Parallel simulation of chip-multiprocessor architectures, ACM Trans. Model. Comput. Simul. 12 (3) (2002) 176–200.

[48] S. Kanaujia, I.E. Papazian, J. Chamberlain, J. Baxter, FastMP: a multi-core simulation methodology, in: MOBS 2006: Workshop on Modeling, Benchmarking and Simulation, 2006.

[49] M.M.K. Martin, D.J. Sorin, B.M. Beckmann, M.R. Marty, M. Xu, A.R. Alameldeen, K.E. Moore, M.D. Hill, D.A. Wood, Multifacet's general execution-driven multiprocessor simulator (GEMS) toolset, SIGARCH Comput. Archit. News 33 (4) (2005) 92–99.

[50] J.E. Miller, H. Kasture, G. Kurian, C. Gruenwald III, N. Beckmann, C. Celio, J. Eastep, A. Agarwal, Graphite: a distributed parallel simulator for multicores, in: HPCA-16, Proceedings of the 16th International Symposium on High-Performance Computer Architecture, 2010.

[51] N. Beckman, et al., Graphite: a distributed parallel simulator for multicores, Computer science and artificial intelligence laboratory technical report, Massachusetts Institute of Technology, 2009. MIT-CSAIL-TR-2009-056.

[52] H. Zeng, M. Yourst, K. Ghose, D. Ponomarev, MPTLsim: a cycle-accurate, full-system simulator for x86-64 multicore architectures with coherent caches, SIGARCH Comput. Archit. News 37 (2) (2009) 2–9. http://doi.acm.org/10.1145/1577129. 1577132.

[53] J. Renau, et al., SESC simulator, 2005. Available online at http://sesc.sourceforge.net.

[54] T. Austin, E. Larson, D. Ernst, SimpleScalar: an infrastructure for computer system modeling, IEEE Comput. 35 (2) (2002) 59–67.

[55] P. Magnusson, M. Christensson, J. Eskilson, D. Forsgren, G. Hallberg, J. Hogberg, F. Larsson, A. Moestedt, B. Werner, Simics: a full system simulation platform, IEEE Comput. 35 (2) (2002) 50–58.

[56] M. Rosenblum, S. Herrod, E. Witchel, A. Gupta, Complete computer system simulation: the SimOS approach, IEEE Parall. Distr. Technol. Syst. Appl. 3 (4) (1995) 34–43. Winter.

[57] J. Chen, M. Annavaram, M. Dubois, SlackSim: a platform for parallel simulations of CMPs on CMPs, SIGARCH Comput. Archit. News 37 (2) (2009) 20–29.

[58] R. Giorgi, C.A. Prete, G. Prina, L. Ricciardi, Trace factory: generating workloads fortrace-driven simulation of shared-bus multiprocessors, IEEE Concurrency, Los Alamitos, CA, USA, vol. 5(4), 1997, pp. 54–68, http://dx.doi.org/10.1109/4434. 641627. ISSN:1092-3063.

[59] S.K. Reinhardt, et al., The Wisconsin wind tunnel: virtual prototyping of parallel computers, in: SIGMETRICS Conference on Measurement and Modeling of Computer Systems, 1993.

[60] N.L. Binkert, R.G. Dreslinski, L.R. Hsu, K.T. Lim, A.G. Saidi, S.K. Reinhardt, The M5 simulator: modeling networked systems, IEEE Micro 26 (4) (2006) 52–60.

[61] S. Das, R. Fujimoto, K. Panesar, D. Allison, M. Hybinette, GTW: a time warp system for shared memory multiprocessors, in: WSC'94: Proceedings of the 26th Conference on Winter Simulation, 1994, pp. 1332–1339.

[62] P.M. Dickens, et al., A distributed memory lapse: parallel simulation of message-passing programs, in: Workshop on Parallel and Distributed Simulation, 1993.

[63] S. Prakash, R.L. Bagrodia, MPI-sim: using parallel simulation to evaluate MPI programs, in: WSC'98, 1998.

[64] S.S. Mukherjee, S.K. Reinhardt, B. Falsafi, M. Litzkow, M.D. Hill, D.A. Wood, S. Huss-Lederman, J.R. Larus, Wisconsin wind tunnel II: a fast, portable parallel architecture simulator, IEEE Concurr. 8 (4) (2000) 12–20.

[65] Xen community overview. https://www.xenproject.org (accessed September 2016).

[66] M. Monchiero, J.H. Ahn, A. Falcon, D. Ortega, P. Faraboschi, How to simulate 1000 cores, SIGARCH Comput. Archit. News 37 (2) (2009) 10–19.

[67] D. Vantrease, R. Schreiber, M. Monchiero, M. McLaren, N.P. Jouppi, M. Fiorentino, A. Davis, N. Binkert, R.G. Beausoleil, J.H. Ahn, Corona: system implications of emerging nanophotonic technology, in: ISCA'08: Proceedings of the 35th International Symposium on Computer Architecture, 2008.

[68] R. Giorgi, C. Prete, PSCR: a coherence protocol for eliminating passive sharing in shared-bus shared-memory multiprocessors, in: IEEE Transactions on Parallel and Distributed Systems, Los Alamitos, CA, USAvol. 10(7), 1999, pp. 742–763.

[69] S. Raghav, M. Ruggiero, D. Atienza, C. Pinto, A. Marongiu, L. Benini, Scalable instruction set simulator for thousand-core architectures running on GPGPUs, in: High Performance Computing and Simulation (HPCS), 2010 International Conference, 2010, pp. 459–466. ISBN:978-1-4244-6827-0.

[70] M.J. Flynn, O. Mencer, V. Milutinovic, G. Rakocevic, P. Stenstrom, R. Trobec, M. Valero, Moving from petaflops to petadata, Commun. ACM 56 (5) (2013) 39–42.

[71] A. Kos, V. Rankovic, S. Tomazic, Sorting networks on Maxeler dataflow super-computing systems, in: Advances in Computers, vol. 96, Elsevier/Academic Press, Amsterdam, 2015, pp. 139–186.

[72] A. Kos, S. Tomazic, J. Salom, N. Trifunovic, M. Valero, V. Milutinovic, New benchmarking methodology and programming model for big data processing, Int. J. Distrib. Sens. Netw. 1550-1477, 2015 (2015) 1–7.

[73] M. Milutinovic, J. Salom, N. Trifunovic, R. Giorgi, Guide to DataFlow Super-computing, Springer, Berlin, DE, 2015, pp. 1–127.

[74] V. Milutinovic (Ed.), Advances in Computers: DataFlow, Elsevier, Cambridge, MA, 2015, (textbook).

[75] P. Evripidou, C. Kyriacou, Data-flow vs control-flow for extreme level computing, Data-Flow Execution Models for Extreme Scale Computing (DFM), 2013, Edinburgh, 2013, pp. 9–13.

[76] http://www.virtualbox.org/, December 2010.

[77] http://www.vmware.com/, December 2010.

[78] http://www.microsoft.com/windows/virtual-pc/, December 2010.

[79] D. Lugones, E. Luque, D. Franco, J.C. Moure, D. Rexach, P. Faraboschi, D. Ortega, G. Giménez, A. Falcón, Initial Studies of Networking Simulation on COTSon, HP Laboratories, 2009. HPL-2009-24, http://www.hpl.hp.com/techreports/2009/HPL-2009-24.html.

[80] J.H. Kelm, D.R. Johnson, M.R. Johnson, N.C. Crago, W. Tuohy, A. Mahesri, S.S. Lumetta, M.I. Frank, S.J. Patel, Rigel: an architecture and scalable programming interface for a 1000-core accelerator, in: Proceedings of the 36th Annual International Symposium on Computer Architecture (ISCA'09), ACM, New York, USA, 2009, pp. 140–151.

[81] D. Sanchez, C. Kozyrakis, ZSim: fast and accurate microarchitectural simulation of thousand-core systems, in: Proceedings of the 40th Annual International Symposium on Computer Architecture (ISCA'13). ACM, New York, NY, USA, 2013, pp. 475–486.

[82] T.G. Mattson, M. Riepen, T. Lehnig, P. Brett, W. Haas, P. Kennedy, J. Howard, S. Vangal, N. Borkar, G. Ruhl, S. Dighe, The 48-core SCC processor: the programmer's view, in: Proceedings of the 2010 ACM/IEEE International Conference for High Performance Computing, Networking, Storage and Analysis (SC '10), IEEE Computer Society, Washington, DC, USA, 2010, pp. 1–11.

[83] T. Mattson, Intel: 1000-Core Processor Possible, PCWorld, 2010 (interview by Joab Jackson).

[84] T. Bunting, W. Kimble, IBM Blade Center JS21 Technical Overview and Introduction, High-Performance Blade Server Ideal for Extremely Dense HPC Clusters, IBM.com/ Redbooks, 2006. http://www.redbooks.ibm.com/abstracts/redp4130.html?Open.

[85] R. Giorgi, R. Badia, F. Bodin, A. Cohen, P. Evripidou, P. Faraboschi, B. Fechner, G. Gao, A. Garbade, R. Gayathri, S. Girbal, D. Goodman, B. Khan, S. Koliaï, J. Landwehr, N. Minh, F. Li, M. Lujàn, A. Mendelson, L. Morin, N. Navarro, T. Patejko, A. Pop, P. Trancoso, T. Ungerer, I. Watson, S. Weis, S. Zuckerman, M. Valero, TERAFLUX: harnessing dataflow in next generation teradevices, Microprocess. Microsyst. 38 (8 Pt B) (2014) 976–990.

[86] AMD White Paper, Virtualizing Server Workloads-Looking Beyond Current Assumptions, 2008. https://www.amd.com/Documents/AMD_WP_Virtualizing_Server_ Workloads-PID.pdf (accessed September 2016).

[87] Intel White Paper, Implementing and Expanding a Virtualized Environment, 2010. http://media10.connectedsocialmedia.com/intel/12/6061/Intel_IT_Best_Practices_ Implementing_Expanding_Virtualized_Environment.pdf (accessed September 2016).

[88] G. Neiger, A. Santoni, F. Leung, D. Rodgers, R. Uhlig, Intel virtualization technology: hardware support for efficient processor virtualization. Intel Technol. J. 10 (3) (2006) 167–178, http://dx.doi.org/10.1535/itj.1003.01. ISSN: 1535–864X.

[89] Website, December 2010. http://www.kerrighed.org/wiki/index.php/Main_Page.

[90] R. Giorgi, P. Faraboschi, An introduction to DF-threads and their execution model, in: IEEE Proceedings of MPP-2014, 2014, pp. 60–65.

[91] M. Gligor, N. Fournel, F. Pétrot, Using Binary Translation in Event Driven Simulation for Fast and Flexible MPSoC Simulation, TIMA, France, 2010.

[92] A. Duran, E. Ayguade, R.M. Badia, J. Labarta, L. Martinell, X. Martorell, J. Planas, OmpSs: a proposal for programming heterogeneous multi-core architectures, Parall. Proc. Lett. 21 (2) (2011) 173–193. http://dx.doi.org/10.1007/978-3-642-37658-0 7.

[93] E. Ayguadé, A. Duran, J. Hoeflinger, F. Massaioli, X. Teruel, An experimental evaluation of the new openMP tasking model, in: Lecture Notes in Computer Science: Proceedings of the 20th International Workshop on Languages and Compilers for Parallel Computing, vol. 5234, Springer, Urbana, IL, USA, 2007, pp. 63–77.

[94] Parallel Studio 2011: Now We Know What Happened to Ct, Cilk++, and RapidMind, Dr. Dobbs Journal (2010-09-02). Retrieved on 2010-09-14.

[95] R.D. Blumofe, C.F. Joerg, B.C. Kuszmaul, C.E. Leiserson, K.H. Randall, Y. Zhou, Cilk: an efficient multithreaded runtime system, in: Proceedings of the Fifth ACM SIGPLAN, 1995.

[96] M. Frigo, C.E. Leiserson, K.H. Randall, The implementation of the Cilk-5 multithreaded language, in: PLDI'98 Proceedings of the ACM SIGPLAN 1998 Conference on Programming Language Design and Implementation, ACM, New York, USA, 1998.

[97] A. Falcon, P. Faraboschi, D. Ortega, Combining simulation and visualization through dynamic sampling, in: ISPASS, 2007, pp. 72–83.

[98] A. Falcon, P. Faraboschi, D. Ortega, An adaptive synchronization technique for parallel simulation of networked clusters, in: Performance Analysis of Systems and Software, 2008. ISPASS 2008. IEEE International Symposium on 20–22 April, 2008, pp. 22–31.

[99] R. Giorgi, Z. Popovic, N. Puzovic, Implementing DTA support in CellSim, in: HiPEAC ACACES-2008, 2008, pp. 159–162. ISBN:978-90-382-1288-3, L'Aquila, Italy.

ABOUT THE AUTHOR

Roberto Giorgi is an associate professor at Department of Information Engineering, University of Siena, Italy. He was a research associate at the University of Alabama in Huntsville, USA. He received his PhD in Computer Engineering and his Master in Electronics Engineering, Summa cum Laude both from University of Pisa, Italy. He is the coordinator of the European Project AXIOM. He coordinated the TERAFLUX project in the area of Future and Emerging Technologies for Teradevice Computing. He is participating in the European projects HiPEAC (High Performance Embedded-system Architecture and Compiler) and SARC (Scalable ARChitectures), ERA (Embedded Reconfigurable Architectures). He took part in ChARM project, developing software for performance evaluation of ARM-processor-based embedded systems with cache memory. He has been selected by the European Commission as an independent expert. His current interests include Computer Architecture themes such as Embedded Systems, Multiprocessors, Memory System Performance, and Workload Characterization. He is a lifetime member of ACM and a senior member of the IEEE, IEEE Computer Society.

CHAPTER THREE

Dataflow-Based Parallelization of Control-Flow Algorithms

N. Korolija*, J. Popović[†], M. Cvetanović*, M. Bojović*
*School of Electrical Engineering, University of Belgrade, Belgrade, Serbia
[†]Microsoft Development Center Serbia, Belgrade, Serbia

Contents

1. Introduction 74
2. Problem Statement 78
3. Dataflow Approaches and the Feynman Paradigm 80
4. Existing Solutions and Their Criticism 88
   4.1 Methods Inherited From the Theory of Systolic Arrays 88
   4.2 Methods Inherited From the Theory of Dataflow Analysis in Compilers 97
   4.3 Methods Inherited From the Theory of Dataflow Programming Tools 99
5. Exploring Dataflow Potentials 103
   5.1 The LBM 103
   5.2 A Lattice–Boltzmann Implementation in the C Programming Language 104
   5.3 Analytical Analysis of Potentials 105
   5.4 A Lattice–Boltzmann Implementation for the Maxeler Dataflow Architecture 106
6. Performance Evaluation 113
   6.1 Case Study: A Control-Flow and a Dataflow Implementation of the LBM 113
   6.2 Dataflow Acceleration for Other Algorithms 116
   6.3 Threat to Validity 117
7. Conclusions 118
Acknowledgments 119
Appendix 119
References 120
About the Authors 123

Abstract

Compared to control-flow architectures, dataflow architectures usually offer better performances in high performance computing. Moreover, dataflow architectures consume less electrical power. However, only since recently, the technology enables the development of dataflow architectures that are competitive with control-flow architectures. From a programming perspective, there are a relatively small number of experienced dataflow programmers. As a result, there is a need of translating control-flow algorithms into the dataflow environment.

Advances in Computers, Volume 104
ISSN 0065-2458
http://dx.doi.org/10.1016/bs.adcom.2016.09.003

73

This chapter focuses on extracting methods from various fields, which could be applied on translating control-flow algorithms to dataflow environment, comparing available programming tools for dataflow architectures with respect to the previously established methods, and finally, evaluating speedups and reductions in power consumption on a dataflow implementation of the Lattice–Boltzmann method, implemented using a specific tool and method. Results show a remarkable speedup (one to two orders of magnitude), and, at the same time, a considerable reduction in power consumption.

ABBREVIATIONS

ALU arithmetic logic unit
CFD computational fluid dynamics
CPU central processing unit
CUDA compute unified device architecture
DRAM dynamic random–access memory
DFEs dataflow engines
EDA electronic design automation
FPU floating-point unit
FPGA field-programmable gate array
GFLOPs giga-floating-point operations per second
ILP instruction level parallelism
I/O input/output
LBM Lattice–Boltzmann method
NS Navier–Stokes
PCIe peripheral component interconnect express
PE processing element
RAM random-access memory
RAW read-after-write
RC reconfigurable computing
ROCCC riverside optimizing compiler for configurable computing
SYS the Lam and Mostow's method
VHDL very high speed integrated circuit hardware description language
VLSI very large-scale integration
WAW write-after-write

1. INTRODUCTION

In past decades, a vast majority of computers were based on the control-flow paradigm. Consequently, programmers were taught how to solve problems by designing control-flow algorithms. As computers gained in speed, they were able to solve more and more complex problems.

The main problem in programming became designing algorithms that use computer resources efficiently, e.g., by exploiting caches and using, whenever possible, main memory instead of hard drives.

Soon, parallelization at various levels has been realized, which resulted in various architectural paradigms, such as: vector processors, pipelining, super-pipelining, super-scalar, multicore, and many-core computers. In the meanwhile, the focus of programmers changed from optimizing algorithms for a single-core computer, over optimizing computations on thread-level and later core-level, to optimizing computations on the level of demand. While the trend is to gradually optimize algorithms on higher levels of abstraction, optimizing the communications in distributed computing remains the main problem.

Not only that this problem does not disappear, but also it rises over time. Increasing the clock speed of a computer is limited by the technology. Therefore, thousands of processors may be available in a single computer nowadays. Despite increasing the memory bandwidth, transferring data from the main memory to processors and between processors remain the main bottleneck. Another technological issue that grows in importance is processors cooling. Recently, computer power consumption has become one of the main concerns in high performance computing. It is estimated that the cost of electrical power that a processor in a cluster consumes annually, may exceed the price of the processor itself [1]. Therefore, it seems that optimizations of architectures tuned to control-flow algorithms are reaching their limits. A potential solution to the problems described earlier is switching to the dataflow paradigm [2,3]. It should be noted that switching paradigms is not rare case. Since the appearance of computers, it had happened many times. We have witnessed switching from machine instructions to assembler, then to higher programming languages, from procedural to object-oriented programming, and recently to functional programming languages. It seems that the dataflow programming, offering superior performances with reduced power consumption, is becoming more and more common.

There are software and hardware dataflow paradigms. Software dataflow assumes an array of processing elements (PEs) similar in functionality to control-flow processors, where, for a given moment, each of them is either executing an instruction or waiting to execute one. The concept behind that is in executing as many independent instructions simultaneously as possible. However, the lack of software dataflow is inherently the same as the one of control-flow processors, and is therefore not in the focus of this chapter.

Therefore, the hardware dataflow will be assumed when explaining dataflow concepts.

Dataflow processor, or dataflow hardware, works on principles of dataflow paradigm. It could basically be seen as a sum of a huge amount of relatively small chip surface parts, each being capable of executing a single instruction, receiving inputs and sending output to parts of the processor executing dependent instructions. While a control-flow processor is capable of executing all kinds of instructions (and therefore having a relatively large chip surface), which will execute only few instructions simultaneously, a dataflow processor could be configured to execute certain algorithm in such a manner that dataflows through him.

Once configured, dataflow hardware could be executing algorithm as soon as needed. However, once it needs to execute another algorithm, it needs to be reconfigured. Due to the need for reconfiguring dataflow processors and technology limitations, dataflow processor should work on lower frequency than today's control-flow processors. The dataflow processor could still have higher instruction throughput, because it would not include complex mechanisms as caches, translation lookaside buffer (TLB) cache register file, and microcode control units, leaving more space for computation parts. A configured dataflow processor could be executing thousands of instructions simultaneously [4], achieving superior performances compared to control-flow processors.

Besides higher instruction throughput, dataflow processors consume less power. Power consumption is approximately proportional to squared frequency, and dataflow processors often have one order of magnitude lower frequencies. Also, dataflow processors do not include previously mentioned complex mechanisms that require power, but rather concentrate power dissipation on instruction execution.

Important property of dataflow processors is that they could adapt to the instructions to be executed in run time [5]. However, since changing the processor itself is much slower than executing an instruction, dataflow processors are useful only for applications that require executing repeatedly the same set of instructions. Even those applications normally include instructions for initializing the data that could not be efficiently processed using the dataflow hardware. Therefore, dataflow processors are usually combined with control-flow processors. These kinds of architectures are known as hardware dataflow architectures [6].

This concept is not new. During 1970s and 1980s, limitations in technology resulted in development of dataflow machines closer to traditional computers [7]. Reconfigurable computing (RC) combines hardware that could be reconfigured to implement application-specific functions and conventional processor or processors. As a result, high performance applications could be accelerated compared to the execution using control-flow processors [8,9]. Dynamically reconfigurable systems adapt their internal structure at run time. Although this concept exists since 1960s, it has become commercially viable only recently. According to some authors [10], the trend is that computers should have both control-flow and dataflow components.

Despite the fact that dataflow processors could enhance performance in high performance computing [11,12], they are still not common in practice. This leads us to exploring main cost factors of computer clusters. The price of processors in clusters is comparable to the price of their few years' power consumption or even less. Therefore, the reduction in power consumption itself may be a valid reason to change infrastructure.

Having technological problems resolved is not enough. Most of the applications are written for control-flow processors, which are conceptually different from dataflow's counterparts. Before they could be executed on dataflow processors, they would have to be reimplemented. Although processing instructions using the dataflow paradigm was faster than using the control-flow paradigm since long time ago, the problem of transforming control-flow source code to the dataflow representation was ignored at the time, while the control-flow processor frequencies were nearly doubling every 2 years, making control-flow processors constantly in advantage over dataflow processors. With increasing popularity of dataflow architectures comes the need for exploring available ways to transform control-flow graph or source code to the dataflow representation.

Hardly any algorithm consists solely of instructions that are repeated over and over again. For other instructions (which usually present most of the source code, but participate in a very small portion of total execution time), conventional processors are more suitable, due to better performances compared to dataflow's counterparts. Therefore, most of application instructions could still be executed on conventional processor, while only parts of application (those instructions executed during very high percentages of the run time) would have to be adapted.

Applications that are being executed in similar forms for decades are well optimized and tested. Some of them are responsible for important calculations, where introduced errors would lead to big financial losses. This makes rewriting them very expensive. Consequently, it is of crucial importance to design tools that will help translating the code to the dataflow paradigm.

This chapter presents an overview of available methods from fields related to the dataflow computing (systolic arrays, dataflow analysis, and compilers), which could be used for transforming control-flow algorithms to dataflow algorithms. All of the methods are presented in a uniform manner, making their direct comparison possible. Each method is first described, then depicted using a figure with the same structure as for all other methods, and finally, discussed. Available tools for compiling source codes to dataflow hardware are discussed with respect to previously presented methods. Furthermore, results of the comparison of an implemented application using the dataflow paradigm and appropriate control-flow application are presented. Section 2 discusses the problem of switching from control-flow to dataflow paradigm. Section 3 presents main differences between control-flow and dataflow paradigms. Section 4 presents selected methods for transforming control-flow algorithms to dataflow algorithms, and in the same section, authors also review the transforming methods inherited from related fields. In Section 5, authors discuss exploiting these methods in transforming the Lattice–Boltzmann method (LBM) from a control-flow application available in open literature to the corresponding dataflow application. Section 6 evaluates performance of dataflow implementation of the LBM, as well as results from other researchers that have implemented various algorithms using similar technologies. Finally, Section 7 includes conclusions and prognosis on the future of dataflow systems, as a viable alternative to control-flow systems.

2. PROBLEM STATEMENT

Switching from control-flow paradigm to dataflow paradigm could improve performance of computation-intensive applications [4,9–12]. In order to achieve this, dataflow compilers would have to be capable of running applications written for control-flow architectures. Some of the principles of this approach will be discussed in this section. Another approach is that programmers adjust their applications. Vast of the code base of applications and algorithms is dedicated to control-flow computers. Also, programmers are mostly taught how to solve problems using control-flow computers. As a result, rewriting all high performance applications would be expensive, error-prone, and long-lasting task. This research focuses on providing tools and methods for programmers to adapt their applications.

One possible solution to the problem is developing compilers that would run control-flow applications on dataflow hardware. This would require a compiler to determine which parts of the application are suitable for dataflow hardware. It seems that the worst case would be if the compiler would not be able to find any part of the application suitable for dataflow hardware. Let's assume that we want to design a compiler. As already mentioned, portions of code that are repeatedly executed are potentially suitable for dataflow hardware. For example, a loop that executes many times mutually independent iterations could be transformed to dataflow hardware. This transformation could be achieved using the same principles that could be found in dataflow compilers. Dataflow compiler could transform dataflow kernel code written in higher level language into the appropriate dataflow representation. A kernel would consist of those statements that form a loop that should be executed using the dataflow hardware. Except defining kernel inputs and outputs, the logic might not have to be changed at all. The main concern is that executing a *for* loop with only few iterations would be much slower using a dataflow hardware, because the dataflow hardware would be only partially utilized (only few instructions could be executed in parallel).

Possible solution to the problem of underutilizing the dataflow hardware because of small problem sizes is storing number of iterations to the log file in the run time, and using this information for recompiling the application. A compiler could work pretty much like typical compilers, except that it could put logging instructions in loops. Also, at the very beginning, it would have to check if given number of application executions for training purposes is already done, and force recompiling. During recompiling, loops that would found to be not suitable for dataflow hardware would be compiled the same way as first time, except that logging instructions would not be needed any more. Other loops, having mutually independent iterations, would be transformed to dataflow representation. However, storing number of iterations in run time imposes numerous problems. For example, logging instructions might affect application behavior. Also, compiler would have to be integrated into the firstly compiled application, or it would have to be ensured that the compiler would still be available at the time of recompiling (note that a computer executing an application might have different architecture than the one that compiles the application). Besides these technical issues, a compiler would recompile the application based on historical behavior. Let us imagine the scenario where a real-time application is written in such a manner that the worst case scenario of a *for* loop does not lead to missing deadlines. Optimizing the average execution time by using the dataflow hardware could lead to missing deadlines, which could possibly lead to a disaster, e.g., in case the real-time application is a self-drive or a rocket application.

Even if we leave both technological constraints and corner cases aside, this compiler might fail in case of the need to translate the loop that does not have mutually independent iterations, but could be transformed to such a loop.

It is not the first time that software engineers encounter the problem of switching paradigms. When designing a many-core system like compute unified device architecture (CUDA) [13], compilers had to be capable of running applications written for such architecture, but also programmers had to change their coding. If the application has to be rewritten for the architecture that is conceptually different, source code that should run in parallel should be explicitly defined. Therefore, a programmer needs to determine what segments of code are most computation-intensive and, consequently, which of them should be executed in parallel.

Therefore, the goal of this research is not to enable the computer to understand the application that it is running, but rather to provide methods and tools that would make the transformation of applications easier. In order to do this, the survey of available methods for dataflow computing from related fields was conducted. Secondly, a tool had to be chosen for the problem in hand. For each available tool, it will be considered which methods for control-flow algorithm transformation it incorporates, as well as what are the algorithmic and hardware constraints of using that tool. From the algorithms point of view, it will considered what constraints have to be solved in order to execute the algorithm using the chosen tool and which methods should be applied directly by the programmer to the algorithm.

3. DATAFLOW APPROACHES AND THE FEYNMAN PARADIGM

Although the Nobel Laureate Richard Feynman did not work on dataflow computing himself, his observations made many researchers (both in universities and in industries) to work on dataflow computing [14]. This fact justifies that his name is being used as reference to the paradigm that is more and more used in supercomputing. Here, the general dataflow approach that follows the Feynman paradigm is presented.

Maximizing the performance of control-flow application execution assumes activities in two fields. One is the algorithm itself and the other one is the underlying hardware. The bottom line of modifying the control–flow algorithm is that it can be executed in less clock cycles. If the algorithm should be executed on a single core, this could be done by simple algorithmic transformations. Otherwise, one could optimize the communication between processors executing the algorithm. Optimizing the hardware could also be done in two ways. One is making the processor as fast as possible. Another one is using as many cores as possible to execute an algorithm suitable for such computer architecture. Following are the main principles and their limits:

1. Reducing the number of clock cycles: once the algorithm is as optimal as it can get, no further progress is possible using this approach.

2. Optimizing the communications: once the algorithm is as optimal as it can get, no further progress is possible using this approach.

3. Increasing the central processing unit (CPU) clock speed: technology limits are close to being reached, limiting us from scaling performances in this direction.

4. Adding more processors: although this could speed-up the executing parts of the algorithm that are not dependent from each other, at the end, one needs to collect all of the data, limiting us from dividing the algorithm into smaller pieces.

Fig. 1 depicts the above-defined four scenarios.

On the other hand, dataflow optimization focuses on the speed of the signal flowing through the wire. The human brain processes more information per second than today's computers, although it is not known that humans can calculate even closely fast as any modern computer. Therefore, in order to really speed-up the algorithm execution, we might need to return to the beginning.

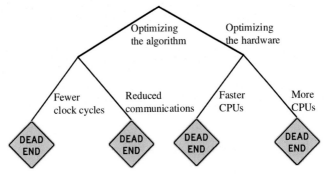

Fig. 1 Optimizing control-flow applications.

Since computers first appeared, they were expanding their performances at a relatively fast rate, approximately doubling the number of executed instructions per second every 2 years. Instruction level parallelism (ILP) dates back from 1940s and 1950s, when the parallelism was first exploited in the form of horizontal microcode. This trend continued up till today. It has become difficult to maintain the same increase in speed, while there is usually a limited amount of available ILP parallelism in an application. Later, in 1960s, more gates were available than it was necessary for a general-purpose processor, leading to various improvements. One of the most known up to today are cache memories that had a crucial effect on computation performance, especially since 1980s, as the gap between speed of processors and memories started to increase rapidly. The growth in speed of processors continued increasing. Once the technology limits were nearly reached, it was not possible to increase the speed of the CPU at the same pace, even at the cost of energy growing exponentially. Wavelength of the speed of light is equal to the speed of light divided by frequency. Today's computers have frequencies around 3 GHz, which makes the wavelength around 10 cm. The size of transistors of today's computers could not be much lowered, since it would heavily affect their function. This leaves not much space for long-term improvements in single chips using existing technology.

Let us consider a simple example algorithm in order to explore possibilities for accelerating the execution using both multicore and dataflow paradigms. A sample code and the computing paradigm of single-core processors are depicted in Fig. 2, where loop iterations are mutually independent, and each statement in one iteration except the first one depends on the previous one.

Multicore and multiprocessor paradigms solve this problem by introducing many cores instead of one. Main problem in making application execution faster naturally shifted from designing the fastest single-core applications to parallelizing application execution. Nevertheless, the increase in speed is limited by communication delays, energy consumption of many cores, and the size of each core. Enhancements of multiprocessors are often not

```
for(i=0;i<1024;i++)
    for(j=0;j<5000;j++){
        doIndependentStatement1();
        doDependentStatement1();
        ...
        doDependentStatementN();
    }
```

Fig. 2 Single-core computing paradigm.

followed anymore by faster application execution [15,16]. Execution of the same sample code using multiprocessors is depicted in Fig. 3, where each of 64 processors executes only a small portion of the outer loop. Multiprocessing used to be implemented using MPI and OpenMP, and nowadays is usually implemented using the CUDA computing paradigm.

Dataflow paradigm offers spatial computing, a natural solution to the previously mentioned problems, by treating computer processing as a factory of production lines instead of one or many specialized workers. The fundamental differences between spatial computing and temporal computing lays in the fact that spatial computing assumes operations being executed in parallel, with storage distributed throughout the circuit, and scheduling driven by dataflow. For special computation-intensive and data-intensive applications, one can design a dataflow and one can program a dataflow computer accordingly. Applications from various domains exhibited performance increase, achieving better price-performance and power-performance ratios compared to their Von Neumann's counterparts [17].

Vast of dataflow architectures consist of interconnected PEs. Many algorithms can be implemented using the dataflow approach, including artificial intelligence, simulating fluid dynamics, signal processing, image processing, pattern recognition, feature extraction, dynamic programming algorithms, graph algorithms, matrix arithmetic, etc. One of the many advantages of this approach is that the data-flows from one PE to another, without a need to access the main memory. This way, a high computational output is achieved with a relatively small network bandwidth. This eliminates the need for broadcast buses. By connecting PEs to each other, one can draw a dataflow diagram. Many data item streams can flow in parallel, joining, and splitting in PEs. Execution flow of the dataflow paradigm is depicted in Fig. 4, where each PE except elements from the first row executes only one *doStatement()* after receiving the required input from previous PE.

In general case, an application does not consist only of a loop or two nested loops. However, everything previously mentioned still applies. Fig. 5 depicts dataflow paradigm algorithm execution in general case.

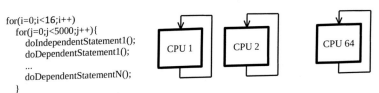

```
for(i=0;i<16;i++)
  for(j=0;j<5000;j++){
    doIndependentStatement1();
    doDependentStatement1();
    ...
    doDependentStatementN();
  }
}
```

Fig. 3 Multiprocessor computing paradigm.

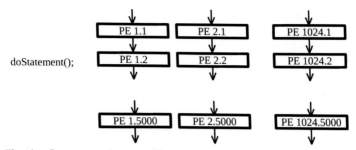

Fig. 4 The dataflow computing paradigm.

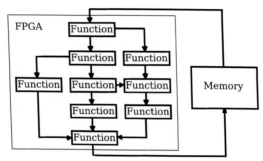

Fig. 5 Comparing control-flow and dataflow.

One can see that for the same amount of computation, one will need a much smaller number of memory accesses. Also, functions implemented in field-programmable gate arrays (FPGAs) are simpler than the processor that can execute any instruction. Therefore, one can think of the dataflow counterpart from the picture as having a pipeline of depth 10, without stalls and without any need for synchronization.

Since the dataflow paradigm is not as widely spread as the control-flow paradigm is, dataflow architectures are still relatively expensive and are often customized for particular applications. Another problem is that there is a limited code base of applications and algorithms for them. By noticing the advantage of pipelined execution of *for* loops, industries have developed various tools that ease the process of transforming applications for Von Neumann architecture into dataflow applications. The main challenge in transforming is in overcoming fundamental differences between architectures. One of the most important problems to solve is developing a methodology for transforming an algorithm represented in some of the high-level programming languages into an algorithm that can be efficiently executed on dataflow architecture. This imposes taking care about timing of data movements and interconnections between PEs in such a way that the data throughput is maximized.

So, why are the dataflow computers not as spread as the control-flow ones, or even more? Of course, this is because this paradigm also has its limitations. Again, accelerating an algorithm execution using the dataflow paradigm assumes activities in two fields: hardware and algorithms. From the very beginning, technology limits in creating efficient dataflow computers were present. Nowadays, the technology allows creating fast dataflow computers. However, most of the tools and human skills are oriented toward creating faster control-flow computers. In the early history of computers, algorithms used to be relatively small in the amount of computation, compared to today's algorithms. They were usually designed in order to release the human brain, and to enable it to work on more complicated issues than calculating and simple information processing. Today, it is not as easy to find a dataflow computer programmer as to find a control-flow computer programmer. Therefore, accelerating dataflow algorithm execution limitations could be roughly divided into:

1. Available problems to be algorithmically solved using dataflow computers, at the beginning.
2. Lack of algorithms written for dataflow paradigm due to the inertia, later.
3. Available technology for implementing efficient dataflow computers, at the beginning.
4. Necessity for changing the technology, later.

Luckily, we are living in a world with an ever faster development rate. Therefore, it is to be expected that the available potential for accelerating algorithms execution using the dataflow paradigm will be achieved soon. Fig. 6 depicts the scenarios mentioned earlier.

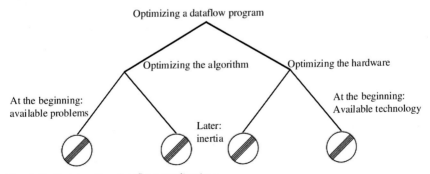

Fig. 6 Optimizing the dataflow applications.

Input tasks queue

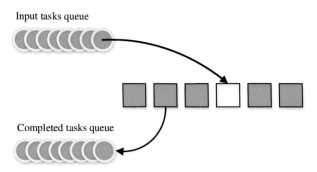

Completed tasks queue

Fig. 7 Processing bag of tasks using the control-flow paradigm.

Fig. 7 demonstrates typical processing of a bag of tasks. Tasks queue contains tasks that should be processed. If a single-core or multicore processor has to run these tasks using multithreading, each thread will continuously execute the following procedure: take the first task from the Task Queue, process it, and write the output to the Completed Tasks queue. Obviously, additional effort is required for scheduling these events. Also, accessing each queue would have to be an atomic operation, requiring semaphores, or some other mechanism to be introduced.

Let us assume that there are six processors being used to process a set of tasks that require the same type of processing, and that each processor is responsible for a single part of each task. Obviously, they would have to communicate, but the synchronization could be fairly simple. In each iteration, the first processor would receive task from the *Input tasks queue*, process its part, and pass the result to the next processor. The following processors would receive input from the previous one, and pass result to the next one, except for the last one that would pass the result into the *Completed tasks queue*. This way, instead of relatively complex computer architecture, relatively simple PEs would be enough. Also, instead of using a bus for the processors to communicate, the PEs could be directly connected to each other. Since these PEs would process only about 1/6 of whole tasks each, one could introduce a simpler PE, being capable of executing only a subset of instructions. This way, all necessary PEs could fit onto a single chip. As a result, a steady stream of tasks could be processed with a relative small amount of computing resources (transistors, buses, etc.), saving the energy and space at the same time, but also increasing the speed, as a result of parallel processing of many elements without a need to fetch from and store to memory more data than necessary. This approach is the dataflow approach. Appropriate diagram is shown in Fig. 8.

However, there are certain limitations when using dataflow architectures. First, dataflow architecture has to be configured for a specific job. As already said, one would have to write an application that will repeatedly execute the same set of instructions. Also, PEs of an iteration of a *for* loop should not depend on results of the previous iteration. Otherwise, the dataflow processor would have to stall, waiting for the input to be ready. Another issue is the factor between the number of bytes that has to be sent for processing and the amount of processing. In order to use dataflow architecture efficiently, time spent for sending the data to and from the dataflow processor has to be less than time for processing the same data using the CPU. Even if the data are loaded on the memory chip on the dataflow hardware, the order of processing data would affect the speed of execution to the great extent. For example, if the application should parse data that models road network, parsing successive edges in a row would bring many dependencies between iterations [18]. However,

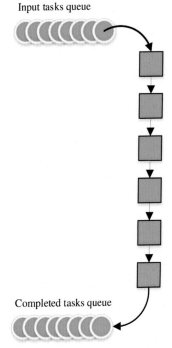

Fig. 8 Processing bag of tasks using the dataflow paradigm.

if the algorithm could be executed in such a manner that data from relatively far edges is parsed simultaneously, the data needed for processing an edge could already be ready. Therefore, there is a need for methods and tools that would efficiently transform control-flow applications to dataflow applications.

4. EXISTING SOLUTIONS AND THEIR CRITICISM

Solutions to the problem of transforming algorithms from control-flow to dataflow paradigm could be found in related research fields. Presented solutions may be seen as implantation of methods that were originally invented for other purposes, especially from the field of very large-scale integration (VLSI) design, or, more precisely, from using multiple regularly connected PEs known as systolic array processors. Transforming control-flow algorithms to dataflow computer architecture is conceptually analog to transforming algorithms to systolic array processors. Just like systolic arrays consist of regularly connected PEs, FPGAs have logic elements and look-up tables connected by routing resources, and configurable input/output (I/O) [19]. We further analyze the methods used in compilers, and finally, we analyze with respect to previous methods available tools (e.g., compilers) for transforming control-flow algorithms into dataflow algorithms.

Table 1 summarizes methods that are going to be presented, showing for each of them their inputs, result that they produce, their applicability, constraints, and whether they require user interaction.

Following frameworks will be briefly discussed in respect to previously discussed methods:
— Mitrionics-C [39],
— StreamsC [40],
— ImpulseC [41],
— SystemC [42],
— SPARK [43],
— The automatic memory partitioning method [44], and
— SoftWare Synthesis for network lookup [45].

4.1 Methods Inherited From the Theory of Systolic Arrays

The systolic array processor concept was introduced by Kung, Leiserson, and Lehman [46,47]. Systolic arrays effectively exploit massive parallelism in computation-intensive applications [48]. Systolic array processor consists of interconnected PEs, where one PE consumes results of arbitrary number

Table 1 Comparison of Methods for Transforming Algorithms From Control-Flow to Dataflow

Method	Input	Produces	Applicability	Constraints	Requires user interaction
The Cohen, Johnson, Weiser, and Davis [20–22]	Mathematical expressions	Systolic array	Could be included in a tool, e.g., for string matching	Translation of mathematical expressions	No
The Lam and Mostow's method (SYS) [23]	Algorithm, optionally obtained by software transformation	Systolic array	Could be included in a tool	Simple for loops	For optimization
The Gannon's method [24]	Algorithm	Algorithm	Deriving functional specification using vector operators representing parallelism	Transforming algorithms involving vector operations	Yes
The H. T. Kung and Lin's method [25]	Canonical mathematical representation of an algorithm	Algorithm	Helping in defining the functionality of PEs and calculating timing constraints	Translation of mathematical expressions	No
The Kuhn's method [26,27] and The Miranker and Winkler's method [28]	Algorithm given in a mathematical expression or as a *for* loop application	Algorithm	Useful for transforming certain algorithms and mathematical expressions, freeing the engineer from calculating the time constraints	A systematic design seems to be possible only for applications with loops	No

Continued

Table 1 Comparison of Methods for Transforming Algorithms From Control-Flow to Dataflow—cont'd

Method	Input	Produces	Applicability	Constraints	Requires user interaction
The Moldovan and Fortes' method [29–34]	An application or a set of recurrence equations	Algebraic model of the algorithm	Suited for high performance applications that consist of loops with recurrence equations	Applications that consist of loops with recurrence equations	No
The Lerner's method [35]	Code	Optimized code	Optimizes the code and eliminates unreachable code	Optimizing the code	No
The ROCCC system [36]	Application written in C to RTL VHDL	Generates highly optimized circuits for portions of C	Subsets of application should be written in C to RTL VHDL	User does not have enough control. Subsets of application should be written in C	At least a rudimentary understanding of how optimization and mapping processes work, and must take part in the process of transforming the control-flow application
The Maxeler framework [37,38]	Application written in C or Java or Python, and kernel(s) written in MaxJ Java-like language	Generates highly optimized circuits for kernels	Suited for high performance applications that consist of loops. Optimize the code and to eliminate unreachable code	User must take part in the process of transforming the control-flow application	Yes

of PEs and produces results for those PEs that need them. Each PE can be a special purpose cell with hardwired functions, a cell with a simple instruction set for processing vector elements, or a cell with a control unit and a processing unit. Systolic array processors were first used for complex computing problems, e.g., matrix multiplication, which is exactly the same computation as graphic cards nowadays do. Systolic arrays can be classified as semisystolic arrays, having global data communication lines to each PE, and pure systolic arrays that are analog to dataflow computer architectures with PEs. We will focus only on pure systolic arrays. All PEs operate simultaneously and necessary operands must be available at the corresponding clock cycle in order for the processing to start in the desired cycle.

As is the case with the dataflow paradigm, one of the most important problems with systolic arrays was designing a methodology for transforming control-flow algorithms to systolic array algorithms. Many methods were designed. They could be roughly divided into the following groups:

1. Methods allowing direct mapping of algorithms onto systolic arrays.
2. Methods for transforming algorithms into those more suitable for systolic arrays; additional work is required in order to be able to execute the transformed algorithms on systolic array processors.
3. Methods for transforming an already designed architecture into a new architecture.
4. Methods for proving the correctness of already implemented systolic array algorithms.

The last two groups of methods are out of scope of this research, since we focus on transforming control-flow applications into dataflow applications and not checking correctness of dataflow implementations.

Methods inherited from the theory of systolic arrays and the theory of dataflow analysis in compilers will be described using the model shown in Fig. 9. Methods inherited from the theory of dataflow programming tools contain much more elements, so we are not going to present them with the same model. Three straight lines present three axes: the algorithm specification, the computing model, and the dataflow architecture. Axes are used for denoting the level of the abstraction. Each method is described as a set of transformations leading from the starting point until the ending point or points. Each point must belong to one of the axes. The farther the point is from the center, the higher is the level of abstraction of the algorithm, model, or the architecture. For example, the starting point might be an algorithm in a form that one mathematician or one programmer would write it.

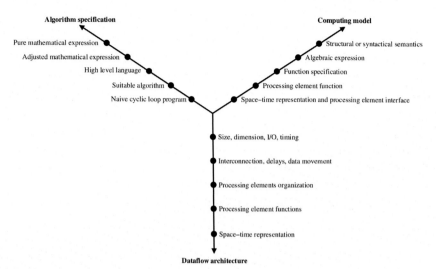

Fig. 9 Generalized model for presenting specific methods.

Using algorithmic transformations, it might become hard to read, thus the arrow would mark leaping toward the center of the three-axes system.

The Cohen, Johnson, Weiser, and Davis method [20–22] allows mapping mathematical expressions onto systolic arrays. It starts from transforming well-defined mathematical expressions including subscripted variables (variables with indexes) using subscript analysis and symbolic manipulation. It further applies Z operator for modeling displacement in time or space. The order of operations execution of the transformed expression is derived using precedence rules. Timing requirements are determined by the specification of PEs, and storage requirements depend on the available architecture of PEs.

The method is useful in dataflow computing, but limited to translation of mathematical expressions, not the whole higher language application. This method was successfully used in string matching, a common function of today's cloud computers that use Hadoop. Fig. 10 demonstrates this method applied to the problem of dataflow programming.

The limitation of this method is that it could only translate mathematical expressions. Therefore, it could only serve as a method that might be included in a tool that helps translate a control-flow application into a dataflow application.

The Lam and Mostow's method (SYS) [23] also maps an algorithm onto a systolic array. However, it starts from already produced software code in a

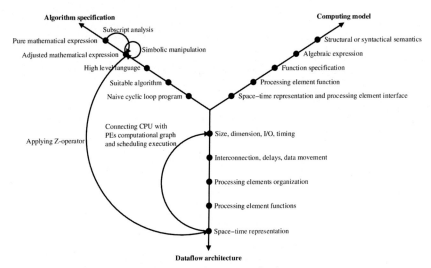

Fig. 10 The Cohen, Johnson, Weiser, and Davis method.

Pascal-like language that provides annotations that make the program suitable for automatic translation. It includes *for* loops with ranges known in compile time, not dependent on variables that become known only in run time. No conditional expressions are allowed. Loops may include only simple begin–end blocks. The SYS accepts as input an algorithm obtained by software transformation from high-level specification that consists of regularly repeating code. The algorithm is mapped onto a systolic array described by structure that determines architecture of PEs and the driver that determines the timing constraints and mapping of streams onto the generated hardware. This approach was used in implementation of the systolic array for finding the greatest divisor of two polynomials. Fig. 11 demonstrates this method applied to the problem of dataflow programming.

Limitations of this method are: (a) it is focused only on algorithms with simple *for* loops and (b) it requires user transformations in order to optimize the output. Portions of this method could be included in a tool that translates both algorithms with simple *for* loops and more complex processing.

The following methods are used for transforming algorithms into other algorithms, more suitable for systolic arrays.

The Gannon's method [24] starts from the algorithm. It defines vector operators as logical units that include functions that could be implemented using PEs. For example, one could define multiplication of two integer numbers that will further be used for integer vector multiplication. Another

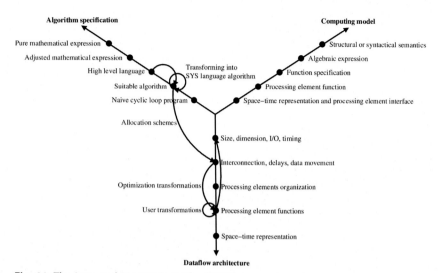

Fig. 11 The Lam and Mostow's method (SYS).

example is data movement or permutation, which could be used for multiplying big binary numbers. They also include a chain operator representing a composition of other operators. Functional specification is derived using vector operators representing parallelism. The functional specification of the algorithm could be transformed to the dataflow graph that could be further transformed to a systolic array using this method. As expected, this method is suitable for transforming algorithms involving vector operations. Fig. 12 demonstrates this method applied to the problem of dataflow programming.

Unfortunately, human interaction may be needed, which makes this method unsuitable for transforming big applications automatically, but the paradigm that this method uses could be applied to similar problems in dataflow computing. Unlike previous two methods that are focusing on translating specific portions of algorithms to the dataflow, this one is closer to high language programmability. It allows defining a functionality that would be executed for each element of an array. Again, an engineer is responsible for parallelism and dataflow, but the method helps in applying required functionality on array elements.

The H. T. Kung and Lin's method [25] generates an algorithmic representation from a canonical mathematical representation of an algorithm. Authors explain the principle on a FIR filter example, where a simple function that sums weighted inputs has to be calculated. Starting from a design C in z-graph

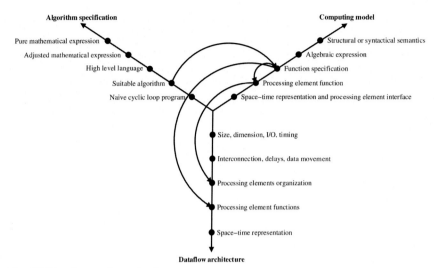

Fig. 12 The Gannon's method.

representation, where all products of appropriate inputs and weights would have to be added in a single cycle, they first create the algebraic representation of the algorithm. Given the fact that they provide algebraic representation of basic blocks, authors of this chapter could claim that this process could be done automatically for more complex designs. They further apply algorithmic transformations, producing a z-graph representation, and further, systolic design that executes only one operation in a cycle. From a z-graph, timing and PEs specification could be obtained. Fig. 13 demonstrates this method applied to the problem of dataflow programming.

As one can see from the figure, this method translates only mathematical expressions, by applying algebraic transformations and it is concentrated primarily on dataflow architectures, helping in defining the functionality of PEs and calculating timing constraints.

The Kuhn's method [26,27] is best suited for algorithms consisting of loops with constant execution time and data dependencies within iterations. Therefore, it is able to process matrix–vector and matrix–matrix multiplications, sorting, etc.

The Miranker and Winkler's method [28] is an extension of the Kuhn's method. It starts from an algorithm that can be given in a mathematical expression or as an algorithm with *for* loop. Given an expression, this method adjusts it, and transforms it to the naïve cyclic loop program. From the loop body, functional specification is obtained, and further, space–time

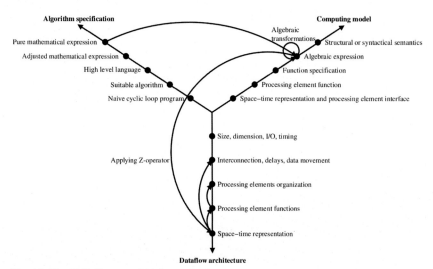

Fig. 13 The H. T. Kung and Lin's method.

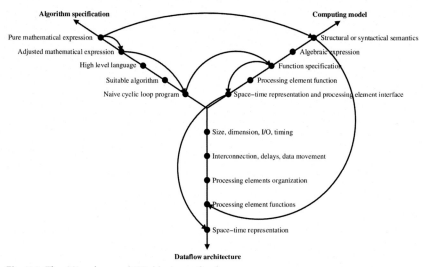

Fig. 14 The Miranker and Winkler's method.

representation and interfaces for PE are obtained. From the point of view of dataflow programming, these could define both PEs functions and space–time representation, as demonstrated in Fig. 14.

This method supports other algorithms as well, but a systematic design seems to be possible only for applications with loops. Therefore, it is useful for transforming certain algorithms and mathematical expressions, freeing the engineer from calculating the time constraints.

4.2 Methods Inherited From the Theory of Dataflow Analysis in Compilers

Optimization methods in conventional compilers have benefited from several decades of extensive research. The same applies for electronic design automation (EDA) tools. As a result, we have powerful compiler tools and powerful tools that can translate VHSIC hardware description language (VHDL) and Verilog code, as well as SystemC code into efficient circuits. However, little research has been done in combining these approaches [49]. Several researchers focused on high-level language to hardware description language translations [50–53], mostly translating C or C++ to hardware description languages with optimizations supporting simple loops and vectors.

The Moldovan and Fortes' method [29–34] uses techniques similar to those used in compilers for deriving an algebraic model of the algorithm from an application or a set of recurrence equations. The model consists of indexed computations that produce results of given formulas or application statements. This model is further transformed using local transformations that rewrite computations and map into functional and structural specifications of PEs, as well as global transformations that restructure the algorithm in such a way that a new set of dependencies fits better the underlying hardware, which is VLSI implementation. Time transformations are responsible for determining moments of data arrival to and from PEs, while space transformations determine interconnections between PEs and data movement. Fig. 15 demonstrates this method applied to the problem of dataflow programming.

This method is suited for high performance applications that consist of loops with recurrence equations. However, in order to provide greater flexibility in supporting translation of other algorithms to dataflow as well, additional work has to be done.

Many researchers active in compilers for the Von Neumann computer architecture worked on dataflow analysis and transformations, in order to optimize the machine code. Lerner *et al.* [35] introduced the Propagate and Replace actions that are able to optimize the code and to eliminate unreachable code. Fig. 16 demonstrates this method, where only the algorithm specification and the computing model axes are in use.

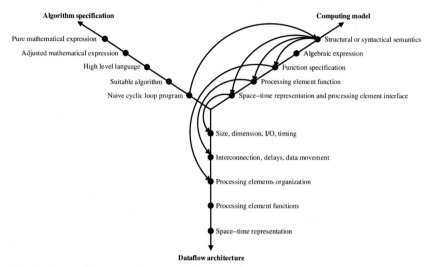

Fig. 15 The Moldovan and Fortes' method.

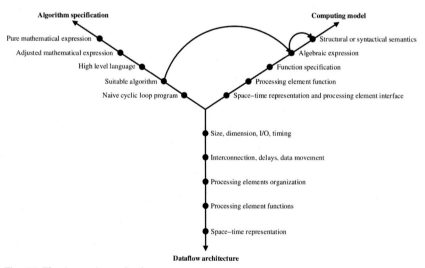

Fig. 16 The Lerner's method.

This is an obvious example of using dataflow analysis in optimizing the code for execution, but it can also help in dataflow programming. Although Lerner's focus was not on preparing an algorithm for dataflow architecture, his work can be applied to the dataflow paradigm, as well.

Unfortunately, unlike specialized dataflow compilers and tools, conventional compilers do not compile applications for dataflow architectures.

Therefore, they could only serve as a guideline in transforming control-flow algorithms to dataflow algorithms.

4.3 Methods Inherited From the Theory of Dataflow Programming Tools

The dataflow solution to the problem of programming for multiprocessors [54] was pioneered by Adams [55], Chamberlin [56], and Rodriguez [57]. Since then, many tools have been introduced, helping in programming dataflow architectures, as well as programming the abstractions (e.g., [58]).

Besides, the mechanical process of converting applications from high-level description (e.g., C or Java) or a dataflow diagram into an optimized low-level equivalent dedicated to the target platform, software development tools improve the application development process, providing an appropriate abstraction of a target platform, hiding details that programmers do not need to know. However, in practice, anyone programming high performance applications must have at least a rudimentary understanding of how optimization and mapping processes work, and must take part in the process of transforming the control-flow application (e.g., by adjusting the flow or by optimizing the original application) [19].

As is the case with most available tools, the riverside optimizing compiler for configurable computing (ROCCC) compilation framework [36] maps only subsets of applications written in C (particularly *for* loops processing arrays) to RTL VHDL. For most of the computation-intensive applications, it is enough to generate highly optimized circuits for portions of applications written in C programming language, which are executed over and over again. Compared to providing support for executing whole applications on FPGAs, this enables efficient usage of FPGAs, leaving space for parallelizing computation-intensive portions of applications. Authors have developed their own SUIF2 level optimizations. The following loop transformations are applied by the ROCCC system: normalization, invariant code motion, peeling, unrolling, fusion, tiling (blocking), strip mining, interchange, unswitching, skewing, induction variable, and forward substitution. The following procedure transformations are applied: code hoisting, code sinking, constant propagation, algebraic identities simplification, constant folding (removing division by one and multiplication by zero), copy propagation, dead code elimination, unreachable code elimination, scalar renaming, reduction parallelization, division/multiplication by constant optimization, and *if* conversion and predicated execution. Array transformations applied in ROCCS are: scalar replacement, array read-after-write (RAW) and write-after-write (WAW) elimination, array renaming, feedback reference elimination, and constant array value propagation [43,45,49]. Fig. 17 depicts the ROCCC system.

There are also two other commercial tools that are similar to ROCCC. These are Mitronics-C and ImpulseC.

Mitrionics-C [39] provides the Mitrion-C language that is based on the C programming language, but it has a special loop statement using the keyword foreach. The core is programmed using Mitrion-C. User has to define memory interfaces using keywords (e.g., memread and memwrite) and timing information using the keyword wait. Once the core is implemented, Mitronics-C instantiates a parallel core Mitrion Virtual Processor on the FPGA.

StreamsC [40] and ImpulseC [41] (a commercial version of StreamC) compilers parallelize execution of C code using VHDL. Their focus is on loops that could be mapped to hardware. However, the user is responsible for partitioning the code into hardware and software processes, and setting up communicating sequential processes using communication channels between them. Unlike ROCCC, StreamC and ImpulseC rely on the communicating sequential processes model for communication between processes. Therefore, they are meant for stream-based data structures and thus not convenient for handling multidimensional arrays, since serious restructuring of the code would be needed. However, Streams-C programmers sometimes need to manually write data reuse

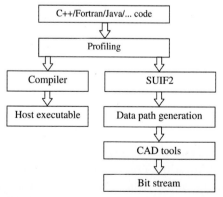

Fig. 17 The ROCCC system.

in the input C code, in order to ensure data retrieval from external memory only once.

SystemC [42] is designed for software–hardware synchronized systems, providing expressive functionality of VHDL or Verilog. Handle-C [56] is a low-level hardware/software construction language with syntax similar to C.

SPARK [43] also transforms C to VHDL. It supports loop unrolling, common subexpression elimination, copy propagation, dead code elimination, copy and constant propagation and dead code elimination, etc. It does not support multidimensional array accesses. SPARK starts from a behavioral description in C, with a constraint that the source code does not define pointers and recursive functions. The transformation starts by data dependency extraction, renaming variables, and pipelining loop instructions. After scheduling, the control synthesis and optimization are done, resulting in a finite state machine controller. The code generation back-end component generates synthesizable RTL VHDL that is further synthesized and verified. The SPARK high-level synthesis system is shown in Fig. 18.

A cross call between a host processor and FPGA is one of the main barriers for supporting automatic translation of high-level languages into VHDL. Some researchers worked on the communication framework between the processor and FPGA, supporting unlimited cross calls and hardware recursive calls [59].

One of the many advantages of FPGA is that the access to the memory can be parallelized. Ben-Ashem and Rotem developed an automatic

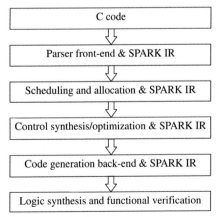

Fig. 18 The SPARK high-level synthesis system.

memory partitioning method for automatically synthesizing general data structures (arrays and pointers) into multiple memory banks for increased parallelism and performance [44].

Unlike most high-level synthesis compilers that focus on loop acceleration, some researchers focused on specialized hardware. For example, Kim *et al.* developed SoftWare Synthesis for network Lookup that generates entire lookup chains performing aggressive pipelining for high throughput [45].

The Maxeler framework [37,38] also maps portions of code to hardware. This framework also provides a possibility to program the kernel that could run on FPGA using MaxJ, a Java-like language that supports functions of the Java programming language needed for computation, but also provides variable types that map to hardware. The MaxCompiler compiler generates VHDL ready for FPGA vendor tools. *Synthesis* transforms VHDL into logical "netlist," which includes basic logic expressions. The *Map* fits basic logic into N-input look-up tables. The *Place* puts look-up tables, digital signal processors, random-access memories (RAMs), flip-flops, etc. at specific locations on the chip. The *Route* sets up wiring between blocks. This is depicted in Fig. 19.

Tools can even provide a programming model that uses a visual programming interface where the programmer can connect blocks of code together to form a high-level representation of a finished circuit, while the tool takes care about the rest (e.g., Starbridge Viva). A list of tools with appropriate web pages are given in the Appendix.

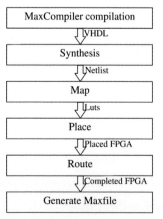

Fig. 19 Stages of compilation using MaxCompiler.

5. EXPLORING DATAFLOW POTENTIALS

Computational fluid dynamics (CFD) simulations are known to be computation intensive. Computational demands of complex simulation tasks can be satisfied only by simulations on modern supercomputers. Both high floating-point performance and high memory to processor chip bandwidth are necessary [60]. For decades, the scientific community has struggled to develop and to optimize suitable algorithms-like finite volume, finite element, or finite difference methods to simulate high Reynolds number Navier–Stokes (NS) problems [61]. An alternative to the NS-based methods for flow computations is the LBM [62]. The LBM is based on the Boltzmann equation and, in principle, is valid over a wider range of flow physics than the NS equations [63]. The LBM has evolved over the last 2 decades and is today widely accepted at universities and industry for solving incompressible flows [63,64].

As a case study of this work, here we present the LBM implemented both in the programming language C and using the dataflow paradigm in the Maxeler framework. We compare both, the speedup of the dataflow version of the algorithm over the control-flow counterpart, and the reduction in energy consumption.

5.1 The LBM

The LBM is a relatively new approach to simulating CFD. It is capable of numerically solving the NS equations, but also of simulating complex physical phenomena, e.g., chemical interactions between elementary cubicles of fluid and the surroundings. It is widely in use due to its efficiency and convenience, as an alternative tool to traditional solvers. The LBM is also a numerical solver of the Boltzmann equation that is the analog of the NS equation at a molecular level. It has the ability to describe fluids in non-hydrodynamic regimes with large molecular mean free paths. Lattice–Boltzmann models evolved from so-called Cellular Automata models, where a state represents the position and the velocity of interacting pseudo-molecular particles of a fluid. This method was designed since the very beginning to run on high performance computers. One of the important advantages of LBM, over some other methods, is that data preprocessing and mesh generation lasts only a small fraction of the total simulation time. Although the method is in some sense hybrid, since the solver is mesh based, it also inherits some aspects of particle-based methods.

Unlike the classical CFD, the LBM might seem resource consuming. The discrete probability distribution functions used in this model require more memory for their storage than the hydrodynamic variables of the NS equations. However, in practice, especially on modern computers, this is greatly compensated by its computational efficiency. The LBM involves only a very limited amount of floating-point operations per computational node. It is well suited for computations on a parallel architecture, even with a slow interconnection network.

We have tested both CPU and Maxeler implementations with a matrix with 112 rows and 320 columns. A number of iterations are algorithmically varied between 1 and 100,000.

5.2 A Lattice–Boltzmann Implementation in the C Programming Language

Fig. 20 presents a compact form of the main loop of the LBM implemented for control-flow architecture in the C programming language. We can see that certain functions are being called over and over again, *maxIter* times in total, where *maxIter* is the required number of iterations for simulation.

The function *stream* requires fetching all matrices. However, it does not require a lot of computing. Function *apply_BCs* is responsible only for updating the edge elements. Function *collide* requires fetching all matrices, but unlike the function *stream*, *collide* has a reasonable amount of processing per each coordinate of the matrices.

Functions *stream* and *collide* are a part of the source code of the Lattice–Boltzmann implementation available online [65]. By analyzing the execution time of each one of the functions of the algorithm, we have noticed that almost all of the execution time is spent on repeatedly executing functions *stream* and *collide*. The total execution time spent on the function *collide* is approximately 50% higher than the total execution time spent on the function *stream*. Having in mind that the function *collide* does almost all of the calculations, one could expect these execution times to differ more.

```
for (iter=0;iter<maxIter;iter++){
    // NOTE: this part of the code should be parallelized,
    // more precisely the functions stream and collide
    stream();
    apply_BCs();
    collide();
    saveData();
}
```

Fig. 20 The critical code of the Lattice–Boltzmann method.

However, fetching the data even from the L3 cache memory lasts quite a lot, compared to multiplying the floating-point numbers. For example, Intel Core i7 Xeon 5500 Series data source latencies are approximately 4 clock cycles for the L1 cache hit, 10 for L2, and 40–65 for L3. Accessing the remote L3 cache would last between 100 and 300 clock cycles. In the case of having big matrices that have to be processed by the LBM, one might end up with a delay of around 60 ns, for fetching the elements from the dynamic random-access memory (DRAM).

5.3 Analytical Analysis of Potentials

For the beginning, an analytical analysis of the potentials for accelerating the LBM using the dataflow approach is given. Since technologies change both in case of control-flow and dataflow processors, our assumed clock speed of the CPU is exactly 10 times the speed of the dataflow clock. We have chosen the following bus speed as representative. Note that this is also our decision and it will eventually be outdated, but the analysis will not change until the paradigm of the underlying hardware changes. Transfer speed between the processor and dataflow engines (DFEs) is the speed of the peripheral component interconnect express (PCIe) V4.0, which is 31.508 GB/s.

The Amdahl's law states that the upper bound on the parallel speedup for any application is given by $1/(1-p)$, where p is the fraction of the application that can be run in parallel [66]. In our case, this means that only instructions that are executed on the DFEs could be accelerated. Luckily, almost all of the LBM processing time is spent on the main loop, resulting in high potentials for the acceleration.

The complexity of the dataflow implementation of the kernel is $O(1)$, since one input is given to DFEs in each clock. On the other hand, control-flow processor executes the kernel in as many cycles as needed for executing all of the instructions that produce the same result as the kernel. Let us call this number n. Note that these instructions are not the same for control-flow and dataflow architectures due to changes in the control-flow algorithm. Therefore, the complexity of the corresponding code on the CPU is $O(n)$, where n is the number of instructions. Advantages of the dataflow approach are already obvious. However, we will try to calculate how high the acceleration could become. By analyzing the CPU code, we have evaluated that the number of cycles that the processor spends, on calculating the same results that a kernel in one cycle produces, is 190, based on the assumption that the 140 assembler instructions including add, sub, mul, and div take one cycle per instruction, and that average length of sqrt is 50 clock cycles. No pipelining is assumed, and no parallel kernels in dataflow architecture are assumed. Obviously, the maximum acceleration we could get under these assumptions is 190 divided by 10, since dataflow processor has exactly 10 times lower frequency. However, we will see that this will be less in our case study. Please note that today's CPUs support multithreading, and that dataflow card may fit more than one kernel, which makes parallelization on both types of processors possible.

Since power consumption is nearly proportional to the squared frequency, the dataflow power consumption has potentials to be 100 times lower in the same circumstances. This assumes only processing power at the VLSI. As we will see later, a computer with Maxeler card consumes almost twice more electrical power, which is to be expected, since both CPU and the Maxeler card are powered, but the dataflow approach assumes running more instructions simultaneously. Therefore, the total power reduction can still be achieved, since the total execution time can be reduced. Generally, there are special clusters consisting of racks with Maxeler cards, which greatly reduce the amount of power that is spend on CPUs, compared to the power spent on Maxeler cards.

By comparing to the frequencies of today's CPUs, we can see that approximately 2.5 bytes can be transferred per each CPU clock cycle, or 25 bytes per one cycle of the Maxeler card. This means that approximately six floating-point numbers can be transferred to the Maxeler per one cycle. This would lead to pipeline stall at the Maxeler card. Fortunately, all matrices can be transferred to the Maxeler card before the calculation starts. Therefore, the time of the transfer is spent only once, which is comparable to the execution time for executing only few iterations from the LBM algorithm.

Please note that the implementation of each instruction of the algorithm directly on hardware instead of running it on the CPU leads to the reduction in number of transistors. However, we could not claim that this leads to power reduction, since comparing transistors that only exist on control-flow processors and those that are in use in dataflow processors is not fair.

5.4 A Lattice–Boltzmann Implementation for the Maxeler Dataflow Architecture

In order to implement LBM using the dataflow paradigm, one could choose appropriate tool that will handle as much as possible of the transforming process from control-flow to dataflow. Following is a brief overview of methods available in the field of systolic arrays, now revisited from the point of view of LBM.

The Cohen, Johnson, Weiser, and Davis method [13–16] maps mathematical expressions to systolic arrays. This is necessary in translating almost any application from control-flow to dataflow paradigm, but it is also included in most of the tools that could help in the process of translation. The LBM includes reasonable amount of computations per each data. SYS [17] also maps an algorithm to a systolic array, but it starts from the software code suitable for translation. As tools need appropriate annotations in order to implement parts of applications on the dataflow hardware, most of them include appropriate libraries and statements needed in the process of compiling the code to the dataflow hardware or producing some other dataflow representation. The Gannon's method [19] derives functional specification from the algorithm. In case of the LBM, a programmer would be required to define the functionality that has to be executed on the dataflow hardware. The H. T. Kung and Lin's method [20] transforms a mathematical expression to an algebraic expression, further defining PEs specification and timing. In case of the LBM, the method cannot be used without major modifications, because implementing only mathematical expressions in hardware would lead to excessive communication between the main memory and the dataflow hardware. The Kuhn's method [21] and The Miranker and Winkler's method [22] are best suited for algorithms consisting of loops with constant execution time and data dependencies within iterations. The method is useful in general case, but the LBM requires more complex methods in order to cover corner cases. To be precise, the LBM requires different processing of elements belonging to the edges of matrices. The Moldovan and Fortes' method [23–28] derives an algebraic model of the algorithm from an application or a set of recurrence equations. Authors find it not being particularly useful in translating the LBM. The Lerner's method optimizes the code by propagating the results of previous statements to the following statements.

As a tool, authors have chosen the Maxeler framework for the following characteristics, in respect to the previously described methods:

- transforming mathematical expressions automatically,
- transforming *for* loops with fixed ranges automatically; also supporting loop unrolling,
- handling the control–flow processor and the dataflow processor communication, and
- handling the elimination of unreachable code.

Besides these, it also has high language programmability, it supports invariant code motion, peeling, fusion, tiling (blocking), interchange, scalar variables, forward substitution, array RAW and WAW elimination, and constant value propagation.

Maxeler requires a programmer to implement a kernel that will be responsible for processing the element(s) of the array(s) using the dataflow hardware, where a stream will be given as an input to the kernel, and stream(s) will be the result of kernel's processing. A kernel needs input and output parameters to be defined by the programmer. Everything in-between is almost the same as in Java applications. All mathematical operations are allowed. The only constraint is that once a variable is stored as a hardware variable, it could not be translated to a Java variable any more. We can think of it as follows: a floating-point variable set to zero, and later stored to hardware variable, changes due to the fact that wires are not ideal. Therefore, a voltage on that wire will not be zero, but rather close to zero, due to the noise on the wire. If we try to store this voltage as a Java *float* variable, since the voltage is not exactly zero, the value would differ from the starting one. Since programmers would hardly adapt to unpredictability of the application execution, this may not be allowed. Data could be streamed either from the main memory, or from the dataflow hardware memory.

The rest of the Maxeler framework specifics will be described on the example of LBM. Most of the execution time spent in executing LBM on a CPU is spent executing the function *collide*. Therefore, *authors* have first implemented this function as a kernel that would process all elements of matrices, passed from the main memory. In both control-flow and dataflow LBM implementations, matrices are stored as vectors, where the first row is placed at the beginning of the vector, followed by the second row, etc. Fig. 21 presents the kernel code that is responsible for updating the matrix elements, where some lines responsible for working with vectors 1–9 are omitted due to redundancy, and replaced with dots.

Compared to the control-flow implementation of the LBM *collide* method, we have applied transformations that would execute faster on a dataflow architecture [67]. Namely, almost all mathematical operations differ from those in the control-flow implementation of the algorithm. For this reason, this algorithm is one of the best suited for demonstrating the application of the presented methods in transforming an algorithm from control-flow to dataflow.

Since LBM has *for* loops with constant execution time, we have achieved what was introduced in the Kuhn's method and the Miranker and Winkler's

```
public class CollideKernel extends Kernel{
  public CollideKernel (KernelParameters parameters){
    super(parameters);
    HWVar rtau = io.scalarInput("rtau" ,hwFloat(8, 24));
    ...
    HWVar f0  = io.input("f0i", hwFloat(8, 24));
    ...
    // Do the summations needed to evaluate the density and components of velocity
    HWVar ro = f0 + ...;
    HWVar rovx = f1 - f3 + f5 - f6 - f7 + f8;
    HWVar rovy = f2 - f4 + f5 + f6 - f7 - f8;
    HWVar vx = rovx/ro;
    HWVar vy = rovy/ro;
    // Also load the velocity magnitude into plotvar - this is what we will display using OpenGL later
    HWVar v2x = vx * vx;
    HWVar v2y = vy * vy;
    HWVar plotvar = KernelMath.sqrt(v2x + v2y);
    HWVar v_sq_term = 1.5f*(v2x + v2y);
    // Evaluate the local equilibrium f values in all directions
    HWVar vxmvy = vx - vy;
    HWVar vxpvy = vx + vy;
    HWVar rortau = ro * rtau;
    HWVar rortaufaceq2 = rortau * faceq2;
    HWVar rortaufaceq3 = rortau * faceq3;
    HWVar vxpvyp3 = 3.f*vxpvy;
    HWVar vxmvyp3 = 3.f*vxmvy;
    HWVar vxp3 = 3.f*vx;
    HWVar vyp3 = 3.f*vy;
    HWVar v2xp45 = 4.5f*v2x;
    HWVar v2yp45 = 4.5f*v2y;
    HWVar mv_sq_term = 1.f - v_sq_term;
    HWVar mv_sq_termpv2xp45 = mv_sq_term + v2xp45;
    HWVar mv_sq_termpv2yp45 = mv_sq_term + v2yp45;
    HWVar vxpvyp45vxpvy = 4.5f*vxpvy*vxpvy;
    HWVar vxmvyp45vxmvy = 4.5f*vxmvy*vxmvy;
    HWVar mv_sq_termpvxpvyp45vxpvy = mv_sq_term + vxpvyp45vxpvy;
    HWVar mv_sq_termpvxmvyp45vxmvy = mv_sq_term - vxmvyp45vxmvy;
    HWVar f0eq = rortau * faceq1 * mv_sq_term;
    ...
    f0 = rtau1 * f0 + f0eq;
    ...
    io.output("f0o", f0, hwFloat(8, 24));
    ...
  }
}
```

Fig. 21 The Lattice–Boltzmann collide kernel.

method by using the Maxeler framework and implementing the functionality of DFEs. The Maxeler framework further derived a functional specification from this kernel, as in the Gannon's method. While the Cohen, Johnson, Weiser, and Davis method transforms mathematical expressions to PEs and timing specification, SYS more closely describes what was achieved using the Maxeler framework, since we had to write the code in the MaxJ programming language, in order to have it mapped to the

FPGAs. Unfortunately, while the Moldovan and Fortes' method is capable of automatically deriving an algebraic model of the algorithm from an application or a set of recurrence equations, we had to think about streams of data and element indices. The Maxeler framework is responsible for handling the functionality defined in the H. T. Kung and Lin's method. Using techniques available in compilers, we have optimized the signal propagation, as it is proposed in the Lerner's method.

As we can see from this figure, there is a considerable amount of processing that has to be done for each element. Having in mind the advantages of dataflow programming, including executing hundreds or thousands of instructions in parallel, and not needing to fetch each input variable from the memory, but rather exchanging inputs and outputs with neighborhood elements responsible for processing dependable instructions, it is to be expected that this kernel will execute faster on a Maxeler card than on a processor. However, in order to speed-up the execution, other functions have to be executed at Maxeler card, as well.

The function *stream* is given in Fig. 22. Again, some parts are replaced with dots due to redundancy. The main reason for long-lasting execution of the function *stream* is that elements have to be fetched. Computing that has to be done on each element is rather simple. Please, notice that this kernel also implies execution of instructions from the *apply_BCs()* function.

We must admit that besides great functionality provided by tools and methods, the responsibility for optimizing the execution of the algorithm on the dataflow architecture is still dependent on the programmer. Fig. 23 demonstrates the main principle of the LBM implementation for the chosen dataflow architecture. In order to calculate parameters in a single finite volume of space (either 2D or 3D), the kernel has to know the parameters of its surrounding finite elements. Therefore, the result of execution of the kernel depends not only on the stream of the column containing the finite element it processes, but also the two neighborhood streams. Additionally, the element of the stream will depend from its predecessor and its successor, which could be handled using the Maxeler framework, by introducing indexes into streams (in our case −1 and +1, denoting the previous and the next element of a stream, respectively).

Fig. 24 depicts the purpose of that LBM manager. The manager is responsible for connecting kernels to the CPUs and between themselves. Although the Maxeler framework automatically develops a manager for an application, any customization requires that a programmer modifies

```
public class StreamKernel extends Kernel {
    public StreamKernel (KernelParameters parameters) {
        super(parameters);
        HWVar f1new = io.scalarInput("f1new" ,hwFloat(8, 24));
        HWVar f5new = io.scalarInput("f5new" ,hwFloat(8, 24));
        HWVar f8new = io.scalarInput("f8new" ,hwFloat(8, 24));
        ...
        HWVar f1  = io.input("f1", hwFloat(8, 24)); // j
        HWVar f2m = io.input("f2m", hwFloat(8, 24)); // j-1
        HWVar f3  = io.input("f3", hwFloat(8, 24)); // j
        HWVar f4p = io.input("f4p", hwFloat(8, 24)); // j+1
        ...
        //Boundary conditions
        //HWVar cnt = control.count.simpleCounter(32);//.cast(hwFloat(8, 24));
        HWVar cntMod = control.count.simpleCounter(32, 320); // 32 bit counter with module 320
        HWVar cond318temp = cntMod > 317;
        HWVar cond318 = cntMod < 319 ? cond318temp : 0; // k5
        HWVar sel_l = cntMod > 0;
        HWVar sel_h = cntMod < 320;
        HWVar pom1tmpf1 = cond318 ? f1 : stream.offset(f1, -1);  // tmpf1[i0] = f1[I2D(ni,im1,j)];
        HWVar tmpf1 = sel_l ? pom1tmpf1 : f1new;  // tmpf1[i0] = f1[I2D(ni,im1,j)];
        HWVar tmpf2 = cond318 ? stream.offset(f2m, 1) : f2m; // tmpf2[i0] = f2[I2D(ni,i,jm1)];
        HWVar tmpf3pom = cond318 ? stream.offset(f3, +2) : stream.offset(f3, +2);
        HWVar tmpf3 = sel_h ? tmpf3pom : f3;  // tmpf3[i0] = f3[I2D(ni,ip1,j)];
        ...
        HWVar tmpf8pom = cond318 ? f8p : stream.offset(f8p,-1); // tmpf8[i0] = f8[I2D(ni,im1,jp1)];
        HWVar tmpf8 = sel_l ? tmpf8pom : f8new; // tmpf8[i0] = f8[I2D(ni,im1,jp1)];
        ...
        io.output("tmpf1", tmpf1, hwFloat(8, 24));
        io.output("tmpf2", tmpf2, hwFloat(8, 24));
        ...
} }
```

Fig. 22 Dataflow implementation of the Lattice–Boltzmann stream function.

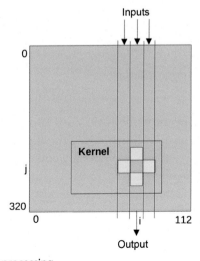

Fig. 23 Stream-based processing.

```
public class LBMManager extends CustomManager {
  LBMManager(MAXBoardModel board_model, String name, Target is_simulation) {
    super(board_model, name, is_simulation);
    KernelBlock k1 = addKernel(new StreamKernel(makeKernelParameters("StreamKernel")));
    KernelBlock k6 = addKernel(new CollideKernel(makeKernelParameters("CollideKernel")));
    Demux split1 = demux("split1");
    ...
    split1.getInput() <== addStreamFromHost("u1"); // Stream k1_f1 = split1.addOutput("f1_u1");
    ...
    Mux join1 = mux("join1");
    ...
    addStreamToHost("i1") <== join1.getOutput();
    ...
    k1.getInput("f1") <== split1.addOutput("k1_u1");
    ...
    join1.addInput("k1_i1") <== k1.getOutput("tmpf1");
    ...
    k6.getInput("f1i") <== split1.addOutput("k6_u1");
    ...
    join1.addInput("k6_i1") <== k6.getOutput("f1o");
    ...
    Stream tread = addStreamFromOnCardMemory("tread", kt.getOutput("rdTest1"));
    kf.getInput("inData") <== tread;
    Stream twrite = addStreamToOnCardMemory("twrite", kt.getOutput("wrTest1"));
    twrite <== kf.getOutput("outData");
    //kernel to host
    Stream toHost = addStreamToHost("outData");
    toHost <== k2.getOutput("outData");
    //DRAM to host
    Stream fromDRAM = addStreamFromOnCardMemory("fromDRAM",
        k2.getOutput("rdInMyDRAM"));
    k2.getInput("inData") <== fromDRAM;
    //host to kernel
    Stream fromHost = addStreamFromHost("inData");
    k1.getInput("inData") <==fromHost;
    //kernel to DRAM
    Stream toDRAM =
        addStreamToOnCardMemory("toDRAM",k1.getOutput("wrOutMyDRAM"));
    toDRAM <== k1.getOutput("outData");
  }
}
```

Fig. 24 The Lattice–Boltzmann manager.

the manager provided by the framework. The LBM iterates through all finite elements many times (*maxIter* times). Only the final result is what a user is interested in. Therefore, all of the processing could be done at the dataflow hardware, since the dataflow hardware has enough memory. In this case, important decision was to keep all semi-results within the memory on the Maxeler card, in order to spare the time that would be needed for transferring these back and forth between the processor and the DFEs. This means that a kernel should be fed from the main memory at the very beginning, while the input should be fetched from the dataflow hardware memory during the execution of all iterations. Similarly, results of iterations have to be stored to the dataflow hardware memory, while only as the very end, data have to be passed to the main memory. Therefore, besides defining the streams between kernels and the CPU, multiplexers had to be introduced, telling the DFEs when to load the data from the processor over the PCIe and when to load it from the DRAM memory that is on the card.

6. PERFORMANCE EVALUATION

Results of the comparison of control-flow implementations and our dataflow implementation of the LBM are given in three domains: speed, complexity, and power.

6.1 Case Study: A Control-Flow and a Dataflow Implementation of the LBM

As we can see from a brief review of the LBM implemented for control-flow architecture in the C programming language, available in the previous chapter, the main loop consists of two functions that are being executed in most of the total execution time. The function *stream* requires fetching all elements of all matrices, which presents a memory bottleneck. However, it does not require a lot of computing. The function *collide* requires both fetching all elements and a reasonable amount of processing per each element. The total application execution time can be roughly divided into sums of the total execution time of these two functions. The execution time of the function *collide* is roughly 1.5 times higher than the execution time of the function *stream*. By comparing execution times of these two functions, we can see that PEs in the function *collide* takes approximately 50% of the time needed for fetching the elements.

We have compared execution time using the MAX2 card with 6 GB of RAM and using Intel i5 650 processor with the clock speed of 3.2 GHz. The computer used 4 GB RAM memory at the speed of 1333 MHz. Our study showed that the acceleration of the dataflow implementation over the control-flow implementation of the LBM is in real case scenarios around 17. Fig. 25 presents the comparison of the execution time of the CPU and the Maxeler implementation of the LBM algorithm for different numbers of iterations.

Fig. 26 demonstrates the extracted acceleration. Compared to the algorithm execution using CPU only, results show acceleration factor of about 17 in a real case scenario. Without taking into account the time needed for

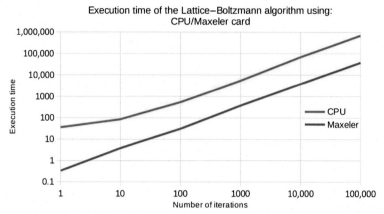

Fig. 25 Comparison of execution times of CPU and Maxeler implementation of the Lattice–Boltzmann algorithm.

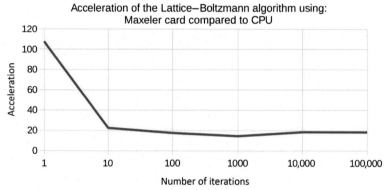

Fig. 26 Achieved speedup of executing the Lattice–Boltzmann algorithm on FPGA, compared to the execution on CPU.

sending the data to the Maxeler card and returning results, in case the application is started with a single iteration, the acceleration factor is more than 100. The execution time on the Maxeler card is nearly proportional to the number of iterations, while the processor after the first iteration executes iterations significantly faster. This can be explained by the time needed for the CPU to fetch the data from the main memory into the cache memory. Please note that for a large enough problem size, it would not be possible to accommodate all of the data into the cache. In that case, the acceleration factor would be around 100. Note that the problem of cache size could also be solved using control-flow paradigm, using a cluster or CUDA. However, that would require transmitting data between processors and the main memory.

We estimate the power consumption using the following method. Based on Ref. [68], we assume that the desktop computer power consumption without MAX2 card is 61 W when idle, and 76 W under workload. The consumption with MAX2 card is 86 W when idle, and 118 W under workload. The processor itself consumes around 51 W when idle, and 91 W when fully loaded. By comparing the execution times of functions *stream* and *collide*, we calculate that the CPU is idle around 20% of time, leading to the estimated average consumption of 64 W. The desktop with Maxeler card MAX2 consumes 118 W. Therefore, calculated power factor is around 1.84. This way, the graph from Fig. 27 is obtained.

The achieved reduction in power consumption is around 8.5. Although the reduction in power consumption is not as big as the potential reduction when switching from control-flow to dataflow paradigm, a lot of power is still consumed on the CPU. However, if DFEs would be optimally occupied by the algorithm (e.g., by updating manager so that the dataflow hardware processes many rows in parallel), we could expect further reductions in energy consumption. For example, the dataflow supercomputer Maxeler MPC-X is capable of executing 8.97 GFLOPs/Watt, which is a performance per Watt comparable to the top Green500 today.

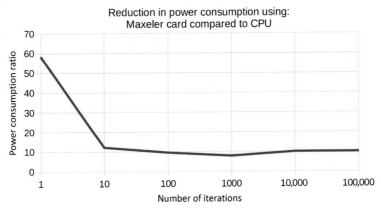

Fig. 27 Comparison of the power consumptions of CPU and Maxeler executing the Lattice–Boltzmann algorithm.

6.2 Dataflow Acceleration for Other Algorithms

Researchers achieved significant speedups using the dataflow paradigm. We present some of them that are also implemented using the Maxeler framework. For each one of them, we present the methods used in the transformation of the algorithm from control-flow to dataflow.

Stojanovic *et al.* solved the Gross–Pitaevskii equation using the dataflow paradigm, achieving the speedup of 8.2, compared to the control-flow counterpart [68]. In order to achieve this speedup, rearranging of the data was necessary. As already described, this method assumes calculating elements that do not depend on each other in a row. If the problem is big enough, elements whose calculation depends on the previously calculated one will have the data ready once the processing is scheduled. For example, if each element, except the first one in a row of a table, depends on the previous element in the same row, but rows are mutually independent, instead of calculating the elements row by row, elements could be calculated column by column.

Kos *et al.* achieved the speedup of 100–150 for sorting more than 1000 arrays consecutively using the dataflow implementation of the Odd–even merge network sort algorithm [69,70]. Arrays consisted of 16–128 elements; speedup is calculated as a ratio between the execution time of sorting on the CPU and the execution time of sorting on DFE. The Odd–even merge sort algorithm sorts elements of an array in 10–28 steps by cyclic splitting the array into two halves, sorting each half independently, and then merging the results. The speedup was achieved by parallelizing all calculations of every step of the Odd–even merge network sort algorithm.

Stanojevic *et al.* [71] achieved the speedup of 18–24 times, compared to the control-flow implementation of the spherical code design based on the variable repulsion force method. The majority of operations are performed in one loop and the fetching can be done in parallel with processing. In the presented implementation, the authors have modified the algorithm itself making it more scalable, so that it is not the same as the original one, but it also iterates toward the solution.

Bezanic *et al.* [72] implemented the RSA algorithm using the Maxeler framework. They recorded speedups of 25–30% for file sizes higher than 40 MB. Although the speedup of DFEs is not as remarkable as in previous cases, this is still a good result, since according to Amdahl's law, only a part of the execution time that is spent on instructions that are parallelized could be accelerated.

Table 2 summarizes the achieved speedups of these algorithms using the dataflow hardware that includes a memory chip.

Trifunovic *et al.* report, in their paper "Paradigm Shift in Big Data Super-Computing: DataFlow vs ControlFlow," speedups of various applications compared to both CPUs and CUDA [73], using both the Maxeler framework and other available technologies.

By comparing the acceleration factors of presented applications, we can see that execution times achieved using dataflow approach are one to two orders of magnitude lower compared to the control-flow implementations. Algorithms that include frequent data exchanging between PEs (e.g., Odd–even merge network sort) tend to have higher potentials for acceleration, while all these data transfers can be done in parallel, while the processor must fetch and store each variable in the memory.

6.3 Threat to Validity

This work presents differences between control-flow and dataflow paradigms, exposing obvious potentials for accelerating certain types of applications using the dataflow paradigm. However, presented results are subject to the comparison of different computer architectures using different types of memories, etc. Authors of presented applications tried to compare the execution times of algorithms on Maxeler cards and CPUs that are similar by production date, usually executing the control-flow and dataflow versions of algorithms on the same computer, with and without using dataflow hardware.

Table 2 The Speedups of Algorithms Implemented for Dataflow Paradigm

Author	Algorithm	Speedup	Conditions
Stojanovic et al. [68]	Gross–Pitaevskii	8.2 ×	–
Kos et al. [69]	Odd–even merge network sort	100–150 ×	More than 1000 arrays
Korolija et al. [67]	Lattice–Boltzmann	17 ×	Matrix dimensions 320×112
Stanojevic et al. [71]	Spherical code design	18–24 ×	$3 \leq D \leq 6$
Bezanic et al. [72]	RSA	25–30%	Size of file >40 MB

In our work, we have used matrices that can fit into the cache memory. If the problem size grows above the size of the cache memory, the acceleration factor of the dataflow implementation of the Lattice–Boltzmann algorithm would be much higher.

The goal of this work was to present the potentials of the dataflow paradigm. Since the achieved acceleration is much higher than the acceleration factor of two consecutive processor generations, we believe that the reader may comprehend presented results with caution, and simply acknowledge the difference in these computing paradigms.

7. CONCLUSIONS

As a result of our work, we feel that the control-flow architectures might soon be outdated as a single architectural type used for high performance computing. Many cores are not always enough for accelerating applications due to the distance between processing units, while the power consumption is remarkably higher than what is theoretically needed for the functionality that they provide. Dataflow solution solves these issues, but the limitation is that it is not feasible for general-purpose computing. Therefore, the optimal solution for most high performance computing problems is a hybrid solution.

The LBM is one of the most widely used methods for fluid dynamics. It can be easily transformed in order to run in parallel. Starting from the C++ code, we have analyzed potentials for acceleration and found a repetitive loop whose execution represents most of the execution time. During the execution of each iteration, certain matrices are accessed by functions *stream* and *collide*. We have presented the dataflow implementation of the LBM that is developed using the Maxeler framework as a tool that combines many methods available from the theory of systolic arrays. As the following step, we have designed kernels to execute iterations on a Maxeler card and transfer data to and from the CPU after each iteration. However, the mid–results were kept in the main memory. Next modification of the algorithm was to use the Maxeler card memory instead of sending the data between the CPU and Maxeler card after each iteration.

Using the dataflow paradigm, fluid flow simulations can be done faster with less power consumption, even though the FPGA run at lower clock frequencies and the part of the chip responsible for executing a single instruction is not capable of doing much more. In addition to greater speed of execution on FPGAs, less power consumption is also achieved. We have also shown that many other algorithms can be accelerated using the dataflow paradigm.

Future work is needed in order to make dataflow programming even easier, relaxing the programmer from needing to know hardware details.

Sometimes, the workforce of ant colony might suit the job better than the elephant workforce. And in computing, the general rule usually applies: the closer—the faster.

ACKNOWLEDGMENTS

This work has been partially funded by the Ministry of Education and Science of the Republic of Serbia (TR32047 and III44006). The authors are thankful to Mr. Borivoje Andric for English language editing of this text.

APPENDIX

SystemC	Open SystemC Initiative (OSCI)	http://www.systemc.org/
Catapult C	Mentor Graphics	http://www.mentor.com/products/c-based_design/
Impulse C	Impulse Accelerated Technologies	http://www.impulsec.com/
Carte	SRC Computers	http://www.srccomp.com/CarteProgEnv.htm
Dime C	Nallatech	http://www.nallatech.com/?node_id=1.2.2&id=19
Streams C	Los Alamos National Laboratory	http://www.streams-c.lanl.gov/
AccelChip	MATLAB DSP Synthesis	http://www.accelchip.com/
Starbridge	VIVA	http://www.starbridgesystems.com/
NAPA-C	National Semiconductor	http://portal.acm.org/citation.cfm?id=795813
SA-C	Colorado State University	http://www.cs.colostate.edu/cameron/compiler.html
CoreFire	Annapolis Micro Systems	http://www.annapmicro.com/
Maxeler Technologies	–	http://www.maxeler.com/

REFERENCES

[1] J.G. Koomey, C. Belady, M. Patterson, A. Santos, K.-D. Lange, Assessing Trends over Time in Performance, Costs, and Energy Use for Servers, Analytics Press, Oakland, CA, 2009.

[2] M. Flynn, O. Mencer, V. Milutinovic, G. Rakocevic, P. Stenstrom, M. Valero, R. Trobec, Moving from PetaFlops to PetaData, Commun. ACM Comput. Surv. 56 (5) (2013) 39–42.

[3] A. Kos, S. Tomazic, J. Salom, N. Trifunovic, M. Valero, V. Milutinovic, New benchmarking methodology and programming model for big data processing, Int. J. Sens. Netw. 11 (8) (2015) 1–7.

[4] T. Nowatzki, V. Gangadhar, K. Sankaralingam, Exploring the potential of heterogeneous von neumann/dataflow execution models, in: Proceedings of the 42nd Annual International Symposium on Computer Architecture, ACM, 2015, pp. 298–310.

[5] A. DeHon, J. Wawrzynek, Reconfigurable computing: what, why, and implications for design automation, in: Proceedings of the 36th annual ACM/IEEE Design Automation Conference, ACM, New York, 1999, pp. 610–615.

[6] A.H. Veen, Dataflow machine architecture, ACM Comput. Surv. 18 (4) (1986) 365–396. ACM.

[7] B.K. Essink, Using FPGAs as fine-grained static dataflow machines, in: 21st Twente Student Conference on IT, June 23rd, 2014 Enschede, The Netherlands, 2014.

[8] C. Schryver, H. Marxen, S. Weithoffer, N. Wehn, High-performance hardware acceleration of asset simulations, High-Performance Computing Using FPGAs, Springer, New York, 2013, pp. 3–32.

[9] S. Stojanovic, D. Bojic, M. Bojovic, An overview of selected heterogeneous and reconfigurable architectures, in: A. Hurson, V. Milutinovic (Eds.), Advances in Computers, 96, Academic Press, Burlington, 2015, pp. 1–45.

[10] A. Hurson, V. Milutinovic, Special issue on dataflow supercomputing, Adv. Comput. 96 (2015) 1–234.

[11] V. Milutinovic, J. Salom, N. Trifunovic, R. Giorgi, Guide to DataFlow Supercomputing, Springer International Publishing, Switzerland, 2015, pp. 1–129.

[12] V. Milutinovic, A. Hurson, Dataflow Processing, first ed., Academic Press, 2015, pp. 1–266.

[13] D. Kirk, NVIDIA cuda software and gpu parallel computing architecture, in: ISMM 7 Proceedings of the 6th International Symposium on Memory Management, 2007, pp. 103–104.

[14] R.P. Feynman, Lectures on Computation, The ACM Digital Library, 1998.

[15] K. Olukotun, L. Hammond, The future of microprocessors, ACM Queue 3 (7) (2005) 26–29.

[16] H. Esmaeilzadeh, E. Blem, R. Amant, K. Sankaralingam, D. Burger, Power challenges may end the multicore era, Commun. ACM 56 (2) (2013) 93–102.

[17] C. Yang, H. Wu, Q. Huang, Z. Li, J. Li, Using spatial principles to optimize distributed computing for enabling the physical science discoveries, PNAS 108 (1) (2011) 5498–5503.

[18] L. Heendaliya, M. Wisely, D. Lin, S.S. Sarvestani, A. Hurson, Influence-aware predictive density queries under road-network constraints, in: Advances in Spatial and Temporal Databases, Springer International Publishing, 2015, pp. 80–97.

[19] D. Pellerin, S. Tibault, Practical FPGA Programming in C, Prentice Hall Press, Upper Saddle River, NJ, 2005.

[20] D. Cohen, Mathematical approach to iterative computation networks, in: Proceedings of Fourth Symposium on Computer Arithmetic, IEEE, 1978, pp. 226–238.

[21] L. Johnsson, D. Cohen, Mathematical approach to modeling the flow of data and control in computational networks, in: VLSI Systems and Computations, Computer Science Press, Rockville, MD, 1981, pp. 213–225.

[22] U. Weiser, A. Davis, A wavefront notion tool for VLSI array design, in: VLSI Systems and Computations, Computer Science Press, Rockville, MD, 1981.

[23] M. Lam, J. Mostow, A transformational model of VLSI systolic design, in: IFIP Sixth International Symposium on Computer Hardware Descriptive Languages and Their Applications, Carnegie-Mellon University, Pittsburg, PA, 1983.

[24] D. Gannon, Pipelining array computations for MIMD parallelism: a functional specification, in: Proceedings of International Conference on Parallel Processing, 1982, pp. 284–286.

[25] H.T. Kung, W.T. Lin, An algebra for VLSI algorithm design, in: Proceedings of Conference on Elliptic Problem Solvers, Monterey, CA, 1983.

[26] R.H. Kuhn, Transforming algorithms for single-stage and VLSI architectures, in: Proceedings of Workshop on Interconnection Networks for Parallel and Distributed Processing, 1980, pp. 11–19.

[27] R.H. Kuhn, Optimization and interconnection complexity for parallel processors, single stage networks and decision trees, PhD thesis, Technical Report 80-1009, University of Illinois, Urbana-Champaign, IL, 1980.

[28] W.L. Miranker, A. Winkler, Space–time representations of computational structures, Computing 32 (1984) 93–114.

[29] J.A.B. Fortes, F. Parisi-Presicce, Optimal linear schedules for the parallel execution of algorithms, in: Proceedings of International Conference on Parallel Processing, IEEE, 1984.

[30] J.A.B. Fortes, C.S. Raghavendra, Dynamically reconfigurable fault-tolerant array processors, in: Proceedings of 14th International Conference on Fault-tolerant Computing, IEEE, 1984.

[31] J.A.B. Fortes, D.I. Moldovan, Parallelism detection and transformation techniques useful for VLSI algorithms, J. Parallel Distrib. Comput. 2 (1985) 277–301. Academic Press.

[32] J.A.B. Fortes, D.I. Moldovan, Data broadcasting in linearly scheduled array processors, in: Proceedings of 11th Annual Symposium on Computer Architecture, ACM/IEEE, 1984, pp. 224–231.

[33] D.I. Moldovan, On the design of algorithms for VLSI systolic arrays, Proc. IEEE 71 (1) (1983) 113–120.

[34] D.I. Moldovan, A. Varma, Design of algorithmically specialized VLSI devices, in: Proceedings of International Conference on Computer Design: VLSI in Computers, 1983, pp. 88–91.

[35] S. Lerner, D. Grove, C. Chambers, Composing dataflow analyses and transformations, in: The 29th Annual ACM SIGPLAN-SIGACT Symposium on Principles of Programming Languages, Portland Oregon, USA, ACM, 2002.

[36] J. Villarreal, A. Park, W. Najjar, R. Halstead, Designing modular hardware accelerators in C with ROCCC 2.0, in: 18th IEEE Annual International Symposium on Field-Programmable Custom Computing Machines, 2010.

[37] M.J. Flynn, O. Pell, O. Mencer, Dataflow supercomputing, in: 22nd International Conference on Field Programmable Logic and Applications, 2012, pp. 1–3.

[38] R. Dimond, S. Racanière, O. Pell, Accelerating large-scale HPC applications using FPGAs, in: 20th IEEE Symposium on Computer Arithmetic, 2011, pp. 191–192.

[39] A. Dellson, G. Sandberg, S. Mohl, Turning FPGAs into supercomputers—debunking the myths about FPGA-based software acceleration, in: Proceedings of the 48th Cray User Group meeting, 2006.

[40] D.J. William, The end of denial architecture and the rise of throughput computing, in: Keynote Speech at Design Automation Conference, 2010.

[41] K. Georgia, N.S. Voros, K. Masselos, System level design of complex hardware applications using ImpulseC, in: 2010 IEEE Annual Symposium on VLSI, IEEE, 2010.

[42] T. Grtker, S. Liao, G. Martin, S. Swan, System Design with SystemC, first ed., Springer, USA, 2010.

[43] S. Gupta, R.K. Gupta, N. Dutt, A. Nicolau, Coordinated parallelizing compiler optimizations and high-level synthesis, ACM Trans. Des. Autom. Electron. Syst. 9 (4) (2004) 441–470.

[44] Y. Ben-Asher, N. Rotem, Using memory profile analysis for automatic synthesis of pointers code, ACM Trans. Embedd. Comput. Syst. 12 (3) (2013). Article No. 68.

[45] S.J. Kim, L. De Carli, K. Sankaralingam, C. Estan, SWSL: software synthesis for network lookup, in: ANCS'13 Proceedings of the Ninth ACM/IEEE Symposium on Architectures for Networking and Communications Systems, 2013, pp. 191–202.

[46] H.T. Kung, C.E. Leiserson, Systolic arrays (for VLSI), in: Proceedings of Sparse Matrix, 1978, pp. 256–282.

[47] H.T. Kung, P.L. Lehman, Systolic (VLSI) arrays for relational database operations, in: Proceedings of International Conference Management of Data, ACM SIGMOD, 1980, pp. 105–116.

[48] K.T. Johnson, A.R. Hurson, B. Shirazi, General-purpose systolic arrays, IEEE Computer 26 (11) (1993) 20–31.

[49] W.A. Najjar, B.A. Buyukkurt, Z. Guo, J. Villareal, J. Cortes, A. Mitra, Compiled code acceleration on FPGAs, Department of Computer Science and Engineering University of California-Riverside, Riverside, CA, 2008.

[50] T.J. Callahan, J.R. Hauser, J. Wawrzynek, The Garp architecture and C compiler, IEEE Computer 33 (4) (2000).

[51] M.B. Gokhale, J.M. Stone, J. Arnold, M. Lalinowski, Stream-oriented FPGA computing in the Streams-C high level language, in: IEEE Symposium on Field-Programmable Custom Computing Machines, 2000.

[52] M. Hall, P. Diniz, K. Bondalapati, H. Zeigler, P. Duncan, R. Jain, J. Granacki, DEFACTO: a design environment for adaptive computing technology, in: Proceedings of the 6th Reconfigurable Architectures Workshop, 1999.

[53] W.A. Najjar, A. Bohm, B. Draper, J. Hammes, R. Rinker, R. Beveridge, M. Chawathe, C. Ross, From algorithms to hardware—a high-level language abstraction for reconfigurable computing, IEEE Computer 36 (8) (2003) 63–69.

[54] R.A. Arvind, R.A. Iannucci, Two Fundamental Issues in Multiprocessing: The Dataflow Solutions, MIT Laboratory for Computer Science, 1983. MIT/LCS/MT-241.

[55] D.A. Adams, A computation model with data flow sequencing, Technical Report CS117, Computer Science Department, Stanford University, Stanford, CA, 1968.

[56] D.D. Chamberlin, Parallel Implementation of a Single-Assignment Language, PhD thesis, Stanford University, Computer Science, 1971.

[57] J.E. Rodriguez, A graph model for parallel computation, Technical Report ESL1-R-398, MAC-TR-64, Laboratory for Computer Science, Massachusetts Institute of Technology, Cambridge, MA, 1969.

[58] K. Stavrou, D. Pavlou, M. Nikolaides, P. Petrides, Z. Popovic, R. Giorgi, Programming abstractions and toolchain for dataflow multithreading architectures, in: Eighth International Symposium on Parallel and Distributed Computing, 2009, pp. 107–114.

[59] G.N.T. Huong, Y. Na, S.W. Kim, Applying frame layout to hardware design in FPGA for seamless support of cross calls in CPU-FPGA coupling architecture, Microprocess. Microsy. 35 (5) (2011) 462–472.

[60] C. Feichtinger, J. Habich, H. Köstler, U. Rüde, T. Aoki, Performance modeling and analysis of heterogeneous Lattice Boltzmann simulations on CPU-GPU clusters, Parallel Comput. 46 (2015) 1–13.

[61] M. Krafczyk, J. Tölke, E. Rank, M. Schulz, Two-dimensional simulation of fluid–structure interaction using Lattice–Boltzmann methods, Comput. Struct. 79 (22–25) (2001) 2031–2037.

[62] G.R. McNamara, G. Zanetti, Use of the Boltzmann equation to simulate lattice–gas automata, Phys. Rev. Lett. 61 (1988) 2332–2335.

[63] H. Yua, S.S. Girimajia, L. Luob, DNS and LES of decaying isotropic turbulence with and without frame rotation using Lattice Boltzmann method, J. Comput. Phys. 209 (2) (2005) 599–616.

[64] C. Feichtinger, Design and performance evaluation of a software framework for multiphysics simulations on heterogeneous supercomputers, Doctoral thesis, Erlangen, 2012.

[65] Lattice–Boltzmann Source Code, Web Page Visited in June, 2015. http://www.pbx-brasil.com/Pesquisa/Ferramentas/cuda/dia02/aulasCuda/exemplos/programas/latticeBoltzman/LB_Demo/2dLB_C.c

[66] G.M. Amdah, Validity of the single processor approach to achieving large scale computing capabilities, in: Proceedings of the April 18-20, 1967, Spring Joint Computer Conference, AFIPS'67 (Spring), ACM, New York, NY, 1967, pp. 483–485.

[67] N. Korolija, T. Djukic, V. Milutinovic, N. Filipovic, Accelerating Lattice–Boltzmann method using the Maxeler dataflow approach, Trans. Internet Res. 9 (2) (2013) 5–10.

[68] S. Stojanovic, D. Bojic, V. Milutinovic, Solving Gross Pitaevskii equation using dataflow paradigm, Trans. Internet Res. 9 (2) (2013) 17–22.

[69] A. Kos, V. Rankovic, S. Tomazic, Sorting networks on Maxeler dataflow supercomputing systems, in: A. Hurson, V. Milutinovic (Eds.), Advances in Computers, 96 Elsevier, Academic Press, Amsterdam, 2015, pp. 139–186.

[70] V. Rankovic, A. Kos, V. Milutinovic, Bitonic merge sort implementation on the Maxeler dataflow supercomputing system, Trans. Internet Res. 9 (2) (2013) 34–42.

[71] I. Stanojevic, V. Senk, V. Milutinovic, Application of Maxeler dataflow supercomputing to spherical code design, Trans. Internet Res. 9 (2) (2013) 1–4.

[72] N. Bezanic, J. Popovic-Bozovic, V. Milutinovic, I. Popovic, Implementation of the RSA algorithm on a dataflow architecture, Trans. Internet Res. 9 (2) (2013) 11–16.

[73] N. Trifunovic, V. Milutinovic, J. Salom, A. Kos, Paradigm shift in big data supercomputing: dataflow vs. controlflow, J. Big Data 2 (4) (2015) 1–9.

ABOUT THE AUTHORS

Nenad Korolija is with the Faculty of the School of Electrical Engineering, University of Belgrade, Serbia. He received an MSc in Electrical Engineering and Computer Science in 2009. He was a Teaching Assistant for Software Project Management and Business Communication Principles: A Practical Course. His interests and experiences include developing software for high performance computer architectures and dataflow architectures. During 2008, he worked on the HIPEAC FP7 project at the University of Siena, Italy. In 2013, he was an intern at the Google Inc., Mountain View, CA, USA.

Jovan Popović is a Program Manager at the Microsoft Development Center Serbia. He received an MSc in Electrical Engineering and Computer Science from the University of Belgrade in 2010. He is a Software Practitioner specialized in project management, big data processing, and web application development. Before, he was with the School of Electrical Engineering, University of Belgrade. He also worked in software industry. The main focus of his research is application of software metrics and applied business intelligence in the software development process.

Miloš Cvetanović is with the School of Electrical Engineering, University of Belgrade, Serbia. He holds a PhD in Computer Engineering from the University of Belgrade. He teaches database systems. His research interests include computer architecture, reverse engineering, information systems, and simulators.

Miroslav Bojović is with the School of Electrical Engineering, University of Belgrade, Serbia. His PhD in Computer Engineering from the University of Belgrade was announced as the best in the school in 1988. He teaches database systems. He held talks at prestigious Universities, including: UCLA, Purdue, and Brown, as well as in companies: McDonnell Douglasand Boeing, Medsite, and Medec. His research interests include database systems, software engineering, and fault tolerant computing.

CHAPTER FOUR

Data Flow Computing in Geoscience Applications

L. Gan*,†,‡, H. Fu*,‡, O. Mencer§, W. Luk¶, G. Yang*,†,‡

*Ministry of Education Key Laboratory for Earth System Modeling, Center for Earth System Science, Tsinghua University, Beijing, China

†Tsinghua University, Beijing, China

‡National Supercomputing Center in Wuxi, Wuxi, China

§Maxeler Technologies, London, United Kingdom

¶Imperial College London, London, United Kingdom

Contents

1. Introduction	126
2. Data Flow Computing in HPC	128
2.1 Brief Summary of Data Flow Computing Model	128
2.2 Maxeler DFE	130
3. Geoscience Applications in HPC	131
3.1 Brief Summary	131
3.2 Climate Modeling	132
3.3 Exploration Geophysics	132
4. Case Study 1: Global Shallow Water Equations	133
4.1 Problem Description	133
4.2 Hybrid Domain Partition Scheme	136
4.3 Mixed Precision Arithmetic	137
4.4 Performance and Power Efficiency	140
5. Case Study 2: Euler Atmospheric Equations	140
5.1 Problem Description	140
5.2 Algorithmic Offsetting	143
5.3 Fast Memory Table and Mixed Precision Arithmetic	145
5.4 Performance and Power Efficiency	145
6. Case Study 3: Reverse Time Migration	147
6.1 Problem Description	147
6.2 Random Boundary	148
6.3 A Customized Window Buffer	148
6.4 Cascading Multiple Computations	149
6.5 Number Representations	149
6.6 Hardware (De)compression Scheme	151
6.7 Performance and Power Efficiency	151

Advances in Computers, Volume 104
ISSN 0065-2458
http://dx.doi.org/10.1016/bs.adcom.2016.09.005

7. Summary and Concluding Remarks 153
Acknowledgments 153
Appendix 154
References 155
About the Authors 156

Abstract

Geoscience research is one of the major fields that calls for the support of high-performance computers (HPC). With the algorithms of geoscience application becoming more complex, and the ever-increasing demands for better performance and finer resolutions, technical innovations from both algorithmic and architectural perspectives are highly desired. In recent years, data flow computing engines based on reconfigurable computing systems such as FPGAs have been introduced into HPC area, and start to show some inspiringly good results in many important applications. In this chapter, we summarize our initial efforts and experiences of using Maxeler Data Flow Engines as high-performance platforms, and target at eliminating the main bottlenecks and obtaining higher efficiencies for solving geoscience problems. Choosing three computing kernels from two popular geoscience application domains (climate modeling and exploration geophysics), we present a set of customization and optimization techniques based on the reconfigurable hardware platforms. Through building highly efficient computing pipelines that fit well to both the algorithm and the architecture, we manage to achieve better results in both the performance and power efficiency over traditional multi-core and many-core architectures. Our work demonstrates that data flow computing engines are promising candidates to make contributions to the development of geoscience applications.

ABBREVIATIONS

BRAM Block Random Access Memory
CPU Central Processing Unit
CUDA Compute Unified Device Architecture
DFE Data Flow Engine
DRAM Dynamic Random Access Memory
FPGA Field Programmable Gate Array
GPU Graphic Processing Unit
MIC Many Integrated Core
RTM Reverse Time Migration
SWEs Shallow Water Equations

1. INTRODUCTION

The geoscience disciplines cover the scientific studies on a wide range of different applications related to earth science. In recent decades, as influences of human activity on the Earth getting more and more significant, problems such as global warming and energy crisis have brought tough challenges to the development of our society, and become key factors that can determine the quality of our future life. Therefore, it is very important to look deep into these geoscience applications and to better understand the basic evolving mechanism of our planet.

In the meantime, the fast development of high-performance computing (HPC) technology has greatly contributed to the progress of geoscience study. Due to the fact that geoscience applications such as climate modeling and exploration geophysics generally require complex simulation algorithms and huge data to process, numerical computing methods based on high-performance computer system become the most efficient ways to acquire satisfying simulation results. Computers based on CPU processors have dominated the field of HPC for decades, and are still the most popular providers of computing power among different geoscience applications. However, as heat dissipation becomes the main bottleneck, it is now expensive and unrealistic to further increase the clock frequency of traditional chips. Modern HPC systems start to exploit new architectural features for further performance boost, such as the integration of more computing cores within single chip and the performance scalings over more computing chips. Graphic Processing Unit (GPU) and Many Integrated Core (MIC) architectures are two representatives using many-core technology. They have achieved good performance results in many applications.

Even though that petascale computing power already becomes available by current supercomputers, bottlenecks from memory bandwidth, cache capability, imperfections on data representations, and the ever-increasing algorithmic complexity of geoscience applications still severely prevent the simulation performance from further improvement. Geoscience scientists and researchers are engaged in looking for highly efficient solutions and innovations from both algorithmic and architectural perspectives.

In recent decades, reconfigurable platforms such as the Field Programmable Gate Arrays (FPGAs) have been brought into HPC field and already demonstrated promising performance results in many applications, such as financing numerical methods [1]. Unlike traditional platforms such as CPU, GPU, and MIC, reconfigurable platform can achieve high efficiency through building an algorithm-oriental data flow engine (DFE) with a long pipeline of concurrent computing units, and employing a set of customizable features such as data representations and cache mechanisms. Moreover, the magnitude of lower clock frequency of the FPGA chips can generally lead to dramatic reductions in power consumptions, and provide a more green and environmentally friendly way for high-performance computing.

There has been many inspiring work that manages to solve geoscience problems using reconfigurable DFEs so far. In this chapter, we will give a brief introduction to the basic background and latest development of DFEs and geoscience applications. Then we will summarize our initial efforts and experiences in Refs. [2–4] that apply Maxeler Data Flow Engines, a highly efficient and user-friendly data flow computing platform, to solve various key issues for geoscience applications. We are choosing three geoscience computing kernels as the study cases, namely, the *Shallow Water Equations (SWEs) Solver* and the *Euler Equations Solver* from atmospheric modeling, and the *Reverse Time Migration (RTM)* kernel from exploration geophysics. For each study case, we present in detail the approaches to build the data flow pipeline corresponding to the algorithm, including the hardware implementation and a set of customizable optimizing techniques. Comparisons with other platforms such as multi-core CPUs, GPUs, and MICs demonstrate sustainable better performance and higher power efficiency, and prove that data flow computing models are promising candidates that can contribute greatly to the development of geoscience applications.

The innovation presented in our chapter can be treated as a combination of the creativity methods #2, #3, #6, and #8 of the work by Blagojevic *et al.* [5]. And the structure of this chapter is as follows: Sections 2 and 3 briefly introduce the background of data flow computing and geoscience applications with respect to high-performance computing; Sections 4–6 present case studies including the data flow design, optimization methods, and the performance results; and Section 7 concludes the chapter.

2. DATA FLOW COMPUTING IN HPC

2.1 Brief Summary of Data Flow Computing Model

As briefly introduced in the previous section, there are many big challenges that prevent traditional high-performance computing platforms (e.g., CPU, GPU, and MIC) from achieving good performance when dealing with complex application kernels. On one hand, the cache misses when processing discontinues data layout and the memory wall [6] greatly degrades the computing efficiencies, and as a result cut down the effect of the inspiringly high-computing performance. On the other hand, traditional platforms are generally only in good support for single-precision (sp) and double-precision (dp) number formats, which further restrict the overall performance when dealing with numerical applications. Therefore, even though inspiringly high peak performance can be provided, the practical efficiency when accelerating application kernels is still not satisfactory. Those low-efficient implementations, when further being scaled over thousands of supercomputer nodes such as Tianhe-2 and Titan-1A supercomputers, would cause huge amount of power consumption despite of the good time to solution.

Therefore, researchers are eager to look for architectural innovations that could provide users with higher performance, lower power loss, and easier-to-use interfaces. The FPGAs have been studied and widely applied in industry for decades. Especially in the area of data processing and telecommunications, we can see many implementations of FPGA-based technology to meet the diversity of demands. However, preliminary work that selects FPGAs as accelerators and performance boosters is still less to be seen and only covers a small number of areas. The major obstacle lies in the inconvenience in hardware programming and hardware compiling. With the fast development of reconfigurable technologies, we start to see more successful accelerations that manage to break the performance walls by wisely integrating FPGAs into modern HPC systems [7, 8]. One inspiring idea is to use reconfigurable platforms such as FPGAs to form a DFE with a long pipeline of concurrent computing units. Data stored in memory can go through the engines and get computed across each computing unit. Through fully pipelining the operations corresponding to the algorithm, DFE model can achieve high computing efficiency [9].

Fig. 1 shows the general architecture of the data flow computing model, which contains two major parts, memory (shown as DRAM) and the

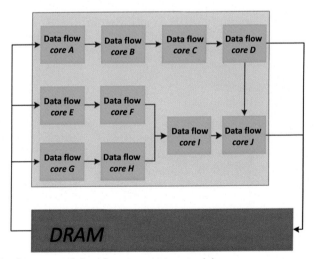

Fig. 1 The architecture of data flow computing model.

computing kernel. Inside the computing kernel there is a set of different data flow cores (marked as green boxes) that each representing a certain kind of operations, such as addition, multiplications, or some more complex nonlinear operations. The data flow cores are connected through pipelines with arrows in the figure depicting the directions of the data flow. Therefore, data required to be processed will go along the pipeline and get computed when it goes through each of the data flow cores. The reconfigurable feature of such platforms enables the general architecture to be customized precisely based on the algorithm, and is therefore specifically fitting well to the problem.

2.2 Maxeler DFE

The Maxeler DFE is a high-performance processing system that combines reconfigurable FPGAs to provide high efficiency and easy-to-use programming interfaces. There are some successful implementations and accelerations of serial applications using Maxeler systems [10–13]. Thus, in the rest of this section, we give a brief introduction to the Maxeler DFE systems. More details can be found in Ref. [14].

Fig. 2 depicts the architecture of a Maxeler Data Flow processing system (Maxeler DFE), which contains both memory and the reconfigurable data processing engine. The engine (marked as the Data Flow Engine in Fig. 2) is able to implement multiple kernels and performs the computation as data flows between the CPU, DFE, and its associated memories. The date flow computing model is the key part in providing higher performance and better efficiency. The local memory (marked as LMem in Fig. 2) of the system is

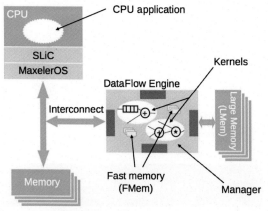

Fig. 2 The architecture of Maxeler DFE [14].

connected to the CPU host memory through PCIe. The DFE itself contains two types of memories. One is the on-board large memory (LMem) that can store few gigabytes of data, and the other one is the on-chip fast memory (FMem) that is capable of providing terabytes/second of data accessing bandwidth.

Note that the bandwidth and flexibility of FMem is a key reason that the DFEs can provide high computing efficiency for complex algorithm, due to the fact that data would otherwise be stalled in memory and greatly slow down the computation. FMem makes the data closer to the computing kernels, breaking the memory wall and hence achieving a high computing efficiency.

As the key computing part, each engine itself contains two major components, *Kernels* and *Manager*. *Kernels* implement computations by deploying a set of different computing unit using the on-chip computing resources, while *Manager* orchestrates the data movement within each *kernel* and between two different *kernels*. When designing a DFE for a given algorithm, users can build different *Kernels* according to the algorithm, and then interconnect the *Kernels* through operating the layout of the *Manager*. Apart from the engine part, a complete DFE system also involves CPU processors that work as controllers, and the CPU-DFE interface that is managed by *MaxelerOS*, which sits within Linux and also within the *Manger* of the engine.

In terms of the user interfaces, Maxeler provides a user-friendly interface that supports high-level programming languages such as C and Java so as to facilitate the hardware programming of *Manager* and *Kernels*. The IDE also contains tools such as resource analysis and software simulation that can assist the performance profiling and optimizations.

3. GEOSCIENCE APPLICATIONS IN HPC

3.1 Brief Summary

Geoscience application covers a large range of research areas that are closely related to the Earth. The earth science discipline, which aims at better understanding the Earth, has long been an important issue as it can protect the quality of our life and to continue benefiting the future generations. Our planet contains an extremely large scale of complicated natural rules that almost apply to all subjects and theories human beings have discovered so far, so the discipline of earth science contains a variety of different subjects. Among them, we choose two representatives to discuss in this chapter, and target at high performance solutions through fully pipelining the algorithms and wisely alternating the customizable optimizations.

In recent decades, the fast development of science and technology has improved the resolution and accuracy of algorithms in geoscience applications. However, the surge in algorithmic complexity and data size also greatly challenges both the numerical methods and the capacity of modern computer systems. Therefore, employing high-performance computing technology becomes the major solution in earth science study. There has been a lot of successes that apply modern HPC platforms to achieve good performance on geoscience kernels. More studies based on heterogeneous platforms such as CPU-GPU, CPU-MIC are frequently to be seen, including the usage of the world's most powerful supercomputers. We even start to see some supercomputers that are specifically built for geoscience research, such as the Earth Simulator Supercomputer in Japan.

3.2 Climate Modeling

For a long time, climate issues have been the key factors that affect our way of life. Especially in recent decades, the increasing interactions between human activities and climate rules further demand a better understanding of the climate. As a result, investigating the climate changing mechanism will continue to be one of the most important research issues, and will continue to serve and protect us in a variety of ways.

There is a number of atmospheric studies based on traditional platforms such as CPUs [15], GPUs [16–18], and MIC [19, 20], and good results have been achieved in terms of both performance and scalability. However, due to the constraint from data presentations, the huge power consumption out of high clock frequency, and the fact that modern algorithms are becoming more computationally intensive and more fine-grained, the overall efficiency of traditional platforms is not satisfactory.

There has been related work on mapping atmospheric simulation onto reconfigurable platforms. Wilhelm [21] analyze a high-level approach for programming preconditioners for an ocean model in climate simulations on FPGAs but do not manage any actual acceleration. Oriato *et al.* [22] accelerate a realistic dynamic core of LAM model using FPGAs. It is a successful trial on reducing resource usage through fixed-point arithmetic.

3.3 Exploration Geophysics

Compared with climate modeling that intends to understand the climate rules, exploration geophysics targets at exploring the underground or undersea geologies and obtaining fine-grained image of the structure inside the Earth. In exploration geophysics, employing high-performance computing technologies can help provide finer resolution and better performance.

In industrial practice, exploration geophysics applications are still largely using CPU-based clusters for data processing and imaging [23]. Employing GPUs as accelerators for exploration geophysics kernels such as the RTM has recently drew more and more attention as some work [24] has achieved promising performance results. However, the relatively low efficiency and the huge power consumption are still big obstacles. On the other hand, preliminary work on using reconfigurable platforms [4] demonstrates a promising result that can keep the performance benefits while solving problems in terms of efficiency and power consumption.

4. CASE STUDY 1: GLOBAL SHALLOW WATER EQUATIONS

4.1 Problem Description

4.1.1 Equations and Discretization

In atmospheric modeling, there are different equations available to simulate the wave propagation and model the essential characteristics of the atmosphere. Among them, SWEs, a set of conservation laws, are the most basic one that is widely used. Cubed-sphere mesh, which is obtained by mapping a cube to the surface of the sphere (Fig. 3A), is chosen as the computational mesh. Compared with other meshes such as the latitude–longitude mesh, cubed-sphere mesh has better load balance in pole regions.

When written in local coordinates, SWEs have an identical expression on the six patches, that is

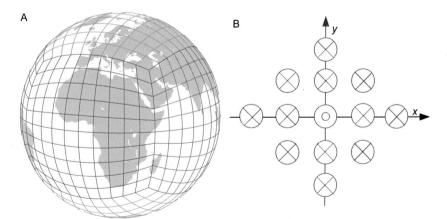

Fig. 3 Mesh and stencil of Shallow Water Equations. (A) Cubed-sphere mesh. (B) The 13-point upwind stencil.

$$\frac{\partial Q}{\partial t} + \frac{1}{\Lambda}\frac{\partial(\Lambda F^1)}{\partial x^1} + \frac{1}{\Lambda}\frac{\partial(\Lambda F^1)}{\partial x^2} + S = 0, \tag{1}$$

where $(x^1, x^2) \in [-\pi/4, \pi/4]$ are the local coordinates, $Q = (h, hu^1, hu^2)^T$ is the prognostic variable, $F^i = u^i Q$ $(i = 1, 2)$ are the convective fluxes, and S is the source term.

Spatially discretized with a cell-centered finite volume method and integrated with a second-order accurate TVD Runge–Kutta method [25], kernels to solve the SWEs are transformed into the computation of a 13-point upwind stencil (Fig. 3B). To compute the prognostic components $(h, hu^1$ and $hu^2)$ of the central point, its neighboring 12 points need to be accessed.

4.1.2 SWE Algorithm and Challenges

Procedure for the CPU algorithm to solve the SWEs at each stencil sweep is shown in Algorithm 1. For each of the six cubed-sphere patches (Fig. 4), first, boundary conditions are applied. The halos is updated with other neighboring patches (line 2). We use the neighboring communication functions from the framework of PETSc (Portable Extensible Toolkit for Scientific computation [26]) to help finish the update. A linear interpolation (line 3) is carried out on the halo across patch interfaces to properly transfer halo information for stencil computations. Second, we do the stencil calculation (lines 4–8), which includes the computation of local coordinate based on global index j and i, and the computation of Flux variables, State Reconstruction, Riemann Solver, and Source Terms (h, hu^1, hu^2). The work flow of the CPU-only algorithm is shown in Fig. 5A, where all the steps are doing in serial (from ① to ④).

Algorithm 1 Original SWEs Algorithm per Stencil Sweep

1: **For** all the six patches **do**
2:     Halo Updating
3:     Interpolations on halos when necessary
4:     **For** all the mesh cells in each patch **do**   //Upwind Stencil
5:         Compute Local Coordinate based on global index (j, i)
6:         Compute Flux, State Reconstruction, and Riemann Solver
7:         Compute Source Terms for h, hu^1, hu^2
8:     **EndFor**
9: **EndFor**

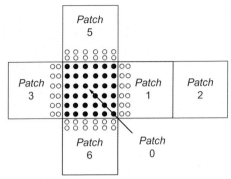

Fig. 4 Mesh points (*solid dots*) to be calculated inside a patch and its halo meshes (*empty dots*) from other patches.

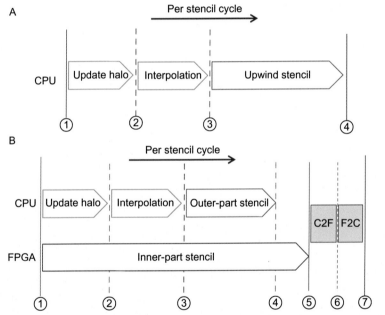

Fig. 5 Work flow of different SWEs algorithms. C2F: CPU to FPGA. F2C: FPGA to CPU. (A) CPU-only work flow. (B) Hybrid work flow.

The SWEs algorithm brings serious design challenges for efficient solutions on DFE platform. Halo updating and interpolations bring data communication between patches. The communication must be carefully handled because it would be extremely heavy and greatly impact the overall performance when the mesh points increase to a large scale. Boundary interpolation also includes a lot of complex conditional statements, which would consume a lot of the limited FPGA resources. Moreover, although the upwind stencil from SWEs only involves 13 points (Fig. 3B), the computational complexity is much higher than normal stencil kernels. To compute one mesh point, we will need at least 434 ADD/SUB operations, 570 multiplications, 99 divisions, 25 square roots, and 20 sine/cosine operations. The high arithmetic density and the irregular operations bring further challenge for the limited on-chip resources.

4.2 Hybrid Domain Partition Scheme

4.2.1 Hybrid Domain Decomposition Methodology

Instead of deploying the whole computational domain into the DFE, we design a hybrid algorithm that utilizes both the host CPU and the DFE simultaneously. We decompose each of the cubed-sphere patch into the inner part and two layers ($L = 2$) of outer part according to Fig. 6A. Then we can find that all the halo exchanges (Comm. between patches arrow in Fig. 6A) and boundary interpolation in Algorithm 1 only happen in the outer part. Therefore, we assign CPU to process the communication and the outer-part computations, and assign DFE to perform the more regular inner-part stencil computations. Fig. 5B shows the work flow of the hybrid design. The CPU will process the halo exchanges (①→②), interpolations (②→③), and the outer-part stencil computing (③→④), while at the same time, DFE will process the inner-part stencil computation (①→⑤). When both the inner part and the outer part are finished (⑥), meshes along the inner–outer boundary will be exchanged (⑥→⑦) (Comm. between CPU and FPGA arrow in Fig. 5).

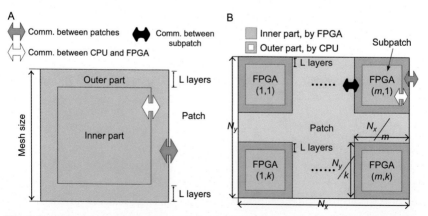

Fig. 6 Domain decomposition of our hybrid CPU-DFE algorithm. (A) CPU and 1 FPGA. (B) CPU and $m \times k$ FPGAs.

Our proposed decomposition methodology has the following advantages:

(1) CPU is now working simultaneously with DFE to solve the problem, which achieves an efficient usage of both computing resources.

(2) The CPU time for communication and computation is hidden in the DFE computing, a well computation–communication overlapping.

(3) Specifically for SWEs, all the complex conditional statements, which are expensive in resources for DFE to implement, are now assigned to CPU.

Note that with small modification, the hybrid algorithm can also be applied to platforms with multiple DFEs, as shown in Fig. 6B. Supposing we have a computing node with $m \times k$ DFEs and multi-core CPUs, and are handling a problem with the mesh size of $N_x \times N_y$, we first decompose the original patch into $m \times k$ subpatches, so that the mesh size for each subpatch is $(N_x/m) \times (N_y/k)$. Such inner patch decomposition will bring extra communications between subpatches (Comm. between subpatch arrow in Fig. 6B). Therefore, now each subpatch has the similar computational and communicating mechanism with the original patch, with only $1/(m \times k)$ of the computing area.

4.2.2 Adjustable Task Partition

Based on the hybrid decomposition methodology, we can further improve the performance through adjusting the area of inner part and outer part in balanced workloads. When the CPU time and the DFE time are most close, the overall performance will increase accordingly. For example, when we set the outer part in Fig. 5 with two outer layers, the inner part processed by DFE would be much larger and the time of computation would be longer. Therefore, by increasing the area of the outer part and carefully tracking both CPU and DFE computing time, we can find the optimal point where the CPU time and DFE time are most close.

According to different computing size of the problem, the optimal point could be different. The DFE performance for processing the inner part is predicted based on the methodology proposed in Ref. [4].

4.3 Mixed Precision Arithmetic

In this part, we propose a mixed precision method to decrease the resource requirement, and deploy the whole SWEs kernel into single DFE to improve the performance.

4.3.1 Range Analysis

Current DFEs are generally more efficient for fixed-point arithmetic than for floating-point arithmetic. Therefore, one strategy we take is to locate the region in the program that actually computes in a small range, and replace the region from floating-point arithmetic to fixed-point arithmetic.

For all the different intermediate variables throughout the kernel, we first perform a range analysis to track the range of their absolute values. As shown in Fig. 7A, while some variables (e.g., *xhv*, *q10hv*, and *tm*) cover a wide dynamic range, some other variables (e.g., *xh*, *xhu*, *q10h*, *q10hu*) only change within a small range. As those variables all locate in the process of State Reconstructions, we can extract the four-direction State Reconstruction parts, and use fixed-point data type in that module. As the values of all variables in the State Reconstructions are located in the range of $(2^{-20}, 2^1)$, we set the fractional bit width to be 2, which is big enough to represent all variables.

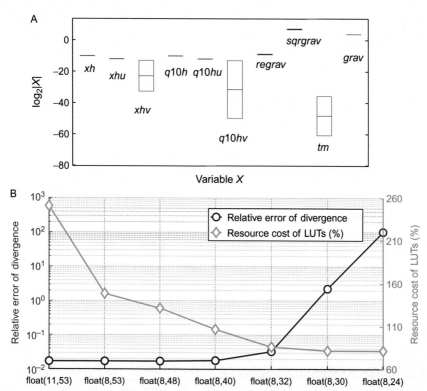

Fig. 7 Mixed precision design for SWEs. (A) Dynamic range of variable $\log_2|X|$. (B) The relative error of divergence and resource cost of LUTs.

For the variables in the rest parts, as they generally cover a wide range, we need to use floating point with reduced precision to represent. We can see that the maximum dynamic range of the base-two logarithmic values of these variables is smaller than 60. Therefore, floating-point number with 8 exponent bits should be good enough to cover the range.

4.3.2 Precision Analysis

As the SWEs kernel generally involves a large number of iterations, it is difficult to achieve meaningful results through analytic precision analysis approaches due to the conservative assumptions. Therefore, in our approach, we determine the precision bit width through bit accurate simulations for different bit-width configurations. Note that the simulation is performed based on the data of a typical benchmark scenario (zonal flow over an isolated mountain), which demonstrates the typical features of numerical atmospheric simulation.

To determine the mantissa bits, we explore a set of different bit widths from 53 to 24 and observe the dynamic trend of the relative error of *divergence* and the on-chip resource cost according to different floating-point bit-width configurations (Fig. 7B). The relative error of *divergence* is computed by comparing the simulated divergence against the standard data set validated in Ref. [27], and can be used as an important indicator to quickly estimate the accuracy. If the relative error is larger than 5%, the result will no longer be true.

For brevity, hereafter float(e, m) denotes floating point with e bits exponent and m bits mantissa, and fixed(i,f) denotes a fixed point with i bits integer and f bits fraction. From Fig. 7B, for float(8,53), float(8,48), and float(8,40) settings, we observe a similar relative error as the double-precision float(11, 53). For float(8,32), we can still achieve a relative error of around 2%. However, when we further reduce the precision to float(8,30), we see a surge of the relative error to a level that is far above the required 5%.

On the resource cost side, float(8,32) is also a suitable choice that reduces the LUTs usage from around 240% to 80% of the total capacity based on a Virtex-6 SX475T FPGA.

For the fixed-point variables in the Reconstruction parts, we apply a similar approach to determine the fractional bit width to be 38. Therefore, we pick float(8,32) and fixed(2,38) as the number representation in the algorithm.

Table 1 Performance and Power Efficiency for Different Platforms of SWEs
Mesh Size: 1024 × 1024 × 6

Platform	Performance (Flops)	Speedup	Power (Watt)	Efficiency (Flops/Watt)	Power Efficiency
6-core CPU	3.2M	1	225	14.1K	1
Tianhe-1A node	75.4M	23×	360	209K	14.8×
MaxWorkstation	319.7M	**100×**	186	1.7M	**121.6×**
MaxNode	1G	**330×**	514	2M	**144.9×**

4.4 Performance and Power Efficiency

Table 1 shows the performance as Flops (floating-point operations get computed per second), and the power efficiency measured on different platforms. Note that the power is measured using a power meter.

The performance of CPU-DFE algorithm using one Virtex-6 FPGA (MaxWorkstation) gains 100 times speedup over 6-core CPU and 4 times over a Tianhe-1A node with 12 CPU cores and a 448-core GPU. With 4 DFEs running simultaneously, the performance of MaxNode gains a speedup of 330 over a 6-core CPU and 14 times over the Tianhe-1A node. The performance of MaxNode is equivalent to 14 nodes in the Tianhe-1A supercomputer.

Even though the FPGA device works at a frequency of 100 MHz, we manage to build the complex kernel on a fully pipelined DFE card, which can perform 428 floating-point and 235 fixed-point operations per cycle. Meanwhile, the fully pipelined design also provides much higher efficiency than that of the CPU- and GPU-based platforms. The combination of the high parallelism and the high efficiency leads to the ultra-high performance of our design.

As for the power efficiency (evaluated by the performance per watt), our CPU-DFE algorithm with 4 DFEs is up to 9 times more power efficient than a hybrid CPU-GPU node of Tianhe-1A supercomputer.

5. CASE STUDY 2: EULER ATMOSPHERIC EQUATIONS

5.1 Problem Description

It is well recognized that the mesoscale atmosphere can be modeled by the fully compressible Euler equations with almost no assumptions made. In a three-dimensional channel with possibly nonsmooth bottom boundary, ignoring the effect of Coriolis force, the Euler equations can be written as the following set of conservation laws:

$$\frac{\partial Q}{\partial t} + \frac{\partial F}{\partial x} + \frac{\partial G}{\partial y} + \frac{\partial H}{\partial z} + S = 0, \tag{2}$$

where

$$\begin{aligned}
Q &= \left(\rho', \rho u, \rho v, \rho w, (\rho\theta)'\right)^T, \\
F &= \left(\rho u, \rho uu + p', \rho uv, \rho uw, \rho u\theta\right)^T, \\
G &= \left(\rho v, \rho vu, \rho vv + p', \rho vw, \rho v\theta\right)^T, \\
H &= \left(\rho w, \rho wu, \rho wv, \rho ww + p', \rho w\theta\right)^T, \\
S &= \left(0, 0, 0, \rho'g, 0\right)^T,
\end{aligned} \tag{3}$$

where ρ, $\mathbf{v} = (u, v, w)$, p, and θ are the density, the velocity, the pressure, and the potential temperature of the atmosphere, respectively. The system is closed with the equation of state

$$p = p_{00} \left(\frac{\rho R\theta}{p_{00}}\right)^\gamma, \tag{4}$$

where $p_{00} = 1013.25$ hPa is the ground-level pressure, $R = 287.04$ J/(kg· K) is the gas constant for dry air, and $\gamma = 1.4$. To minimize roundoff errors, values of $\rho' = \rho - \bar{\rho}$, $(\rho\theta)' = \rho\theta - \bar{\rho}\bar{\theta}$, and $p = p - \bar{p}$ have been shifted according to the hydrostatic state that satisfies $\frac{\partial \bar{p}}{\partial z} = -\bar{\rho}g$.

After using a cell-centered finite volume scheme and an explicit Runge–Kutta time stepping [3] method, each time step in solving the Euler equations requires two stencil sweeps applied at all mesh elements. As shown in the left panel of Fig. 8, to process a mesh element in the 3D channel, 24 neighboring

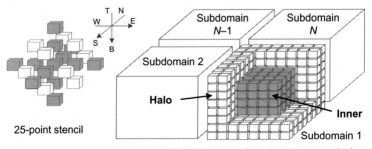

Fig. 8 *Left*: 25-point Euler stencil; *right*: hybrid domain decomposition, each domain is divided into inner and halo areas.

elements need to be accessed. The right panel of Fig. 8 demonstrates the 3D domain decomposition for parallel computing. We first decompose the whole 3D channel into small subdomains according to the number of paralleling resources, and then all the subdomains will be processed in parallel. Based on the diamond stencil, communication is required between subdomains to update the halo elements, which are the two outer layers of the subdomain (e.g., blank elements of subdomain 1 in Fig. 8).

Algorithm 2 Original Euler Algorithm per Stencil Sweep

1: **For (k, j, i)**←$(0, 0, 0)$ to $(N_{k-1}, N_{j-1}, N_{i-1})$ // Loop All Elements
2:     **If (k, j, i)**∈ Boundary   // Boundary Condition
3:          Halo Updating or Boundary Processing
4:     **EndIf**
5:     Calculate Coordinates
6:     Compute Fluxes{
7:          State Reconstruction
8:               Riemann Solver}
9:     Compute Source Terms   // Stencil Ends
10: **EndFor**

The procedure of computation is shown in Algorithm 2. At each stencil sweep and for each mesh point, the first step is to apply the boundary condition (line 3) if the point belongs to the boundary area. The major stencil computation (lines 5–9) contains two steps, namely, the Compute Fluxes and the Compute Source Terms (to count the effect of the gravity force). The Compute Fluxes itself contains two steps, namely, State Reconstruction (to recover values on the interfaces of each mesh element) and Riemann Solver (to estimate the numerical fluxes). We remark here that because of the conservative property of the finite volume scheme, the numerical fluxes on a common edge of two consecutive mesh elements are identical.

Similar to the approach introduced in Section 4.2, we also apply a hybrid domain partition scheme for Euler stencil computation. As shown in the right panel of Fig. 8, we use DFE to process the computations of the inner part, and use CPU to process the computations of the outer part (halo) as well as all the relevant communications. Therefore, more balanced CPU–DFE working mechanism and well communication–computation overlapping are achieved.

5.2 Algorithmic Offsetting

The identical rule to compute the fluxes on a common edge of two consecutive mesh elements (remarked in Section 5.1) offers us a big optimizing space by means of the streaming offsetting model. We thus propose an algorithmic offsetting method to simplify the Euler stencil kernel.

Algorithm 3—Part 1 shows a fragment of the State Reconstruction step to compute east-direction intermediate variables $qe[0]$, $qe[1]$, and west-direction intermediate variable $qw[1]$. We can figure out that computing $qe[0]$ and $qw[1]$ is applying an identical rule on different elements from input stream x, and computing $qe[1]$ and $qe[0]$ is applying similar rules on different elements. We further use Fig. 9 to illustrate the streaming pipelines that are deployed to compute the parts of $qe[0]$ and $qw[1]$ shown in bold in Algorithm 3—Part 1. The operations connected by solid pipelines are deployed to compute the part of $qe[0]$ shown in bold, and the operations connected by dotted pipelines are deployed to compute the part of $qw[1]$ shown in bold. Obviously, the operations in the two pipelines are identical, and the input elements for dotted pipeline are one time step backward of elements for solid pipeline. As a result, all the operations connected by dotted lines can be replaced by offsetting existing stream one time step backward ($offset(-1)$). Similarly, we only need to compute the stream $qe[0]$ in

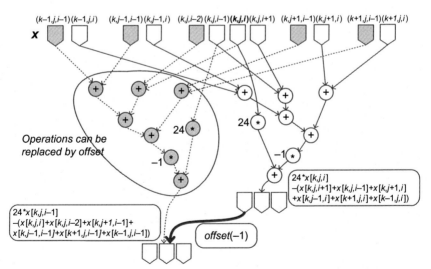

Fig. 9 The streaming pipeline to finish the corresponding calculations of Euler Equations. Operations by *dotted lines* can be replaced by offsetting existing streams.

Table 2 Number of Floating-Point Operations per Sweep of Euler

Part 1	+, −	×	÷	Pow,Sqrt	Offset
Original ALG	1192	697	170	48	132^a
ALG offsetting	619	549	76	21	$30^a + 140^b$
Look-up table	424	460	51	21	$30^a + 140^b$

[a]Offset operations on original input streams.
[b]New offset operations generated after using ALG offsetting.

Algorithm 3. By offsetting stream $qe[0]$ one time step backward, we can get the stream of $qw[1]$ at current time step. As for $qe[1]$, similar offsetting methods could also be applied with few modifications. The approach of algorithmic offsetting is shown in Algorithm 3—Part 2.

By applying algorithmic offsetting on both the State Reconstruction and Riemann Solver steps, we manage to eliminate 40% of the total floating operations ("ALG offsetting" row in Table 2).

Algorithm 3 Demonstration of the Algorithmic Offsetting Method

($q_e[0]$, $q_e[1]$, $q_w[1]$ are intermediate variables in State Reconstruction of Euler algorithm)

Part 1: Original code.

```
qe[0] = 24*x[k,j,i] - (x[k,j,i+1]+x[k,j,i-1]+x[k,j+1,i]+
x[k,j-1,i]+x[k+1,j,i]+x[k-1,j,i]) +
3*(x[k,j,i+1]+x[k,j,i-1]) - 2*(x[k,j,i+1]-x[k,j,i-1]);
qe[1] = 24*x[k,j,i+1] - (x[k,j,i+2]+x[k,j,i]+x[k,j+1,i+1]+
x[k,j-1,i+1]+x[k+1,j,i+1]+x[k-1,j,i+1]) +
3*(x[k,j,i+2]+x[k,j,i]) + 2*(x[k,j,i+2]-x[k,j,i]);
qw[1] = 24*x[k,j,i-1] - (x[k,j,i]+x[k,j,i-2]+x[k,j+1,i-1]+
x[k,j-1,i-1]+x[k+1,j,i-1]+x[k-1,j,i-1]) +
3*(x[k,j,i]+x[k,j,i-2]) - 2*(x[k,j,i]-x[k,j,i-2]);
```

Part 2: Algorithmic offsetting method.

```
tmp1 = 24*x[k,j,i]-(x[k,j,i+1]+x[k,j,i-1]+x[k,j+1,i]+
x[k,j-1,i]+x[k+1,j,i]+x[k-1,j,i])+
3*(x[k,j,i+1]+x[k,j,i-1]);
tmp2 = 2*(x[k,j,i+1]-x[k,j,i-1]);
qe[0](t) =tmp1 - tmp2;
qe[1](t) =tmp1(t+1) + tmp2(t+1);
qw[1](t) =qe[0](t-1);
```

5.3 Fast Memory Table and Mixed Precision Arithmetic

In the Calculate Coordinates step of Algorithm 2, all the variables only rely on the index coordinate (k, j, i). Therefore, those variables can be precalculated during compiling time by CPU and stored as a table in the on-chip fast memory. When needed, those variables can be acquired through looking up the table. If the on-chip fast memory is not big enough to store all the coordinate variables, we can alternatively store extra variables on the large on-board memory as constant variables. Consequentially, we occupy extra on-chip fast memories in exchange of computations, and further eliminate over 10% of the original operations ("Look-up table" row in Table 2).

The customizable feature on data representation provides another method to reduce the resource usage. We can apply reduced-precision floating-point number to replace the original double precision. For the mantissa part, we gradually decrease the bit width and observe the influence on the resource usage and the accuracy. We choose the least mantissa width that could meet the resource requirement and guarantee the accuracy at the same time. The exponent part is decided through tracking the data range of the variables throughout the program, and finding the least exponent width that is still good enough to cover the range of all variables. The method above is introduced in detail in Ref. [2]. Therefore, input streams will be converted into reduced-precision data and then they will be computed. Similarly, they will be converted back to double precision before they are copied back.

5.4 Performance and Power Efficiency

Table 3 shows the performance as Flops (floating-point operations get computed per second), and the power efficiency (performance per Watt) for different implementations. The CPU-MIC rack has the same physical size as the MPC-X FPGA unit, and can provide a more fair comparison based on performance per volume and power efficiency per volume.

The CPU-DFE unit with 8 FPGA chips is 18.5 times faster and 8.3 times more efficient than the multi-core CPU implementation with two 12-core Intel E5-2697 (Ivy Bridge) CPUs, and is 6.2 times faster and 5.2 times more power efficient than a hybrid implementation with two 12-core Intel E5-2697 CPUs and three Intel Xeon Phi 5120d (MIC) cards.

Table 3 Performance and Power Efficiency for Different Platforms of Euler Equations
Mesh Size: 260 × 240 × 228

	Performance (Flops)	Speedup	Power (Watt)	Efficiency (Flops/Watt)	Power Efficiency
CPU 24-core	244.6M	1	427	571.7K	1
CPU-MIC unit	752.7M	3×	815	921K	1.6×
CPU-DFE unit	4.5G	**18.5×**	950	4.8M	**8.3×**

The reference designs based on the most powerful multi-core and many-core architectures have been fully optimized through a series of sophisticated paralleling techniques. However, the overall performance is not scaled ideally, as we have to face the challenges from the complex stencil algorithm, and the bandwidth bottleneck caused by heavy data exchange. The discontinuous data access for the stencil computation leads to a higher rate of cache miss, and further restricts the computing efficiency. As for the DFE design, through applying hybrid mechanism, algorithmic offsetting, fast memory table, and the customizable-precision arithmetic, we manage to map the complex Euler stencil kernel into a single FPGA chip, and build a deep pipeline that can efficiently perform nearly 1000 floating-point operations per cycle. The inputting streams in addition form a cache-like data buffer that provides perfect data access [6]. All above contributions finally lead to the better performance of DFE over the reference designs.

In terms of the power efficiency, due to the low clock frequency, DFE generally consumes a lower energy usage over traditional platforms, and accordingly becomes a better alternative for studying the climate issues in a more environmentally friendly and green way.

Note that the CPU-MIC unit used in the reference implementation can be considered as a replication of one computing node from Tianhe-2, the world's top supercomputer with a theoretical peak performance of 54.9 PFlops. As atmospheric modeling generally desires a large-scale experiment to achieve better resolutions, we can project that our hybrid CPU-DFE design, if scaled to a large-scale supercomputer scenario, would demonstrate a similar speedup as archived in section, and greatly reduce the power consumption.

6. CASE STUDY 3: REVERSE TIME MIGRATION

6.1 Problem Description

6.1.1 The Reverse Time Migration Algorithm

Fig. A.1 shows the pseudo code of the RTM algorithm. In this example, we apply a simple second-order stencil operator to approximate the derivatives.

The RTM algorithm consists of different levels of loops that iterate over shots, time steps, and the 3D grids (lines 5–10 and lines 25–28). The computations for different shots (i.e., different source locations) are completely independent of each other and can be assigned on different nodes for the multiple-node scenario. Therefore, we only focus on the scaling of performance within a single node.

The computation for each shot consists of the forward loop (lines 7–22) that propagates the source wave fields from time step 0 to $nt - 1$, and the reverse loop (lines 25–43) that reverse-propagates the receiver wave fields from time step $nt - 1$ to 0. While reverse-propagating the receiver wave fields, we cross-correlate the source and receiver wave fields of the same time step, and accumulate the results (line 42). These propagations are implemented as finite-difference stencils, which are the most time-consuming parts.

Besides, the forward and reverse propagation loops also need to add the recorded source and receiver signals to the corresponding locations, respectively (line 17, line 35), and to deal with the boundary conditions (line 20, line 38).

6.1.2 Computational Challenges in Reverse Time Migration

The first challenge of RTM comes from the cross correlation of source and receiver wave fields (line 42). The source and receiver wave fields get computed in different directions in time. Depending on the problem dimension size (nx, ny, nz), the typical size of the source wave fields for one time step can be 0.5–4 GB and the algorithm normally involves up to several thousand time steps.

Most existing designs take the checkpointing approach [24] to store the source wave fields at certain time steps, and then recompute the rest time steps when needed.

The second challenge comes from the memory access pattern. The neighboring points are stored in different rows, different columns, or even different slices, and can be far apart in the memory space. The requirement to access all neighboring points incurs a lot of cache misses when the domain gets large.

6.2 Random Boundary

To avoid the data transfer needed for checkpointing source wave fields and encapsulate the computation within the DFE, we propose the idea of adding randomness into the boundary region and making computation of source wave fields reversible.

In the original RTM algorithm, we process BC to absorb the reflections from the simulation boundaries that do not exist in the real world. However, adding the absorbing BC into the computation makes it impossible to reverse the migration of source fields in time. To keep the process reversible, we apply an alternative idea to replace BC computation with the process of adding randomness into the velocity fields. The randomness in the boundary region distorts the artificial reflections, thus removing them from the correlated image.

More technical details and example imaging results can be found in Ref. [28]. In general, the random boundary approach demonstrates the same level of accuracy as the absorbing BC, while removing the data transfer overhead of checkpointing. Note that random boundary is only used for the source wave fields. The receiver wave fields are still propagated using the absorbing BC.

6.3 A Customized Window Buffer

Another advantage that we can take from the DFE is the option to construct customized buffers for the 3D stencil we compute in RTM. An example is shown in Fig. 11, where we compute a second order in space stencil on a 3D $n \times n \times n$ array. We use BRAMs (the programmable buffering units) and registers to construct a window buffer of the input stream.

Through the utilization of BRAMs, which are both larger and more flexible than the L1 cache in CPU, we can achieve perfect data reuse for the stencil. Take a 12th order 37-point star stencil for example, one MAX3 DFE can accommodate 24 concurrent pipelines running at 125 MHz. The window buffer provides concurrent access to 37 points in each cycle, amounting to an internal memory bandwidth of $24 \times 37 \times 4$ bytes $\times 120$ MHz $= 426$ GB/s. In the CPU case, the equivalent effective internal bandwidth provided by the cache is only 14 GB/s (projected from the computation performance). The customized local buffer contributes a lot to the RTM performance on the DFEs.

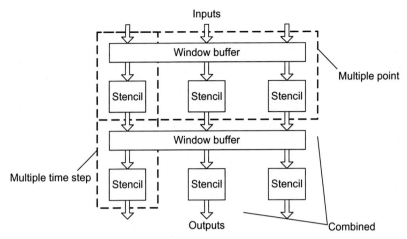

Fig. 10 Different ways to parallelize the RTM computation: (a) process multiple points concurrently; (b) process multiple time steps in one pass; and (c) a combined approach that process multiple time steps for multiple points.

The BRAMs in the current FPGA chips provide storage of several mega bytes, often not enough to store the involved slices completely. Therefore, we need to perform a 2D domain decomposition that decompose a n^3 data cube into smaller data cubes of size $nx \times ny \times n$.

6.4 Cascading Multiple Computations

As one stencil only requires dozens of multipliers and adders, we can further improve the performance by accommodating multiple stencil operators in one DFE.

To multiply the performance, we can either process multiple points concurrently (the top row of Fig. 10), or cascade multiple time steps into one deep pipeline (the left column of Fig. 10). While the multiple–point approach requires multiple times of the memory bandwidth, the multiple-time-step approach costs more buffering units to release the bandwidth bottleneck.

The above different parallelization approaches again provide options to balance the reconfigurable resources and the memory bandwidth of the system.

6.5 Number Representations

In exploration geophysics such as seismic imaging, single–precision floating-point numbers are the standard number representation that people use.

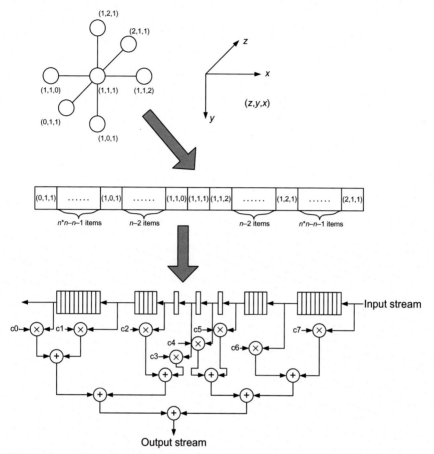

Fig. 11 A streaming design of a 3D convolution engine using a window buffer.

Therefore, in our current RTM design, we do most of the computation in 32-bit floating-point numbers (8-bit exponent, 23-bit mantissa).

However, as the reconfigurable DFEs provide the unique advantage of supporting customized number representations, we can achieve potential performance benefits by exploring different number representations. For the most time-consuming stencil kernel, our previous work [29] shows that using reduced-precision floating-point numbers or even fixed-point numbers can significantly reduce the resource cost and lead to much higher performance per chip.

Our previous work on a 2D downward continuation migration [24] demonstrated that we could achieve the same level of accuracy through fixed-point numbers and controlled shifting at certain time steps. In this work, we apply a similar idea to the stencil part and customize the number representation of the multiply and add operands based on the range of coefficients and wave fields. For most variables, we can use a 24-bit fixed-point representations to get a similar accuracy to 32-bit floating-point representations. For a 12th order in space stencil (37 points, 12 multipliers, and 38 adders), the customization of number representations reduces the resource cost from 16943 luts, 23735 ffs, and 24 DSP48Es down to 3385 luts, 3718 ffs, and 12 DSPs. The precision optimization enables us to fit higher-order stencils and significantly more concurrent pipelines into one chip.

6.6 Hardware (De)compression Scheme

While the number of representation optimizations increases the number of computation kernels we can fit into the chip, the hardware (de)compression scheme is our tool to magnify the number of values that we can stream in and out of the chip in each cycle.

We adopt different compression methods for different types of data. For wave-field data, which needs to be read and written for many times, we use lossy schemes based on block floating point, which has a balanced cost of compression and decompression. The schemes support different compression levels that we can explore in different scenarios. Our experiments show that in most cases 2*times* compression of small blocks of data (i.e., storing each data item in 16 bits compared to the 32-bit single-precision floating point) with a shared exponent produces image results that are geophysically indistinguishable from computation using uncompressed data.

For velocity data (and other read-only earth model parameters), we use a compression method that has a high compression cost and low decompression cost. We quantize the entire 3D volume of velocities into a small number of distinct values stored in a look-up table. Therefore, instead of storing the actual velocity values, we store indices. In most cases, a table of 256 different velocity values (8-bit index) is good enough to describe the model and gives us 4*times* compression for the velocity fields.

6.7 Performance and Power Efficiency

We describe the throughput as the floating-point operations get computed per second (Flops). In this experiment, we are applying a 12th order in space stencil (an enlarged version of the 2nd order in space stencil shown in Fig. 11) with 12 neighboring points on each axis (37 points in total). Compared with the 6th order in space stencil computed in our previous work [6], this one is more similar to what industrial applications are using.

As a base case, we implement a CPU version of the RTM algorithm that uses two 8-core Sandy Bridge CPUs (each running at 2.27 GHz). To make a fair comparison, we apply OpenMP and SIMD vectorization to fully utilize the multiple cores and vector processing units in the CPUs. We also perform different levels of cache blocking to further improve the cache behavior and vectorization efficiency. After a careful optimization, the performance of our CPU version scales to 22.8 GFlops.

Table 4 shows the performance and power efficiency comparison among the CPU design, our previous MAX2 design [6], our current MAX2, MAX3 designs, and the RTM design in Ref. [30]. As Refs. [6], [30], and our current work compute 6th, 8th, and 12th order in space stencils, respectively, we convert the performance of Ref. [6] and Ref. [30] by a ratio of floating-point operation counts. Compared with our previous work [6], with the addition of precision optimization and compression scheme, our current design on MAX3 provides over two times of performance. Compared with other existing FPGA-based designs, our work also improves significantly on both performance and power efficiency. One MAX3 DFE provides equivalent performance to around 72 cores, with 10 times higher power efficiency.

Table 4 Performance and Power Efficiency of RTM

Platform	Sandy Bridge (2×8 cores)	MAX2 [6] (2× Virtex-5)	MAX3 (1× Virtex-6)	Ref. [30] (4× Virtex-5)
Performance (Flops)	22.8G	46.8G	102G	54G
Speedup	1	2.1×	4.5×	2.36×
Power (Watt)	377	186	165	725
Efficiency (Flops/Watt)	60M	251M	618M	74.4M
Power efficiency	1	4.1×	10.2×	1.2×

As Refs. [6], [30], and this work compute 6th, 8th, and 12th order in space stencils, respectively, we convert the performance of Refs. [6] and [30] by a ratio of floating-point operation counts.

7. SUMMARY AND CONCLUDING REMARKS

This chapter summarized our initial efforts and experiences that solved geoscience problems by using data flow computing engines. We have chosen three important stencil-based geoscience kernels, the Global Shallow Water Equation Solver, the Euler Equation Solver, and the Reverse Time Migration Solver as the study cases, and fully pipelined their algorithms onto the reconfigurable high-performance computing platforms. A set of customizable optimizing methods are discussed and applied to achieve inspiring performance improvement and high power efficiency.

In summary, reconfigurable platforms can provide novel optimizing methods out of their customizable features. For example, compared with the imperfections in data presentation of traditional HPC platforms, the mixed precision arithmetics that enables flexibility in data format and precision can greatly improve the computing efficiency of logic units and decrease the consumptions of the on-chip resource. The customizable window buffer is able to perform better caching behaviors, while the hardware data decompression scheme is able to decrease the data transfers. Therefore, we can push data closer to the computing side and break the memory wall restriction. On the other hand, the hybrid domain decomposition mechanism can employ both CPU host and DFE accelerator to work simultaneously, and accordingly provide more balanced computing workload as well as well communication–computation overlapping. In special cases such as the algorithmic offsetting methods applied to optimizing the Euler algorithm, we can also see customizable methods targeting at the feature of a chosen algorithm.

In conclusion, data flow computing model is a promising solution in dealing with algorithms from geoscience applications. Our work in this chapter demonstrates dramatic improvement in both the performance and power efficiency compared with other tradition counterparts such as GPU and MIC. Even though we only present three kernels to study in this chapter, the optimizing approaches based on data flow computing model can be applicable to other geoscience applications with algorithmic similarities.

ACKNOWLEDGMENTS

This work was supported in part by the National Natural Science Foundation of China (grant no. 61303003, 41374113, and 91530323), the National High-Tech R&D (863) Program of China (grant no. 2013AA01A208), Tsinghua University Initiative Scientific Research

Program (no. 20131089356), UK EPSRC, the European Union Seventh Framework Programme (grant agreement no. 257906, 287804, and 318521), HiPEAC NoE, and the Maxeler University Program.

APPENDIX

```
0:// s(nt, nz, ny, nx) : source wave field array
1:// r(nt, nz, ny, nx) : receiver wave field array
2:// v(nz, ny, nx) : velocity array
3:// res(nz, ny, nx) : the resulting image array, initialized as zeros
4:
5:for ( ishot = 0; ishot < nshot; ishot++ ){
6:      //forward migration
7:      for ( it = 0; it < nt; it++ )
8:          for ( iz = 0; iz < nz; iz++ )
9:              for ( iy = 0; iy < ny; iy++ )
10:                 for ( ix = 0; ix < nx; ix++ ){
11:                     s(it,iz,iy,ix)=2*s(it-1,iz,iy,ix)-s(it-2,iz,iy,ix)+
                                     v(iz,iy,ix)*v(iz,iy,ix)*dt*dt*(
12:                                   s(it-1,iz,iy,ix)*(2/dx/dx+2/dy/dy+2/dz/dz)+
13:                                   (-s(it-1,iz,iy,ix-1)-s(it-1,iz,iy,ix+1))/dx/dx+
14:                                   (-s(it-1,iz,iy-1,ix)-s(it-1,iz,iy+1,ix))/dy/dy+
15:                                   (-s(it-1,iz-1,iy,ix)-s(it-1,iz+1,iy,ix))/dz/dz);
16:
17:                     if ( (iz, iy, ix) corresponds to the current source location )
18:                         s(it,iz,iy,ix) += recorded_source(it,iz,iy,ix);
19:
20:                     if ( (iz, iy, ix) is in the boundary range )
21:                         process_boundary_condition();
22:                 }
23:
24:      //reverse migration
25:      for ( it = nt-1; it >= 2; it-- )
26:          for ( iz = 0; iz < nz; iz++ )
27:              for ( iy = 0; iy < ny; iy++ )
28:                  for ( ix = 0; ix < nx; ix++ ){
29:                      r(it-2,iz,iy,ix)=2*r(it-1,iz,iy,ix)-r(it,iz,iy,ix)+
                                      v(iz,iy,ix)*v(iz,iy,ix)*dt*dt*(
30:                                    r(it-1,iz,iy,ix)*(2/dx/dx+2/dy/dy+2/dz/dz)+
31:                                    (-r(it-1,iz,iy,ix-1)-r(it-1,iz,iy,ix+1))/dx/dx+
32:                                    (-r(it-1,iz,iy-1,ix)-r(it-1,iz,iy+1,ix))/dy/dy+
33:                                    (-r(it-1,iz-1,iy,ix)-r(it-1,iz+1,iy,ix))/dz/dz);
34:
35:                      if ( (iz, iy, ix) corresponds to the one of the receiver locations )
36:                          r(it-2,iz,iy,ix) += recorded_receiver(it-2,iz,iy,ix);
37:
38:                      if ( (iz, iy, ix) is in the boundary range )
39:                          process_boundary_condition();
40:
41:                      //correlate the source and receiver wave fields into the imaging results
42:                      res(iz,iy,ix) += s(it-2,iz,iy,ix)*r(it-2,iz,iy,ix);
43:                  }
44:}
```

Fig. A.1 Pseudo code of the RTM algorithm.

REFERENCES

[1] G. Mingas, C. Bouganis, in: 2012 IEEE 20th Annual International Symposium on Field-Programmable Custom Computing Machines (FCCM), A custom precision based architecture for accelerating parallel tempering MCMC on FPGAs without introducing sampling error, IEEE, 2012, pp. 153–156.

[2] L. Gan, H. Fu, W. Luk, C. Yang, W. Xue, X. Huang, Y. Zhang, G. Yang, Accelerating solvers for global atmospheric equations through mixed-precision data flow engine, in: 2013 23rd International Conference on Field Programmable Logic and Applications (FPL), IEEE, 2013, pp. 1–6.

[3] L. Gan, H. Fu, C. Yang, W. Luk, W. Xue, O. Mencer, X. Huang, G. Yang, A highly-efficient and green data flow engine for solving Euler atmospheric equations, in: 2014 24th International Conference on Field Programmable Logic and Applications (FPL), IEEE, 2014, pp. 1–6.

[4] H. Fu, L. Gan, R.G. Clapp, H. Ruan, O. Pell, O. Mencer, M. Flynn, X. Huang, G. Yang, Scaling reverse time migration performance through reconfigurable dataflow engines, IEEE Micro 34 (1) (2014) 30–40.

[5] V. Blagojevi´c, D. Boji´c, et al., A systematic approach to generation of new ideas for PhD research in computing, Comput. Eng. 23 (2012).

[6] H. Fu, R.G. Clapp, Eliminating the memory bottleneck: an FPGA-based solution for 3D reverse time migration, in: Proceedings of the International Symposium on Field Programmable Gate Arrays, 2011, pp. 65–74.

[7] V. Milutinovic, J. Salom, N. Trifunovic, R. Giorgi, Guide to Dataflow Supercomputing, Springer, Switzerland, 2015.

[8] Z. Jovanovic, FPGA accelerator for floating-point matrix multiplication, IET Comput. Digit. Tech. 6 (4) (2012) 249–256.

[9] M.J. Flynn, O. Mencer, V. Milutinovic, G. Rakocevic, P. Stenstrom, R. Trobec, M. Valero, Moving from petaflops to petadata, Commun. ACM 56 (5) (2013) 39–42.

[10] A. Kos, V. Ranković, S. Tomažič, Sorting networks on Maxeler dataflow supercomputing systems, Adv. Comput. 96 (2015) 139–186. Chapter 4.

[11] A. Kos, S. Tomažič, J. Salom, N. Trifunovic, M. Valero, V. Milutinovic, New benchmarking methodology and programming model for big data processing, Int. J. Distrib. Sens. Netw. 501 (2015) 271752.

[12] N. Trifunovic, V. Milutinovic, J. Salom, A. Kos, Paradigm shift in big data supercomputing: dataflow vs. controlflow, J. Big Data 2 (1) (2015) 1–9.

[13] N. Trifunovic, V. Milutinovic, N. Korolija, G. Gaydadjiev, An appgallery for dataflow computing, J. Big Data 3 (1) (2016) 1.

[14] D. Oriato, S. Girdlestone, O. Mencer, Dataflow computing in extreme performance conditions, Adv. Comput. 96 (2015) 105–137.

[15] G. Strand, Community earth system model data management: policies and challenges, Procedia Comput. Sci. 4 (2011) 558–566.

[16] T. Shimokawabe, T. Aoki, J. Ishida, K. Kawano, C. Muroi, 145 TFlops performance on 3990 GPUs of TSUBAME 2.0 supercomputer for an operational weather prediction, Procedia Comput. Sci. 4 (2011) 1535–1544.

[17] J. Mielikainen, B. Huang, H. Huang, M.D. Goldberg, GPU acceleration of the updated Goddard shortwave radiation scheme in the weather research and forecasting (WRF) model, IEEE J. Sel. Topics Appl. Earth Obs. Remote Sens. 5 (2) (2012) 555–562.

[18] C. Yang, W. Xue, H. Fu, L. Gan, L. Li, Y. Xu, Y. Lu, J. Sun, G. Yang, W. Zheng, A peta-scalable CPU-GPU algorithm for global atmospheric simulations, in: Proceedings of the 18th ACM SIGPLAN Symposium on Principles and Practice of Parallel Programming, ACM, 2013, pp. 1–12.

[19] W. Xue, C. Yang, H. Fu, X. Wang, Y. Xu, L. Gan, Y. Lu, X. Zhu, Enabling and scaling a global shallow-water atmospheric model on Tianhe-2, in: 2014 IEEE 28th International Parallel and Distributed Processing Symposium, IEEE, 2014, pp. 745–754.

[20] W. Xue, L. Wang, Ultra-scalable CPU-MIC acceleration of mesoscale atmospheric modeling on Tianhe-2, IEEE Trans. Comput. 64 (8) (2015) 2382–2393.

[21] F. Wilhelm, Parallel preconditioners for an ocean model in climate simulations, Ph.D. thesis, Karlsruhe, Karlsruher Institut für Technologie (KIT), Dissertation 2012.

[22] D. Oriato, S. Tilbury, M. Marrocu, G. Pusceddu, Acceleration of a meteorological limited area model with dataflow engines, in: 2012 Symposium on SAAHPC, 2012, pp. 129–132.

[23] M. Araya-Polo, F. Rubio, R. De la Cruz, M. Hanzich, J.M. Cela, D.P. Scarpazza, 3D seismic imaging through reverse-time migration on homogeneous and heterogeneous multi-core processors, Sci. Program. 17 (1-2) (2009) 185–198.

[24] H. Fu, W. Osborne, R.G. Clapp, O. Mencer, W. Luk, Accelerating seismic computations using customized number representations on FPGAs, EURASIP J. Embed. Syst. 2009 (2009) 3.

[25] S. Gottlieb, C.W. Shu, E. Tadmor, Strong stability-preserving high-order time discretization methods, SIAM Rev. 43 (1) (2001) 89–112.

[26] S. Balay, J. Brown, K. Buschelman, V. Eijkhout, W. Gropp, D. Kaushik, M. Knepley, L. Curfman McInnes, B. Smith, H. Zhang, PETSc Users Manual Revision 3.4, 2013).

[27] D.L. Williamson, J.B. Drake, J.J. Hack, R. Jakob, P.N. Swarztrauber, A standard test set for numerical approximations to the shallow water equations in spherical geometry, J. Comput. Phys. 102 (1) (1992) 211–224.

[28] R.G. Clapp, Reverse time migration with random boundaries, in: SEG Expanded Abstracts, 2009, pp. 2809–2813.

[29] H. Fu, R.G. Clapp, O. Mencer, O. Pell, Accelerating 3D convolution using streaming architectures on FPGAs, in: SEG Expanded Abstracts, 2009, pp. 3035–3039.

[30] M. Araya-Polo, J. Cabezas, M. Hanzich, Assessing accelerator-based HPC reverse time migration, IEEE Trans. Parallel Distrib. Syst. 22 (2011) 147–162.

ABOUT THE AUTHORS

Lin Gan is a postdoctoral research fellow in the Department of Computer Science and Technology at Tsinghua University, and an assistant director of the National Supercomputing Center in Wuxi. His research interests include FPGA-based solutions to global atmospheric modeling and exploration geophysics, and algorithmic development and performance optimizations based on hybrid platforms such as CPUs, FPGAs, and GPUs. Gan has a PhD in computer science from Tsinghua University, and has been awarded the most significant paper award by an international Significant Papers Committee (SPC) at FPL 2015. Email: lingan@tsinghua.edu.cn.

Haohuan Fu is an associate professor in the Ministry of Education Key Laboratory for Earth System Modeling, and the Center for Earth System Science, at Tsinghua University, and a deputy director of the National Supercomputing Center in Wuxi. His research interests include high-performance computing in earth and environmental sciences, computer architectures, performance optimizations, and programming tools in parallel computing. Fu has a PhD in computing from Imperial College London. Please direct all correspondences to Haohuan Fu. Email: haohuan@tsinghua.edu.cn.

Oskar Mencer Prior to founding Maxeler, Oskar was a Member of Technical Staff at the Computing Sciences Center at Bell Labs in Murray Hill, leading the effort in "Stream Computing." He joined Bell Labs after receiving a PhD from Stanford University. Besides driving Maximum Performance Computing (MPC) at Maxeler, Oskar was a Consulting Professor in Geophysics at Stanford University and he is also affiliated with the Computing Department at Imperial College London, having received two Best Paper Awards, an Imperial College Research Excellence Award in 2007, and a Special Award from Com.sult in 2012 for "revolutionizing the world of computers." Email: mencer@maxeler.com.

Wayne Luk is a Professor of Computer Engineering at Imperial College London, and the Director of the EPSRC Centre for Doctoral Training in High Performance Embedded and Distributed Systems. He was a Visiting Professor at Stanford University. His research focuses on theory and practice of customizing hardware and software for specific application domains, such as genomic data analysis, climate modeling, and computational finance. He has a doctorate in engineering and computing science from the University of Oxford. He is a Fellow of the Royal Academy of Engineering, the IEEE, and the BCS. Email: w.luk@imperial.ac.uk.

Guangwen Yang is a professor in the Department of Computer Science and Technology at Tsinghua University, and a director of the National Supercomputing Center in Wuxi. His research interests include parallel algorithms, cloud computing, and the earth system model. Yang has a PhD in computer science from Tsinghua University. Email: ygw@tsinghua.edu.cn

CHAPTER FIVE

A Streaming Dataflow Implementation of Parallel Cocke–Younger–Kasami Parser

D. Bojić, M. Bojović
School of Electrical Engineering, University of Belgrade, Belgrade, Serbia

Contents

1.	Introduction	160
2.	Problem Statement	161
	2.1 Context-Free Languages	162
	2.2 The CYK Algorithm	165
	2.3 Modifications to the CYK Algorithm	166
	2.4 Parallelizing CYK Parsing	169
3.	Existing Solutions and Their Criticism	170
	3.1 Existing Solutions for Shared Memory Multicore Systems	170
	3.2 Existing Solutions for Distributed Memory Systems	171
	3.3 Existing Solutions for Reconfigurable Hardware Systems	172
	3.4 Existing Solutions for Many-Core (GPU) Systems	175
	3.5 Summary of Presented Solutions	178
4.	A Dataflow Implementation of a CYK Parser	180
5.	Performance Analysis	184
	5.1 Modeling Space and Time Requirements	184
	5.2 Experimental Analysis	187
6.	Conclusion	190
	Acknowledgment	191
	Appendix	191
	References	197
	About the Authors	199

Abstract

Parsing is the task of analyzing grammatical structures of an input sentence and deriving its parse tree. Efficient solutions for parsing are needed in many applications such as natural language processing, bioinformatics, and pattern recognition. The Cocke–Younger–Kasami (CYK) algorithm is a well-known parsing algorithm that operates on context-free grammars in Chomsky normal form and has been extensively studied for execution on parallel machines. In this chapter, we analyze the parallelizing

Advances in Computers, Volume 104
ISSN 0065-2458
http://dx.doi.org/10.1016/bs.adcom.2016.09.004

159

opportunities for the CYK algorithm and give an overview of existing implementations on different hardware architectures. We propose a novel, efficient streaming dataflow implementation of the CYK algorithm on reconfigurable hardware (Maxeler dataflow engines), which achieves 18–76× speedup over an optimized sequential implementation for real-life grammars for natural language processing, depending on the length of the input string.

ABBREVIATIONS

CFG Context-free grammar
CKY Cocke–Kasami–Younger
CNF Chomsky normal form
CPU central processing unit
CUDA compute unified device architecture
CYK Cocke–Younger–Kasami
DFE dataflow engine
FPGA field-programmable gate array
GPU graphic processing unit
OpenMP open multiprocessing
PCFG probabilistic context-free grammar
PCIe peripheral component interface express
SLiC interface simple live CPU interface
SM streaming multiprocessor
VHDL VHSIC hardware description language
WSJ Wall Street Journal

1. INTRODUCTION

Languages described by context-free grammars (CFGs) are used in many applications such as natural language processing (NLP) [1], bioinformatics [2], pattern recognition [3], and several others [4–6]. In these applications, syntactic knowledge about the language is acquired by parsing. When huge amounts of data need to be processed, efficient low complexity parsers are required [7].

Parallel algorithms have been studied for decades, mainly in high-performance computing, but they are getting more attention in recent years due to the physical constraints preventing frequency scaling, and due to the intention to reduce power consumption (and consequently heat generation) by computers [8].

A baseline approach for exploiting parallelism in parsing is simply to parse different sentences in parallel on separate instances of the sequential parser. This is likely to be the best way to exploit parallelism with networked clusters and shared memory multicore machines when parsing a large corpus of sentences off-line. However, there are situations where parsing speed of one sentence is subject to real-time constraints, e.g., when parsing is a component of a system that interacts with users [9].

Cocke–Younger–Kasami (CYK, also known as CKY) is a well-known parsing algorithm [10–12]. Parallel CYK parsing has been extensively studied over the last two decades. Solutions were given for various hardware architectures, both for fixed and for reconfigurable hardware domains [9,13–19]. However, we are not aware of any previous solution for explicit dataflow architecture like the one we propose in this chapter. Some recent implementations of various algorithms using the dataflow paradigm show considerable speedups, power reductions, and space savings over their implementation using the control flow paradigm [20].

The structure of the chapter is as follows: In Section 2, we define basic notions and explain the sequential CYK algorithm, analyzing its potential for parallelization. In Section 3, we give an overview of existing solutions of parallel CYK parsing on various hardware architectures, and then we summarize the most important aspects of those existing solutions, comparing them to our solution. In Section 4, we explain details of our solution. The analytical performance model and the experimental results are given in Section 5. Section 6 is the conclusion, where we summarize our findings and give pointers for future development.

2. PROBLEM STATEMENT

Syntactic parsing of natural languages is the task of analyzing the grammatical structure of sentences and predicting their most likely parse trees. These parse trees can then be used in many ways to enable natural language processing applications like machine translation, question answering, and information extraction. The CYK dynamic programming algorithm [10–12] is used to find the parse tree or trees for a given sentence of length n in $O(|G|n^3)$ time, where $|G|$ represents the number of rules in a grammar. While often ignored, the grammar constant $|G|$ typically dominates the runtime in practice. This is because grammars with high accuracies have thousands of nonterminal symbols and many thousands of context-free rules, while most sentences have on average only about n = 20 words. To speed up computation, the CYK algorithm can be efficiently parallelized on specialized hardware, like reconfigurable field-programmable gate array (FPGA) chip.

First, we briefly recall the definition of context-free languages and the sequential CYK algorithm. Then we discuss parallelizing this algorithm, which is the main topic of this chapter.

2.1 Context-Free Languages

A context-free grammar G is specified by the tuple $G = (V, \Sigma, P, S)$, where V is a set of nonterminals (or variables), Σ is a set of terminals, P is a set of production rules (also called rewrite rules, or productions), and S is the start symbol, and must belong to nonterminals [21]. Nonterminals represent different types of phrases or clauses in the sentence, also called syntactic categories, e.g., VP = Verb Phrase, NP = Noun Phrase, PP = Propositional Phrase, etc. Terminals are disjoint from nonterminals and they make the actual content of the sentence (e.g., kids, box, opened).

Each production rule is of the form $A \rightarrow \gamma$, where $A \in V$ (i.e., A is a non-terminal), $\gamma \in (V \cup \Sigma)^*$, that is, γ is a string of nonterminals and/or terminals (star denotes zero or one or more symbols).

Given a CFG $G = (V, \Sigma, P, S)$, let $\alpha A \beta$ be a string, where $A \in V$, and α, β, and γ are strings from $(V \cup \Sigma)^*$. When we use production rule $A \rightarrow \gamma$, we say that A is rewritten to γ and denote this derivation step by $\Rightarrow$ symbol: namely, $\alpha A \beta \Rightarrow \alpha \gamma \beta$. When there are zero or more steps of derivation, we denote this step by $\Rightarrow^*$ symbol. The language L(G) of G is then a set of terminal strings derived from the start symbol S, namely, $L(G) = \{w \in \Sigma^* \mid S \Rightarrow^* w\}$. That is, we can derive each sentence (i.e., string of terminals) in the language L(G) by systematically rewriting each nonterminal using corresponding rules, starting from S.

For example, consider a grammar G_1: Nonterminals are S, VP, NP, TV, IV, and DatV. Terminals are saw, ate, gave, telescopes, Jack, and apples. S is the start symbol. The rules are given in Fig. 1.

1. S → NP VP	6. IV → 'ate'
2. VP → TV NP	7. DatV → 'gave'
3. VP → IV	8. NP → 'telescopes'
4. VP → DatV NP NP	9. NP → 'Jack'
5. TV → 'saw'	10. NP → 'apples'

Fig. 1 Context-free grammar G_1.

We can derive the sentence *Jack saw telescopes* by the application of rules 1, 9, 2, 5, and 8, respectively, in each derivation step:

$$S \Rightarrow NP \;\; VP \Rightarrow Jack \;\; VP \Rightarrow Jack \;\; TV \;\; NP \Rightarrow Jack \; saw$$
$$NP \Rightarrow Jack \; saw \; telescopes$$

A result of parsing can be represented in the form of a treebank or syntax tree. A treebank is a parsed text corpus that annotates syntactic or semantic sentence structure. For example, the following treebank corresponds to the previous derivation example:

$$(S \; (NP \, Jack) \; (VP \; (TV \, saw) \; (NP \, telescopes)))$$

A syntax tree, or parse tree, is an ordered, rooted tree that represents the syntactic structure of a string according to some context-free grammar. The parse tree for our example derivation is given in Fig. 2.

To be able to process some CFG using the CYK algorithm, the CFG needs to be in Chomsky normal form (CNF) [22]. We can say that a CFG $G = (V, \Sigma, P, S)$ is in CNF if every production rule in P is either of the form $A \rightarrow BC$ or $A \rightarrow a$, where A, B, $C \in V$ and $a \in \Sigma$. It is well known that every CFG can be transformed into CNF. To convert a grammar to CNF, a sequence of simple transformations is applied in a certain order; this is described in most textbooks on automata theory [23].

Let us illustrate the process for our sample grammar G_1: We need only two transformations, binarization and elimination of unary productions (these transformations will be of interest to us in a later discussion).

Binarization is the elimination of right-hand sides of rules with more than two nonterminals.

We must replace each rule of the form

$$A \rightarrow X_1 X_2 ... X_n$$

(with more than two nonterminals) $X_1, ..., X_n$ by rules

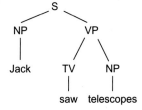

Fig. 2 A parse tree for the sentence: Jack saw telescopes.

$$A \rightarrow X_1 A_1,$$
$$A_1 \rightarrow X_2 A_2,$$
$$\ldots,$$
$$A_{n-2} \rightarrow X_{n-1} X_n,$$

where A_i are new nonterminal symbols. This does not change the grammar's produced language $L(G)$. By applying this rule to G_1, we introduce a new nonterminal NP1 and replace rule 4 with two rules; thus we obtain a new grammar G_2, shown in Fig. 3.

We will now eliminate unary rules from G_2. A unary rule is a rule of the form:

$$A \rightarrow B,$$

where A, B are nonterminal symbols. To remove it, for each rule

$$B \rightarrow X_1 \ldots X_n,$$

where $X_1 \ldots X_n$ is a string of nonterminals and terminals, add rule

$$A \rightarrow X_1 \ldots X_n,$$

unless $A \rightarrow X_1 \ldots X_n$ is a unary rule which has already been removed. By applying the unary removal procedure to rule 3 of G_2, where A = VP, B = IV, we obtain the new grammar G_3, shown in Fig. 4.

Grammar G_3 is now in CNF. Rule 7 can safely be deleted, because no other rule refers to nonterminal IV, so it is not used in derivations. From now on, we assume that an input CFG is in CNF. For more details on these topics, the reader is referred to Ref. [23].

1. S → NP VP
2. VP → TV NP
3. VP → IV
4. VP → DatV NP1
5. NP1 → NP NP
6. TV → 'saw'
7. IV → 'ate'
8. DatV → 'gave'
9. NP → 'telescopes'
10. NP → 'Jack'
11. NP → 'apples'

Fig. 3 Context-free grammar G_2.

1. S → NP VP
2. VP → TV NP
3. VP → 'ate'
4. VP → DatV NP1
5. NP1 → NP NP
6. TV → 'saw'
7. IV → 'ate' (uselessrule)
8. DatV → 'gave'
9. NP → 'telescopes'
10. NP → 'Jack'
11. NP → 'apples'

Fig. 4 Context-free grammar G_3.

2.2 The CYK Algorithm

Given an input string $S = a_1 \ldots a_n \in \Sigma^*$ and a CFG $G = (V, \Sigma, P, S)$, the CYK algorithm, which is based on the bottom-up dynamic programming, determines whether S is in L(G). The standard version of CYK operates only on context-free grammars given in CNF. However, any context-free grammar may be transformed to a CNF grammar expressing the same language [23].

Pseudocode for the CYK algorithm is given in Fig. 5. The main data structure that it builds is a table (or matrix) P. Each cell of P is a set of nonterminal symbols, essentially encoding information about constituent subsequences of the input sequence of words S. This algorithm considers every possible subsequence of the input sequence S and sets a nonterminal R_A to be a member of the matrix array $P[i,j]$ if the subsequence of words of length i starting from j can be generated from R_A. Once it has considered subsequences of length 1, it goes on to subsequences of length 2, and so on.

For subsequences of length 2 and greater, it considers every possible partition of the subsequence into two parts (controlled by variable k) and checks to see if there is some production $P \to Q\,R$ such that Q matches the first part and R matches the second part. If so, it records P as matching the whole subsequence. Once this process is completed, the sentence is recognized by the grammar if the subsequence containing the entire sentence is matched by the start symbol, i.e., $S \in P[n,1]$.

We will illustrate CYK algorithm based on the following grammar G_4 (Fig. 6) with the start symbol S, parsing the sentence *the kids opened the box on the floor.*

```
1   let the input be a string S consisting of n words: a₁ ... aₙ.
2   let the grammar contain r non-terminal symbols R₁ ... Rᵣ.
3   let Rₛ be the start symbol of the grammar.
4   let P[n,n] be a matrix array of sets of non-terminals.
5   Initialize all elements of P to an empty set.
6   for each i = 1 to n
7      for each terminal production Rⱼ -> aᵢ
8      set Rⱼ as a member of P[1,i]
9   for each i = 2 to n -- Length of span
10     for each j = 1 to n-i+1 -- Start of span
11        for each k = 1 to i-1 -- Partition of span
12           for each production Rₐ -> R_B R_C
13              if R_B is a member of P[k,j], and R_C a member of P[i-k,j+k]
14                 then set Rₐ as a member of P[i,j]
15  if Rₛ is a member of P[n,1]
16     then S is member of language
17     else S is not member of language
```

Fig. 5 The sequential CYK algorithm.

1. S → NP VP1	6. VP1 → VNP	11. N → 'floor'
2. S → NP VP2	7. VP2 → VP1 PP	12. V → 'opened'
3. PP → PNP	8. Det → 'the'	13. V → 'box'
4. NP → Det N	9. N → 'kids'	14. P → 'on'
5. NP → NP PP	10. N → 'box'	

Fig. 6 Context-free grammar G_4.

i / j	1	2	3	4	5	6	7	8
8	S							
7								
6			VP1,VP2					
5	S			NP				
4								
3			VP1			PP		
2	NP			NP			NP	
1	Det	N	V	Det	N,V	P	Det	N
	the	kids	opened	the	box	on	the	Floor

Fig. 7 The contents of matrix P for the CYK parse of the sentence *the kids opened the box on the floor*.

Fig. 7 illustrates the CYK matrix P for the aforementioned sentence with respect to the example grammar G_4. The loop in line 6 of the CYK algorithm is used to populate P matrix row for $i=1$. For example, $P[1,1]=\{\text{Det}\}$ because the first word in a sequence is 'the', and there is the rule Det → 'the'. Rows of P matrix for $i \geq 2$ are filled in by the loops in lines 9–11 of the CYK algorithm. For example, in the word sequence starting from position 1 ($j=1$), of length 2 ($i=2$), the algorithm considers the sequence partitioning to the first and the second word for $k=1$. The sequence could be matched by the rule NP → Det N, hence $P[2,1]=\{\text{NP}\}$, because the first word is matched by the rule Det → 'the' (that is, $P[1,1]=\{\text{Det}\}$), and the second word is matched by the rule N → 'kids' (that is, $P[1,2]=\{\text{N}\}$). The whole triangular matrix P is populated by iterating through all remaining values of i, j, and k. Finally, we conclude that the sentence belongs to $L(G_4)$, because the start symbol could match the whole sentence, that is, $S \in P[8,1]$.

2.3 Modifications to the CYK Algorithm

The pair-wise approach of the CYK algorithm limits it to binary context-free grammars. Any grammar can be reduced to a binary grammar using CNF [23]. However, it is better to avoid full CNF, as the transformation loses information about unary rules of the form X → Y, where both X and Y are nonterminals. The elimination of unary rules could result in a quadratic blowup in grammar size measured by number of rules, which consequently affects the performance of some parallel CYK implementations, since it could mean that more hardware resources are needed than physically available to do grammar processing in parallel.

Instead, we used a modified version of the CYK algorithm to support unary rules directly using a unary expansion process [15]. Conceptually, whenever the algorithm adds a nonterminal to a P matrix cell, we expand cell contents by adding other nonterminals that can be derived by unary rules from the original nonterminal. For example, for our sample grammar G_2, if we add IV to some P matrix cell, we should also add VP to the same cell. This process repeats on the newly added nonterminals until no more new expansions can be added.

This calculation is called closure of unary productions and can be implemented using the Warshall algorithm [24] during preprocessing of the grammar, before running the CYK algorithm. Now, the CYK algorithm is changed in line 14, such that instead of adding a unique nonterminal RA to P[i,j] set, a whole closure set of RA is added to P[i,j].

Another optimization to the sequential CYK algorithm concerns the innermost loop. Grammar productions with the same pair of nonterminals on the right-hand side can effectively be merged together in the same memory structure. The left-hand side of those productions is represented with a single set, so that all nonterminals of merged productions are members of that set (or the union of their closure sets if there are unary productions). In this way, algorithm iterates over all different nonterminal pairs on the right-hand side of productions, instead of all binary productions in a grammar, which is on average 20% less for grammars used in NLP. Pseudocode for the extended CYK algorithm, which is the baseline for our parallelization approach, is given in Fig. 8.

The modified CYK algorithm (Fig. 8) is for a recognizer that will only determine if a sentence is in the language. It is simple to extend it into a parser that also constructs a parse tree, by storing parse tree nodes as elements of the array, instead of the Boolean value. The node is linked to the array elements that were used to produce it, so as to build the tree structure. Returning to our example of grammar G_3 and the sentence *the kids opened the box on the floor*, this sentence is actually ambiguous. It has two different parse trees depicted in Fig. 9, corresponding to two different meanings; hence, there are multiple nonterminals recorded in matrix P from Fig. 7.

Because natural language CFGs are highly ambiguous, it is also possible to extend the CYK algorithm to parse strings using weighted and stochastic context-free grammars [25]. Weights (probabilities) are then stored in

```
1   let the input be a string S consisting of n words: a₁ ... aₙ.
2   let the grammar contain r non-terminal symbols R₁ ... Rᵣ.
3   let Rₛ be the start symbol of the grammar.
4   let P[n,n] be an array of sets of non-terminals.
5   let closure[n] be a vector of sets of non-terminals.
6   let map[Rₓ,Rᵧ] be a map collection of sets of non-terminals.
7   Initialize all elements of P and map and closure to an empty set.
8   -- calculation of closure sets
9   for each i = 1 to r
10     set Rᵢ as a member of closure[Rᵢ]
11  for each unary production Rⱼ -> Rᵢ
12     set Rⱼ as a member of closure[Rᵢ]
13  -- apply the Warshall algorithm
14  for each i = 1 to r
15     for each j = 1 to r
16       for each k = 1 to r
17         if Rⱼ is a member of closure[Rᵢ]
18            and Rₖ is a member of closure[Rⱼ]
19         then set Rₖ as a member of closure[Rᵢ]
20  -- calculation of map sets
21  for each production Rₐ -> R_B R_C
22     add all elements of closure[Rₐ] to map[R_B,R_C]
23
24  -- end of preprocessing, start of parsing
25  for each i = 1 to n
26     for each terminal production Rⱼ -> aᵢ
27        add all elements from closure[Rⱼ] to P[1,i]
28  for each i = 2 to n -- Length of span
29    for each j = 1 to n-i+1 -- Start of span
30      for each k = 1 to i-1 -- Partition of span
31        for each element (R_B,R_C) => X from the map collection
32          if R_B is a member of P[k,j], and R_C a member of P[i-k,j+k]
33             then add all elements from X to P[i,j]
34  if Rₛ is a member of P[n,1]
35    then S is member of language
36    else S is not member of language
```

Fig. 8 A modified CYK algorithm that we used as a basis for our parallelization research.

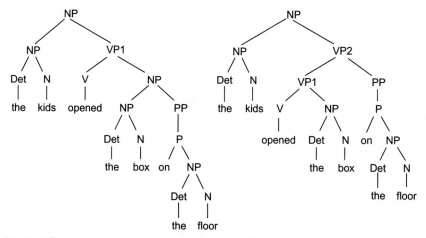

Fig. 9 Different parse trees for the sentence: the kids opened the box on the floor.

P matrix instead of Booleans, so P[i,j] will contain the minimum weight (maximum probability) that the substring from i to j can be derived from A (for every grammar nonterminal). Further extensions of the algorithm allow all parses of a string to be enumerated from lowest to highest weight (highest to lowest probability). These last two extensions of the algorithm (reconstructing the parse tree and handling stochastic grammars) are outside the scope of our research that deals only with recognizing a sentence membership to the language defined by a CFG (Figs. 8 and 9).

2.4 Parallelizing CYK Parsing

When parallelizing any algorithm, it is important to consider the algorithm's work and span [26]. Work is the total amount of computation performed by the algorithm, across all processors (or, equivalently, the total time taken when run on one processor). The span is a theoretical measure of the fastest time an algorithm could execute given an infinite number of processors. An algorithm's span is limited by its critical path, the longest sequence of computations that depend on each other's results. The ratio of an algorithm's work to its span limits its speedup or the performance it can achieve relative to its single-processor performance. An ideal parallel algorithm achieves linear speedup; that is, given P processors, it will execute P times faster than it would on one processor.

CYK is an instance of dynamic programming algorithms; this means that it divides the parsing problem into smaller subproblems that can be solved separately. This structure makes them amenable to parallelization because the separate subproblems can often execute in parallel. CYK parallelizes very well because the dependencies between operations are very sparse and well defined. Because so many of the computations involved in CYK parsing are independent of each other, CYK algorithm gives many opportunities for parallel computation.

The traversal order of the CYK chart itself is underconstrained, a fact we exploit when introducing parallelism later. For example, we can exchange the order of two inner loops (with indices j and k), to make data access more regular (sequential), which results in better cache utilization in shared memory configuration. In fact, we can traverse the CYK chart in any order, as long as each cell is visited after all cells to its left and all cells below it have been visited.

The innermost loop, one that iterates over grammar productions, is a do-all kind of loop. We can process each production independent of others.

This fact is used in several hardware solutions (on reconfigurable FPGA chip) to parallelize and thus speed up processing related to the innermost loop. Elements of P matrix, which are often implemented as bit arrays of several memory words (for large number of nonterminals), could also be processed in a do-all fashion, for union operations.

Important properties of a solution, beside the speedup, are its scalability and extensibility [16]. Scalability refers to tailoring the solution to the characteristics of any given CNF grammar so that no hardware resources are wasted. Extensibility is achieved if the solution does not restrict maximum grammar size, but the size can be increased on demand by using more hardware units.

The exact way a parallel algorithm is constructed from sequential one depends on the underlying hardware architecture. In the following section, we will give an overview of existing solutions for several different hardware architectures. Then we will discuss our innovative way of parallelizing CYK parsing for streaming dataflow architecture.

3. EXISTING SOLUTIONS AND THEIR CRITICISM

First, we give an overview of related techniques classified according to the target architecture, and then we summarize the most important aspects of those existing solutions, comparing them to our solution.

3.1 Existing Solutions for Shared Memory Multicore Systems

Manousopoulou et al. [27] implemented the parallel CYK parser on a multicore system, where the limited parallelization possibilities provided by the systems restrict the speedups that can be achieved (7–$8 \times$). A similar approach from van Lohuizen [28] reports a mere $1.8 \times$ speedup. The best speedup in this category of algorithms of $15.2 \times$ for 16 core processor (nearly linear) is reported by Boyd-Wickizer et al. [15].

Boyd-Wickizer et al. [15] employed several techniques to achieve this level of parallelism: at the P matrix cell level of parallelism (the outer two loops with indices i and j, lines 9 and 10 in Fig. 5), they identified data dependencies between cells and made a transitive reduction of dependency graph (removed transitive arcs, as in Fig. 10).

In the solution [15], each cell value is computed using one thread, with a push model of thread synchronization, where cells do not wait on other cells to complete. Instead, when a cell calculation completes, its thread checks if it is the last dependency of any other cells and, if so, spawns the computations of those cells. This model scales well to a large number of short-lived threads.

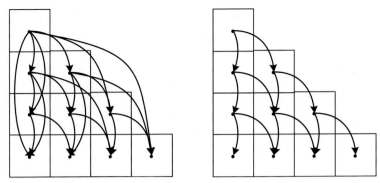

Fig. 10 Full and reduced P matrix cell dependencies.

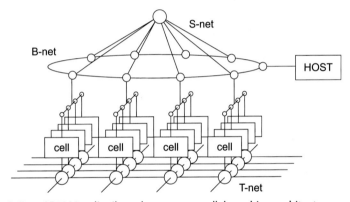

Fig. 11 Fujitsu AP1000+ distributed memory parallel machine architecture.

The technique [15] also uses cache aware partitioning by dividing the CYK inner loop processing into chunks that fit into cache. Other techniques include tracking dependencies on the level of individual rule processing inside each cell.

3.2 Existing Solutions for Distributed Memory Systems

Takashi *et al.* [19] proposed a parallel CKY parser on a distributed memory machine, Fujitsu AP1000+ consisting of 256 nodes, where each node contains a single processor (Super Sparc 50 MHz with 16 MB of memory). AP1000+ architecture is presented in Fig. 11. It has three networks: a broadcast network (B-net; 25 MB/s), a torus network (T-net; 50 MB/s per a link), and a synchronization network (S-net). On the AP1000+ a processing unit is called a cell. Each cell is controlled by a host machine using the B-net and S-net. The AP1000+ offers special instructions which allow remote memory accesses. The remote memory access does not disturb a remote processor (which implements a write through cache policy). Each cell can read remote memory with a get instruction and write with a put instruction.

The operating system of this machine is called Cell-OS, which offers a single user and a single-program operating environment. Under Cell-OS, the machine is reset before launching each parallel program, and the kernel is loaded with the parallel program.

Using a specific parallel language ABCL/f, Takashi et al. [19] parallelized CYK over elements of P matrix. More specifically, although the order of traversing P matrix is somewhat different than in the baseline CYK algorithm from Fig. 5, we can express the algorithm [19] as follows:

First, the outermost loop with index i (line 9 in Fig. 5) has been parallelized, which is the coarsest parallelism in the CYK algorithm. At this level, ideal speedup reaches n for a sentence of length n at the beginning of the parsing and decreases as parsing proceeds.

Next, the loop with index j (line 10 in Fig. 5) has been parallelized, which is the second coarsest parallelism. That is, computation of $P[i,j]$ is a unit of parallel processing.

Next, the inner loops (lines 11 and 12 in Fig. 5) have not been parallelized, but for that loops, computation of the final value of $P[i,j]$ is done after computations of both $P[i-k,j+k]$ and $P[k,j]$ have been completed.

With a grammar of 18,891 rules and 206 nonterminal symbols, a speedup of $45\times$ was achieved compared to an optimized C++ sequential version running on Sun Sparc Station 10 workstation, but for very long input sequences (120 words). For shorter input sequences of about 40 words, that is average length of the real corpus in Japanese of 2173 sentences used, the speedup was less than $5\times$. Since the parallel machine has a distributed memory system, where the synchronization among the nodes is implemented with message passing, the synchronization overhead is significant, preventing parallelization of the inner loops of the CYK algorithm.

3.3 Existing Solutions for Reconfigurable Hardware Systems

Ciressan et al. [16] proposed and implemented an FPGA design that could be considered as a straightforward implementation of the CYK algorithm in hardware (Fig. 12). The general idea of their hardware design is to use n processors to parse a sentence containing at most n words. Each processor is

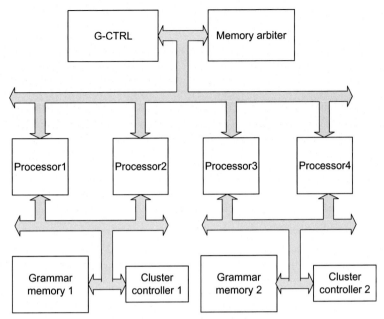

Fig. 12 FPGA design with a processor per input word.

responsible for calculating a column of P matrix. The CYK memory stores the sets P[i,j] and is shared for read and write by all working processors in the system (token passing priority arbiter is used). It is the task of the global controller G-CTRL to activate or deactivate the processors and to synchronize the processors at the end of outer loop iteration. The grammar memories store identical copies of the binary representation of the CNF grammar.

During parsing, the processors intensively access the grammar memories, but due to physical constraints (i.e., the number of I/O pins of an FPGA), it was not possible to have a separate grammar memory bus for each processor in the system. Instead, processors are grouped in clusters that share the same grammar memory (again, priority arbiter is used). They report a speedup of 69.9 × for a real-life grammar with 10,129 nonterminals and 74,350 rules in its CNF form. This is the result of a simulation of the system with 14 processors and 7 clusters (in reality, they could put just 10 processors and 3 memory clusters onto their FPGA chip). The simulation limited the maximum sentence length to 14, corresponding to the number of processors in the design. The real word corpuses have the larger average sentence length, about 25. The design seems to be congested around P memory because all processors simultaneously access it.

Bordim and Nakano [13] studied the CYK algorithm on FPGAs and developed a hardware generator that creates a Verilog HDL source performing CYK parsing for a given CFG. Their approach considers 2048 production rules and 64 variables in an input CFG and shows a speedup factor of almost $750 \times$. The main idea of their approach is to accelerate the inner loop processing of CYK parser by not iterating through rules one by one. Instead, they conceptualized a huge lookup table, where the input address would consist of values of both cells $P[i - k, j + k]$ and $P[k, j]$. The output from this table would be a final result to $P[i, j]$. It needs to be precomputed (once per grammar, before parsing starts) considering all grammar rules for every pair of different values of $P[i - k, j + k]$ and $P[k, j]$. As those values are bit arrays of r bits, a memory capacity of 2^{2r} bits is needed (2^{128} in case that there are 64 nonterminals in the grammar), which is impractically large. As a result, they devised a method to look up pairs of chunks of bit arrays $P[i - k, j + k]$ and $P[k, j]$, which reduced the table capacity to 256 MB for 64 nonterminals, at the expense of 64 table lookups instead of just one.

Even with this optimization, the proposed approach suffers from insufficient memory or logic elements and limits the number of rules in the grammar and the number of nonterminal symbols. Hence, it cannot be applied to real-world, state-of-the-art grammars.

Nevertheless, the idea of trading memory for processing speed via lookup tables motivated us to devise an alternative scheme, where the set of N rules is processed simultaneously by means of lookup table.

The rule processing loop of the CYK algorithm (Fig. 5) consists of two set membership tests, and an update to $P[i, j]$ matrix element:

```
12   for each production RA -> RB RC
13     if R_B is a member of P[k,j], and R_C a member of P[i-k,j+k]
14        then set R_A as a member of P[i,j]
```

The membership tests use the precomputed part of P matrix and are a do-all kind of computation that can be done fully in parallel for all grammar rules (subject to the amount of available hardware on an FPGA chip). $P[i, j]$ set update, on the other hand, is an aggregate function. Theoretically, it could be realized using combinatorial logic elements with a large fan-in. In practice, multiple pipeline stages are required for FPGA synthesis to succeed, effectively decreasing the performance to one rule per clock cycle.

To speed up P[i,j] calculations, and avoid large fan-in logic, we used a special lookup table. The membership test yields one-bit result per each rule. The set of those N bits is used as an address to a lookup table, which returns a precomputed result which is a union of left-hand sides of all rules from the set that has 1 in a lookup address. This approach could be applied regardless of the total number of rules in the grammar; hence, it has excellent scalability. If we use multiple (say M) lookup tables, then we can process M * N rules in parallel. The optimal values of M and N have to be empirically determined. The details of our approach are given in Section 4.

3.4 Existing Solutions for Many-Core (GPU) Systems

Johnson [9] examined the CYK algorithm for dense probabilistic context-free grammars (PCFGs) and constructed a dense PCFG with 32 variables and 32,768 production rules with random probability. The author reported an 18.4 × speedup obtained on NVIDIA Fermi s2050 GPUs (graphic processing units) and suggested a reduction method in one block for calculating the probability.

Dunlop *et al.* [29] presented a matrix encoding of CFGs using a multiplication method for a matrix low-latency parallelized CYK algorithm, with up to 9 × speedup for probabilistic CFGs. They encoded the grammars of CFG in a matrix form in which the rows are the left-hand side variable of the production and the columns are the right-hand side variables (pairs in CNF).

Yi *et al.* [25] proposed an efficient parallel CYK algorithm for natural language parsing of PCFG on GPUs. A PCFG is a CFG in which each production is augmented with the probability. Their algorithm assigns each production rule of an input PCFG to each core in a GPU and finds the valid parsing rules quickly. They claim a 26 × speedup compared to a sequential C implementation.

We will examine a recent (2014) solution for parallel CYK implementation in compute unified device architecture (CUDA) programming model Kim *et al.* [18], because they parallelized the algorithm that is of interest to us.

CUDA allows programmers to utilize NVIDIA GPUs to accelerate applications in domains other than graphics. A CUDA program calls parallel kernels. A kernel executes in parallel across a set of parallel threads. The programmer or a compiler organizes these threads in thread blocks and thread-block grids. The GPU instantiates a kernel program on a grid of parallel thread blocks [30].

Each thread within a thread block executes an instance of the kernel and has a thread ID within its thread block, program counter, registers, per-thread private memory, inputs, and output results. A thread block is a set of concurrently executing threads that can cooperate among themselves through barrier synchronization and shared memory.

In the CUDA parallel programming model (shown in Fig. 13), each thread has a per-thread private memory space used for register spills, function calls, and C automatic array variables. Each thread block has a per-block shared memory space used for interthread communication and for sharing of parallel algorithms' data and results. This shared memory has two orders of magnitude less latency than the off-chip global memory, but is very small (16–64 kB, depending on the architecture). CUDA therefore provides the programmer with the flexibility (and burden) to explicitly manage shared memory (i.e., loading a value from global memory and storing it).

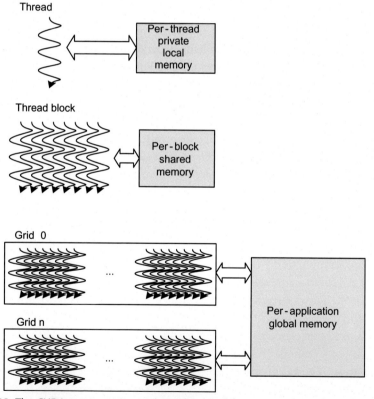

Fig. 13 The CUDA programming and memory models.

Grids of thread blocks share results in Global Memory space after kernel-wide global synchronization [30]. There is also a so-called texture memory for storing constant values, read-only memory for GPU and writable only by the central processing unit (CPU).

The CUDA's hierarchy of threads maps to a hierarchy of processors on the GPU. The GPU executes one or more kernel grids; a streaming multiprocessor (SM) executes one or more thread blocks; and CUDA cores and other execution units in the SM execute threads. To improve performance by memory locality, the SM executes threads in groups called warps [30]. In typical GPUs, a warp consists of 32 threads that share the units for instruction fetching and execution. Thus, a thread cannot advance to the next instruction if other threads in the same warp have not yet completed their own execution. On the other hand, threads in different warps are truly independent: they can be scheduled and executed in any order. Up to two warps are scheduled to execute on each SM.

One of the important factors for designing parallel algorithms is how to map the input data to the threads for fast parallel processing. Kim *et al.* [18] start from a variant of the CYK algorithm where the loop with index k and the loop over rules are interchanged. They map the second loop (with index j) to thread blocks, and the loop over rules to threads. They consider three different methods of mapping grammar rules to threads: rule based (mapping rules in the order they appear in the grammar), left-variable sorting, where rules are grouped by their left-hand sides before mapping to threads (thereby reducing shared memory requirements for intermediate results), and right-variable sorting, where rules are sorted by the first nonterminal on the right-hand side before mapping to threads (thereby increasing thread performance by reducing thread divergence). They also add dummy rules to reduce thread divergence (avoid boundary conditions) and thus improve thread execution performance at the cost of additional memory accesses.

They experimented with different methods of mapping CYK data structures to CUDA memory hierarchy. They tried storing rule data in global memory, in texture memory, and with storing intermediate results (a value of P matrix cell for a particular nonterminal) in shared memory—the final P matrix is in global memory.

They experimented with a grammar obtained from a Penn Treebank with 98 nonterminals and 3840 binary rules, using NVidia 560 Ti GPU with 8 streaming multiprocessors having in total 384 CUDA cores, with 1 GB of global memory, and 48 kB of shared memory size. The CPU was Core i3 3.10 GHz with 8 GB of operating memory. The greatest speedup is

8.41 × over sequential CYK version for a combination of using left-variable sorting, shared memory, and dummy rules, but for a relatively small grammar. With a full size grammar, they obtain 8.21 × speedup using the right-variable sorting, and without using the shared memory. They notice that using texture memory over global memory for storing grammar rules does not increase performance of the algorithm.

3.5 Summary of Presented Solutions

Following the overview of existing solutions to parallelize CYK parser algorithm, Table 1 gives a summary comparison of selected solutions in terms of most important parameters with our solution. We have chosen the best performing solution in terms of speedup to sequential CYK version from each architecture category described in Sections 3.1–3.4. We are mostly interested in solutions that solve exactly the same problem as ours, namely CYK recognizer. However, we also included a few solutions that are dealing with the probabilistic CYK algorithm, because this algorithm is structurally similar to basic algorithm, the main difference being that it needs floating point arithmetic operations instead of logical operations (on bit arrays representing sets of nonterminals). Because of that structural similarity, the basic ideas for parallelization could be reused for both types of algorithms (but hardware needs are different).

In Table 1 for each solution, we list best achieved speedups (it is usually not a single value, but a range of values depending on the parameters such as the grammar size and the length of input), the hardware architecture it is targeted to, the variant of CFG it could directly process, the size of grammar, and the length of input sequences used in experimentation, whether the verification was performed by actually running the parallelized solution or just simulating it, and about the scalability and extensibility properties as we defined them in Section 2.4.

Because the solutions are from different years, implemented on different technology generations, there is no sense of comparing actual runtimes of solutions, but just their speedup values. The speedup is defined as the ratio between parsing runtime on sequential hardware and a parallel one belonging to the same technology generation. The cautionary note is that those values from different solutions are not directly comparable, but should be put in perspective with parameters of grammars and the length of input sequence. The solutions that are measured using real grammars (number of nonterminals at least 1000, number of rules at least several thousands)

Table 1 A Summary of Existing Solutions to Parallel CYK Parsing

Authors and Year	Speedup Range	Parallel Architecture	CFG Type	CFG Vars/Rules/Input Length	Verification	Scalable/ Extensible
Boyd-Wickizer et al. [15]	15.2×	Multicore (16) CPU	CNF/w unary rules	2800/13,400/7–16	Experimental	Yes/yes
Takashi et al. [19]	5–45×	Distributed memory symmetric (256 nodes)	CNF	200/19,000/40–120	Experimental	Yes/yes
Ciressan et al. [16]	10–69.9×	FPGA/VHDL	CNF	10,100/74,000/3–15	Simulation	Yes/ potentially
Bordim and Nakano [13]	750×	FPGA/Verilog	CNF	64/2048/32	Experimental	No/?
Yi et al. [25]	25.8×	GPU (480 cores)	PCFG/CNF	1120/900,000/~20	Experimental	Yes/?
Kim et al. [18]	8.41×	GPU (384 cores)	CNF	98/3840/~20	Experimental	Yes/?

and that are verified by running an actual implementation in parallel are much more credible than solutions using toy examples, too long input sequences or just simulating the algorithm behavior. Also, there is no standard (benchmark) implementation of the sequential CYK algorithm, and it also greatly affects the overall speedup value. We have chosen to present speedup values in comparison to "canonical" CYK implementations as it is described in the literature when introducing it, with the usual set of compiler optimizations and with the choice efficient data structures for representing P matrix, and not some special restructured variants that are using the ideas obtained from parallel implementations (e.g., by introducing huge lookup tables to trade space for runtime, etc.).

4. A DATAFLOW IMPLEMENTATION OF A CYK PARSER

Our solution of parallel CYK parsing is targeted to streaming dataflow architecture of reconfigurable hardware accelerators offered by Maxeler Technologies, a fast-expanding high-performance computing company with roots at Stanford, Bell Labs, in the United States, and Imperial College, London, in the United Kingdom.

Fig. 14 sketches the architecture of a Maxeler hardware acceleration system which equips one or more Dataflow Engines attached to a set of memories and connected to a host CPU via PCIe channels [31]. Accelerating an

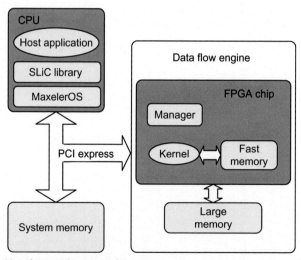

Fig. 14 The Maxeler accelerator architecture.

application involves analyzing the entire application, adapting program structure, and partitioning the execution flow and data layout between CPUs and accelerators. The program of the Dataflow Engines comprises arithmetic data paths for the computations (the kernels) and modules orchestrating the data I/O for these kernels (the manager).

The Maxeler Kernel Compiler generates configuration of hardware, which configured forms the Dataflow Engines used as accelerators to the CPU. Therefore, the program describes computations structurally (computing in space) rather than specifying a sequence of processor instructions (computing in time). The main unit of processing is a kernel, which is a streaming core with a dataflow described by a unidirectional graph. Subsequently, data streams through the arithmetic nodes. Efficient streaming kernels strongly emphasize the regularity of the dataflow, making the actual computations look like a side effect of streaming. These kernels are suitable for deeply pipelined dataflow implementation, which is crucial for achieving good performance.

We could say that our innovation belongs to classes S (specialization) and I (implantation) of the classification given in Ref. [32]. The solution specializes the parallel CYK algorithm to yet unexplored hardware architecture. The solution bears some similarities to the technique of Bordim and Nakano [13], in the sense that we used lookup tables to speed up grammar processing (i.e., trading space for speed), but instead of mapping pair of P matrix cells to a table result, we mapped the conditional results of matching R rules at the same time to P matrix cell. In that way, we eliminated the limits of the existing solution, because our technique could be applied to grammars of any size (adjusting the level of parallelism to available hardware resources), and, at the same time, retained a solid runtime performance.

The complete kernel we developed for a CYK parser is given in the Appendix, written in MaxJ language, which is a variant of Java language used to describe the structure of the kernel. MaxJ could be regarded as a hardware description language, like VHDL or Verilog. However, MaxJ has a higher level of abstraction than those languages, which makes programmer more productive. When programming in MaxJ, a programmer thinks of dataflow graphs, stream variables, arrays, etc, and not hardware entities like registers, signal buses, etc. The MaxJ compiler is effectively a Java software library, and as such, kernel graphs are created by writing a Java program and executing it. A kernel graph behavior could be simulated (for a purpose of program testing) and eventually kernel graphs are directly mapped to hardware, using FPGA hardware synthesis tools.

Fig. 15 depicts the abstracted kernel dataflow graph for the parallel CYK algorithm. Various implementation details have been left out, which produce many more nodes in the actual kernel graph.

The CYK algorithm main data structure, matrix P, is represented in the kernel by chip-internal block memory PMEM (lines 53–56 of the kernel listing in the Appendix). Its capacity is quadratic to the size of the input, and it has three read ports and one write port per clock cycle (internally MaxJ compiler generates duplicate copies of memory blocks to achieve this). PMEM is a linearized representation of P (a vector that corresponds to a row-by-row representation of matrix).

Three address generators that correspond to expressions P[k,j], P[i− k, j+k], and P[i,j] from the sequential algorithm in Fig. 8 are linear combinations of the values of counters i, k, and j. Those three hardware counters are chained together to counter g (g is fastest incrementing per each tick, that is clock cycle of FPGA chip), see lines 41–48 of the kernel listing in

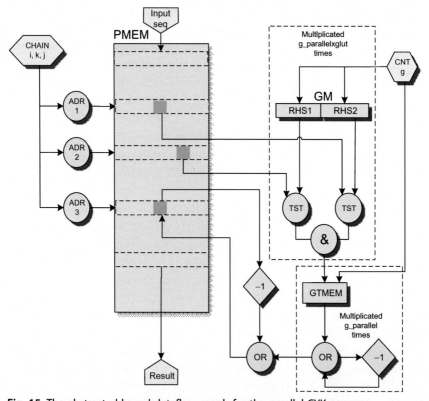

Fig. 15 The abstracted kernel dataflow graph for the parallel CYK parser.

the Appendix. When counter g wraps up, then counter j increments by one, etc. Counters i, k, and j correspond to *for* loops in lines 28–30 of the sequential algorithm in Fig. 8 (with a change in the order of k and j loops as discussed earlier). Counter g roughly corresponds to *for* loop in line 31 of Fig. 8 (taking into account the earlier discussion that an improved sequential algorithm iterates over a set of different nonterminal pairs on the right-hand sides of productions). However, in each g increment, a total of (*g_parallel* x *g_lut*) productions get processed, where *g_parallel* and *g_lut* are kernel compile time constants.

There is exactly the same number (*g_parallel* x *g_lut*) of instances of GM memory (kernel listing lines 68–71); every cell of each GM instance is composed of RHS1 and RHS2 parts that are indices of nonterminal pairs for grammar rules. Every GM instance has a capacity of *g_max* cells, where *g_max* is a kernel compile time constant (it depends on a total number of different nonterminal pairs in grammar rules, divided by a product of *g_parallel* and *g_lut*). A set of *g_lut* instances of GM memory correspond to one instance of GTMEM memory.

There are a total of *g_parallel* instances of GTMEM memory (kernel lines 81–86). Each instance of GTMEM memory holds information for calculating the partial result for P[i,j] calculation (lines 32–33 of the sequential algorithm) for *g_lut* grammar pairs at once (in a particular iteration of g). The capacity of each GTMEM instance is *g_max*. A GTMEM memory instance contains information of the resulting left-hand side set for each possible combination of *g_lut* grammar pairs for *g_max* different sets of those pairs. Suppose, for example, that *g_lut* compile time constant is 5, and an observed GTMEM memory instance holds information for productions 1–5 in a particular iteration of g. Suppose, for example, we give 01001 as the address of GTMEM cell (excluding the part of address linked to the value of g counter), that means that pairs (productions) 2 and 5 are recognized (in a particular iteration of g), so GTMEM cell will contain ORed values of nonterminal sets for the left-hand sides of productions 2 and 5. If we give, e.g., 11111 as the input address, that means that all five pairs are recognized, so the output from GTMEM will be ORed values of nonterminal sets for the left-hand sides of all five productions.

The processing flow for P[i,j] calculation (lines 31 and 32 of the sequential algorithm, kernel listing lines 107–162) is as follows: the output of GM memory instance, that is, indices of nonterminals in a given pair (RHS1, RHS2), is tested against P cells that correspond to P[k,j] and P[i − k, j + k]. If there is a match in both components of (RHS1, RHS2) pair, the meaning is that P[k,j] and P[i − k,j + k] sets contain those nonterminals. It is a one-bit information (one grammar pair is matched), and *g_lut* of those bits are grouped together to form an input address of GT memory instance. It is one part of the address and another part being the value of g counter to account for every of *g_max* iterations. Because there are *g_max* iterations to process all grammar pairs, the outputs from the same GTMEM instance are ORed together and the result is ORed with an old value of P[i,j] to obtain a new value of P[i,j]. Pipeline delays are symbolically represented as −1 nodes in Fig. 15. Actual pipeline depths are dependent on the kernel parameter values, and the actual number of ticks to calculate one P[i,j] value for fixed values of i, k, and j is *g_max* plus the overall pipeline depth.

Some details have been omitted in Fig. 15; during initialization (while the signal *init* is in active state), the input sequence is written into PMEM locations for the first row of matrix P driven by the *inp_cnt* counter. The result P[N,1] is written into the output stream result (controlled by values of counters i, k, and j).

Member functions *SetGmContents()* and *SetGtContents()* of *CykV2ParserKernel* class are used to set contents of memories GMEM and GTMEM during kernel compilation. They implement reading of file *gmem.txt*, generated from the CPU code as a result of the preprocessing of the grammar.

5. PERFORMANCE ANALYSIS

We devised an analytic model for space and time requirements of our implementation. The model helps predicting which CFG size could successfully fit onto a particular hardware, and what efficiency to expect, because there are several generations of dataflow elements. We validated the models and our implementation experimentally.

5.1 Modeling Space and Time Requirements

Analytic modeling of space and time requirements for dataflow CYK kernel helps to determine meaningful combinations of kernel parameters that are "free standing," i.e., not dictated by the CFG. Especially having in mind that the kernel compile time could exceed 10 h for large kernels and particular hardware synthesis options, it is not rational to just try to compile kernel for all different combinations of parameters, and see if the compilation succeeds or not, due to on–chip memory and logic capacity, and signal routing constraints.

Space requirements of the dataflow CYK parser are dictated by the use of on-chip block memory (so-called fast memory, or FMEM in Maxeler documentation). There are three dataflow variables representing data structures mapped to FMEM: PMEM variable holds a matrix P, GM variable holds right-hand side information for grammar productions, and GTMEM variable is used to map sets of productions to resulting left-hand side nonterminal sets as described in the previous section. The overall space requirements are successfully approximated by GTMEM alone because that structure is much bigger than PMEM and GM together.

In the calculation of GTMEM variable size that follows, we use these parameters: ba_bsize is a required number of bytes to store a bit array representing a set of grammar nonterminals, g_lut is a number of grammar productions used in GTMEM mapping, g_max_bits is a required number of bits to hold g_max value, g_max is the number of iterations of g counter, and $g\_parallel$ is a multiplication factor for GTMEM instances.

Parameters ba_bsize, g_max, and g_max_bits are dependent on the properties of the CFG for which we compile the kernel. Parameters g_lut and $g\_parallel$ are a free choice of programmer, taking into account the maximum capacity of the hardware implementing the kernel (they should be as large as on-chip memory capacity and routing constraints permit, because this speeds up processing).

Table 2 gives some properties of the grammars from Penn Treebank used in our experiments and discussed in the next section. The number of iterations is calculated from the number of unique pairs in the grammar and chosen g_lut and $g\_parallel$ values as follows:

$$iterations = \text{ceiling}\left(unique\_pairs / (g\_lut^* g\_parallel)\right).$$

Table 2 Properties of Grammars in Binarized Form Used in the Experimental Analysis

Grammar	Nonterminals	Terminals	Binary Prods	Term. Prods	Unary Prods	Unique Pairs
G05	263	404	338	407	19	294
G20	679	1608	1049	1658	45	842
G40	1238	3144	2026	3320	76	1503
G50	1480	3891	2470	4167	89	1793
G100	2883	7300	4968	8303	163	3356

GTMEM instance address space size g_max is calculated as the first power of two greater than the number of iterations. Finally, we can write down the formula for GTMEM size:

$$GTMEM_{SIZE} = ba\_bsize * 2^{g\_lut} * 2^{g\_max\_bits} * g\_parallel$$

The total number of iterations of the CYK parser kernel num_iter is calculated as follows: recall the nested loops of the CYK algorithm, which are mapped to counter chain in the dataflow kernel (the only difference in the values of kernel counters i, j being one less than in the pseudo-code):

```
1   for each i = 1 to n-1
2     for each j = 0 to n-i
3       for each k = 1 to i
```

We start by summing the number of iterations of inner loops for each value of i.:

$$num\_iter = n \cdot 1 + (n-1)2 + \cdots + (n+1-i)i$$
$$+ \cdots + (n+1-(n-1))(n-1) = \sum_{i=1,n-1} (n+1-i)i$$
$$= \sum_{i=1,n-1} (n+1)i - \sum_{i=1,n-1} i^2$$

Knowing that $\sum_{i=1,m} i = m(m+1)/2$ and $\sum_{i=1,m} i^2 = \frac{1}{3}m(m+1)$ $(m+1/2)$, we get:

$$num\_iter = \sum_{i=1,n-1} (n+1)i - \sum_{i=1,n-1} i^2 = (n+1)(n-1)n/2$$
$$- (n-1)n(n-1/2)/3$$

To get the total number of clock cycles for kernel execution, or "ticks" in Maxeler terminology, we multiply num_iter by g_max plus pipeline delay, and add n ticks for the initial reading of the input sequence:

$$num\_ticks = n + num\_iter * (g\_max + pipeline\_delay)$$

Pipeline delay is dependent on the values of kernel compile time parameters and is obtained as a result of functional simulation of the design. According to Maxeler documentation, an estimation of kernel running time is obtained by multiplying num_ticks with a period of stream clock, which is nominally 10 ns (for a frequency of 100 MHz). Estimated running times for several input grammars are presented in Table 4 along with the experimental results and discussed in the next section.

5.2 Experimental Analysis

The experiments were conducted on Maxeler MPC-C500 system with 2 Vectis (MAX3) dataflow engines (but only a single engine was used in all experiments), 2 Intel Xeon 5650 CPUs with 12 logical cores each, running at 2.67 GHz, with 12 MB cache memory per processor, and with 48 GB of system memory. At the heart of Vectis dataflow engine is Virtex 5 chip (sx475t) with 100 MHz stream clock and about 4 MB of on-chip RAM memory. MaxCompiler 2012.2 was used to compile kernel code. CPU code was compiled with using gcc 4.4.7 compiler with -O3 optimization level.

We used the same benchmark as in Ref. [15], that is a family of Penn Treebank grammars, constructed by processing a different percentage of *Wall Street Journal* (*WSJ*) corpus. G05 is induced by processing 5% of the corpus, G20 is induced by processing 20% of the corpus, and G100 is induced from the full corpus. While G20 and lower percentage grammars could not be used in real applications due to sparsity of their terminal sets, G40 and higher percentage grammars are good representatives of grammars used in real application scenarios. These grammars are publicly freely available at http://pdos.csail.mit.edu/~amdragon/mcchart.tar.gz. Relevant properties of these grammars in binarized form are presented in Table 2.

Kernel compile time parameters were explained in the previous section. It was said that parameters g_lut and $g\_parallel$ are free to choose in order to fit design onto the chip and to achieve efficient parsing. Table 3 presents kernel on-chip memory requirements for various chosen values of g_lut (number of grammar pairs processed simultaneously by GTMEM instance) and $g\_parallel$ (number of GTMEM instances). Formulas for calculating the number of iterations, g_max, and GTMEM size were given in the previous section.

Experimental analyses were conducted for highlighted values in Table 3. Other values fail either because of exceeding maximum on-chip memory capacity of Vectis dataflow unit, or failing synthesis (the typical error is congested design where router fails to route all signals, or routed design fails to meet timing constraints).

The runtime for a dataflow engine (DFE) program (shown in Table 4) does not include a call to *maxload()* in simple live CPU (SLiC) interface (loading bitmap into the FPGA device) because it is done only once, and then the device could be repetitively activated to parse various input sequences. We used precision UNIX time measurement library with a resolution of 1 ns (because of relatively small runtimes). All measurements are averaged from repetitive running of several input sequences of the same length.

Table 3 Kernel On-Chip Memory Requirements

g_lut (bits)	g_parallel	Grammar	g_max	Iterations	GTMEM Size
12	16	G05	8	5	48 MB
12	8	G20	4	4	5.242.880 B
11	8	G05	4	4	2.621.440 B
10	16	G20	8	6	12 MB
10	16	G50	16	12	48 MB
8	4	G20	32	27	3.145.728 B
8	4	G50	64	57	12.582.912 B
8	2	G50	128	113	12.582.912 B
6	5	G50	64	60	3.932.160 B
6	3	G50	128	100	4.718.592 B
6	4	G40	64	63	2.621.440 B
5	4	G50	128	90	3.145.728 B
5	3	G50	128	120	2.359.296 B
5	3	G100	256	224	9.043.968 B
5	2	G100	512	336	12.058.624 B

Table 4 and Fig. 16 depict speedup factors for different lengths of input sequences and for several grammar sizes. The speedup is better for larger grammars and longer input sequences. As we already explained, G40 and larger grammars are representatives of real-life application grammars, and smaller grammars are included just for the sake of performance comparison. The maximum grammar size and the maximum input length are limited by the chip capacity. We did not manage to put larger grammars than G50 onto the dataflow element because hardware synthesis fails, but this problem could be mitigated by using more technologically advanced dataflow elements (Vectis units we used in our experimentation are from year 2012).

From the plot in Fig. 17 of relative errors of estimated versus real runtime for DFE parser for all data points from Table 4, one can conclude that the estimation always underestimates the real runtime, and that the error is below 20% if runtimes are above 5 ms. The underestimation could be explained by the fact that an adopted model of estimation does not take into account overhead imposed by calling DFE element via SLiC interface from C program, and the time of actual transfer of data to and from DFE element.

Table 4 Runtimes, Relative Errors of Estimating Runtimes, and Speedup Factors

CFG	Pipe	Length	EstimTimeDFE	TimeDFE	Rel. Err (%)	TimeCPU	Speedup
G50	17	10	3.025000e−04	1.012999e−03	70.14	1.885896e−02	18.62 ×
G50	17	20	2.189000e−03	2.893649e−03	24.35	1.316913e−01	45.51 ×
G50	17	30	7.099500e−03	7.733790e−03	8.20	4.448955e−01	57.53 ×
G40	24	10	1.828000e−04	8.527000e−04	78.56	1.215706e−02	14.26 ×
G40	24	20	1.322600e−03	2.081429e−03	36.46	8.995527e−02	43.22 ×
G40	24	30	4.289400e−03	5.086453e−03	15.67	2.927572e−01	57.56 ×
G40	24	40	9.953200e−03	1.081398e−02	7.96	7.848344e−01	72.58 ×
G40	24	50	1.918400e−02	1.998208e−02	3.99	1.529233e+00	76.53 ×
G20	24	10	1.072000e−04	7.933540e−04	86.49	4.020108e−03	5.07 ×
G20	24	20	7.754000e−04	1.509060e−03	48.62	2.982419e−02	19.76 ×
G20	24	30	2.514600e−03	3.216202e−03	21.81	9.566635e−02	29.75 ×
G20	24	40	5.834800e−03	6.574839e−03	11.26	2.316708e−01	35.24 ×
G20	24	50	1.124600e−02	1.369639e−02	17.89	5.521245e−01	40.31 ×
G05	21	10	5.890000e−05	8.095410e−04	92.72	4.870600e−04	0.60 ×
G05	21	20	4.258000e−04	1.096989e−03	61.18	3.572204e−03	3.26 ×
G05	21	30	1.380700e−03	1.998695e−03	30.92	1.152191e−02	5.76 ×
G05	21	40	3.203600e−03	3.652385e−03	12.29	2.953434e−02	8.09 ×
G05	21	50	6.174500e−03	6.318746e−03	2.28	5.163583e−02	8.17 ×
G05	21	60	1.057340e−02	1.046341e−02	1.05	8.578888e−02	8.20 ×

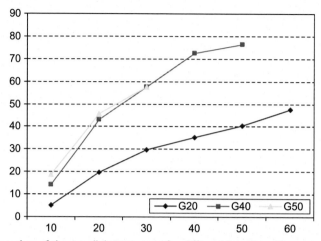

Fig. 16 Speedup of the parallel CYK parser for different lengths of input.

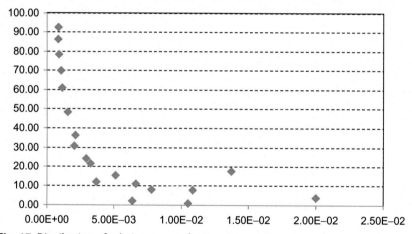

Fig. 17 Distribution of relative errors of estimating runtimes.

This overhead has some fixed component, so when the number of data processed is too small, this overhead is not negligible. It is consistent with the claim in Maxeler documentation that the system should be used for big data processing, and the warning that communicating with DFE has some overhead components.

6. CONCLUSION

Parallelizing CYK parsing has been of great interest to research community, especially with recent advanced in natural language processing and other application areas. We presented a solution to parallel CYK parsing that is realized in an innovative parallel model, namely Maxeler streaming dataflow, which is targeted to reconfigurable hardware accelerators (FPGA based). We already analyzed [8] the potential benefits and risks of Maxeler model compared to other competing parallel technologies. Considering the level of abstraction and programming productivity, the streaming dataflow model described in MaxJ language stands in half way between software parallel models like OpenMP or CUDA, and hardware description languages like VHDL.

In case of parallel CYK parsing, we managed to achieve an efficient solution of the problem with speedup factors from $18 \times$ to $76 \times$ on real-life grammars, and for different input lengths, which is the same or better than other solutions of the same problem. The solution, which is for one dataflow hardware element (or node), could be extended to multiple dataflow elements in order to be able to efficiently process even larger grammars that emerge in practical applications.

Finally, as the author of [9] points out, the hardware and software support for modern parallel architectures is rapidly growing. CPUs are produced with more and more cores, CUDA model is getting new features with each generation, and FPGA chips make constant advances in capacity and speed. Therefore, there is a clear path for constant improvements of all kinds of solutions for parallel parsing.

ACKNOWLEDGMENT

This work has been partially funded by the Ministry of Education and Science of the Republic of Serbia (TR32047).

APPENDIX

A complete kernel of the parallel CYK parser, in the MaxJ dialect of the java language:

```
1 package cykparserv2;
2
3 import java.io.BufferedReader;
4 import java.io.FileReader;
5 import java.util.ArrayList;
6 import java.util.List;
7
8 import com.maxeler.maxcompiler.v2.kernelcompiler.Kernel;
9 import com.maxeler.maxcompiler.v2.kernelcompiler.KernelParameters;
```

```
10 import com.maxeler.maxcompiler.v2.kernelcompiler.stdlib.core.
   CounterChain;
11 import com.maxeler.maxcompiler.v2.kernelcompiler.stdlib.memory.
   Memory;
12 import com.maxeler.maxcompiler.v2.kernelcompiler.types.base.DFEType;
13 import com.maxeler.maxcompiler.v2.kernelcompiler.types.base.DFEVar;
14 import com.maxeler.maxcompiler.v2.kernelcompiler.types.
   composite.DFEArray;
15 import com.maxeler.maxcompiler.v2.kernelcompiler.types.
   composite.DFEArrayType;
16 import com.maxeler.maxcompiler.v2.utils.Bits;
17 import com.maxeler.maxcompiler.v2.utils.MathUtils;
18
19 class CykParserV2Kernel extends Kernel {
20
21   private static final DFEType type = dfeUInt(32);
22   private static final DFEType type64 = dfeUInt(64);
23
24   private BufferedReader br;
25
26   protected CykParserV2Kernel(KernelParameters parameters,
27       int ba_size, int g_max, int G_PARALLEL, int g_lut, int
       seq_max) {
28    super(parameters);
29
30    DFEArrayType<DFEVar> resultType =
31      new DFEArrayType<DFEVar>(type, ba_size);
32
33  DFEArrayType<DFEVar>  type_glut  =  new  DFEArrayType<DFEVar>
   (dfeUInt(1),g_lut);
34
35    DFEVar seq_len = io.scalarInput("seq_len", type64);
36
37    DFEVar init = control.count.pulse(seq_max);
38
39    DFEVar inp_cnt = control.count.simpleCounter(8);
40
41    DFEArray<DFEVar> input_seq = io.input("input_seq",resultType,
       init);
42    CounterChain chain = control.count.makeCounterChain(~init);
```

```
43    DFEVar ii = chain.addCounter(seq_len-1,1);
44    DFEVar kk = chain.addCounter(stream.offset(ii+1, -1),1);
45    DFEVar k = kk+1;
46    DFEVar j = chain.addCounter(stream.offset(seq_len-ii, -1),1);
47    DFEVar i = ii+1;
48    DFEVar gg = chain.addCounter(g_max+24,1);
49
50    int padr_bits = MathUtils.bitsToAddress(seq_max * seq_max);
51    DFEType padrt = dfeUInt(padr_bits);
52
53    List<Memory<DFEVar>>  p  =  new  ArrayList<Memory<DFEVar>>
      (ba_size);
54    for (int b=0; b< ba_size-1; b++) {
55      Memory<DFEVar> pm = mem.alloc(type, seq_max * seq_max);
56      p.add(pm);
57      //pm.mapToCPU("pmem"+(b+100));
58    }
59
60    int g_mems = G_PARALLEL * g_lut;
61    List<Memory<DFEVar>>  g  =  new  ArrayList<Memory<DFEVar>>
      (g_mems);
62    List<Memory<DFEVar>> gt =
63            new ArrayList<Memory<DFEVar>>(G_PARALLEL * (ba_size-
            1));
64    try {
65      br = new BufferedReader(new FileReader(
66              System.getProperty("user.dir")+"/src/
              cykparserv2/gmem.txt"));
67
68    for (int gi=0; gi< g_mems; gi++) {
69      Memory<DFEVar> gm = mem.alloc(type, g_max);
70      setGmContents(gm, g_max);
71      g.add(gm);
72    }
73
74    if ( ! br.readLine().equals("Check") ) {
75      System.out.println("Error: GMEM file corrupted\n");
76      System.exit(1);
77    }
78      int g_max_bits = -1;
```

```
79      while ( 1<<(++g_max_bits) < g_max )
80        ;
81    for (int gi=0; gi< G_PARALLEL; gi++) {
82      for (int b=0; b< ba_size-1; b++) {
83        Memory<DFEVar> gtmem = mem.alloc(type, (1<<g_max_bits)*
           (1<<g_lut));
84        setGtContents(gtmem, (1<<g_lut)*(1<<g_max_bits));
85        gt.add(gtmem);
86      }
87    }
88
89    br.close();
90  } catch (java.io.IOException e) {
91          System.out.println("Error reading memory contents:"+e.
             getMessage());
92          System.exit(1);
93    }
94
95    Bits[] masks = new Bits[32];
96    for (int b=0; b < 32; b++)
97      masks[b] = new Bits(32,1<<b);
98
99    Memory<DFEVar> mask = mem.alloc(type, 32);
100   mask.setContents(masks);
101
102   DFEArray<DFEVar> result = io.output("result", resultType,
103       (i === (seq_len -1)) & (k === i )
104       & (j === 0)
105       & chain.getCounterWrap(gg) );
106
107 int ba_bits = MathUtils.bitsToAddress(ba_size-1);
108 int gmax_bits = MathUtils.bitsToAddress(g_max);
109   List<DFEVar> p_rhs1 = new ArrayList<DFEVar>(ba_size);
110   List<DFEVar> p_rhs2 = new ArrayList<DFEVar>(ba_size);
111   List<DFEVar> has_lhs = new ArrayList<DFEVar>(G_PARALLEL);
112   for (int b=0; b< ba_size-1; b++) {
113     DFEVar p_rhs1_tmp = p[b].read(((k-1)* seq_max + j).
         cast(padrt));
114     p_rhs1.add( p_rhs1_tmp );
```

```
115    DFEVar p_rhs2_tmp = p[b].read(((i - k)* seq_max + j + k).
       cast(padrt));
116    p_rhs2.add( p_rhs2_tmp );
117    }
118    for (int gi=0; gi < G_PARALLEL; gi++) {
119     DFEArray<DFEVar> has_lhs_gi = type_glut.newInstance(this);
120     for (int gj=0; gj < g_lut; gj++) {
121      DFEVar g_last = g[gi * g_lut + gj].read(gg.slice
         (0,gmax_bits));
122      DFEVar rhs1w = control.mux(g_last.slice(5,ba_bits),
         p_rhs1);
123      DFEVar rhs2w = control.mux(g_last.slice(21,ba_bits),
         p_rhs2);
124      DFEVar has_rhs1 = ( rhs1w & mask.read(g_last.slice(0,5)) );
125      DFEVar has_rhs2 = ( rhs2w & mask.read(g_last.slice(16,5)) );
126      has_lhs_gi[gj] <==
127             optimization.pipeline((has_rhs1 !== 0 ) & (has_rhs2
                !== 0 )) ;
128     }
129    DFEVar has_lhs_tmp = has_lhs_gi.pack();
130      has_lhs.add( has_lhs_tmp );
131    }
132
133    for (int b=0; b< ba_size-1; b++) {
134
135     DFEVar oldp = ((k===1)|(kk===0))
136          ? constant.var(type,0)
137          : p[b].read((i * seq_max + j).cast(padrt));
138
139     for (int gi=0; gi < G_PARALLEL; gi++) {
140
141     DFEVar gt_gi = gt[gi*(ba_size-1)+b].read(
142                       gg.slice(0,gmax_bits).cat(has_lhs
                          [gi]));
143
144     DFEVar gt_tmp0 = type.newInstance(this);
145      DFEVar gt_tmp1 = type.newInstance(this);
146            gt_tmp0 <== (gg.slice(0) === 0)
147                       ? constant.var(type,0)
```

```
148                                   : (stream.offset(gt_tmp0,-2)
                                      | gt_gi);
149
150              gt_tmp1 <== (gg.slice(0) === 1)
151                            ? constant.var(type,0)
152                            : (stream.offset(gt_tmp1,-2)
                                      | gt_gi);
153
154      DFEVar gt_tmp = stream.offset(gt_tmp0,-1) | gt_tmp1;
155      // if even g_max exchange gt_tmp1 and gt_tmp0
156
157      oldp |= stream.offset(gt_tmp,-14);
158    }
159    DFEVar ooldp = stream.offset(oldp,-10);
160    p[b].write( (init) ? (inp_cnt).cast(padrt) : (i * seq_max + j).
       cast(padrt),
161               (init)? input_seq[b] : ooldp ,init | chain.
                  getCounterWrap(gg));
162    }
163
164    result[ba_size-1] <== input_seq[ba_size-1];
165
166 }
167
168 protected void setGmContents(Memory<DFEVar> gm, int gm_size)
169          throws java.io.IOException {
170    String g_str = null;
171    g_str = br.readLine();
172    //g_str = new String(new char[gm_size*8]).replace("\0", "0");
173    Bits[] gm_bits = new Bits[gm_size];
174    for (int gi=0; gi < gm_size; gi++) {
175       gm_bits[gi] = new Bits(32,g_str.substring(gi*8,gi*8+8));
176    }
177    gm.setContents(gm_bits);
178 }
179
180  protected void setGtContents(Memory<DFEVar> gtmem, int gt_size)
181          throws java.io.IOException {
182    String g_str = null;
```

```
183    g_str = br.readLine();
184    //g_str = new String(new char[gt_size*8]).replace("\0", "0");
185    Bits[] gt_bits = new Bits[gt_size];
186    for (int gi=0; gi < gt_size; gi++) {
187        gt_bits[gi] = new Bits(32,g_str.substring(gi*8,gi*8+8));
188    }
189    gtmem.setContents(gt_bits);
190  }
191 }
```

REFERENCES

[1] D. Jurafsky, M.H. James, Speech & Language Processing, Pearson Education, India, 2000.

[2] R. Durbin, S. Eddy, A. Krogh, G. Mitchinson (Eds.), Biological Sequence Analysis: Probabilistic Models of Proteins and Nucleic Acids, Cambridge University Press, Cambridge, ISBN: 978-0-521-62971-3, 1998.

[3] A.H. Toselli, E. Vidal, F. Casacuberta, Multimodal Interactive Pattern Recognition and Applications, Springer Science & Business Media, London, 2011.

[4] J. Moscola, J.W. Lockwood, Y.H. Cho, Reconfigurable content-based router using hardware-accelerated language parser, ACM Trans. Des. Autom. Electron. Syst. (TODAES) 13 (2) (2008) 28.

[5] P. Schüller, Flexible combinatory categorial grammar parsing using the CYK algorithm and answer set programming, in: P. Cabalar, T.C. Son (Eds.), Logic Programming and Nonmonotonic Reasoning, Springer, Berlin Heidelberg, 2013, pp. 499–511.

[6] P. Shukla, S. Tokekar, S. Jain, Finding fuzzy reasoning path using CYK algorithm, in: IEEE Conference Anthology, 1–8 January, 2013. pp. 1, 5.

[7] S. Clark, A. Copestake, J.R. Curran, Y. Zhang, A. Herbelot, Large-scale syntactic processing: parsing the web, in: Final Report of the 2009 JHU CLSP Workshop, 2009.

[8] S. Stojanović, D. Bojić, M. Bojović, An overview of selected heterogeneous and reconfigurable architectures, Adv. Comput. 96 (2015) 1–45.

[9] M. Johnson, Parsing in parallel on multiple cores and GPUs, in: Australasian Language Technology Association Workshop, 2011.

[10] J. Cocke, Programming Languages and their Compilers: Preliminary Notes, Courant Institute of Mathematical Sciences, New York University, New York, 1969. ISBN: B0007F4UOA.

[11] D.H. Younger, Recognition and parsing of context-free languages in time $O(N^3)$, Inform. Control 10 (2) (1967) 189–208.

[12] T. Kasami, An efficient recognition and syntax-analysis algorithm for context-free languages: Technical report, Hawaii Univ. Honolulu Dept. of Electrical Engineering, Hawaii, 1965.

[13] J.L. Bordim, K. Nakano, Accelerating the CKY parsing using FPGAs, IEICE Trans. Inf. Syst. 86 (5) (2003) 803–810.

[14] J.L. Bordim, O.H. Ibarra, Y. Ito, K. Nakano, Instance-specific solutions for accelerating the CKY parsing of large context-free grammars, Int. J. Found. Comput. Sci. 15 (02) (2004) 403–415.

[15] S. Boyd-Wickizer, A. Clements, N. Narula, Parallelizing the CKY and Earley parsing algorithms, Online: http://www.mit.edu/~6.863/fall2012/projects/writeups/parallelckypaper.pdf, 2009 (accessed 13.08.15).

[16] C. Ciressan, E. Sanchez, M. Rajman, J.C. Chappelier, An FPGA-based coprocessor for the parsing of context-free grammars, in: Proc. of the IEEE Symposium on Field-Programmable Custom Computing Machines, 2000.

[17] S. Guodong, G. Yuwan, S. Yuqiang, W. Xiaokang, Y. Aling, Word-lattice parsing parallel algorithm, in: 2nd International Workshop on Database Technology and Applications (DBTA), 27–28 November, 2010, pp. 1–4.

[18] K.H. Kim, S.M. Choi, H. Lee, K.L. Man, Y.S. Han, Parallel CYK membership test on GPUs, in: C.-H. Hsu, X. Shi, V. Salapura (Eds.), Network and Parallel Computing, Springer, Berlin, Heidelberg, 2014, pp. 157–168.

[19] N. Takashi, T. Kentaro, K. Taura, J. Tsujii, A parallel CKY parsing algorithm on large-scale distributed-memory parallel machines, in: Proceedings of the Pacific Association for Computational Linguistics, 1997, pp. 223–231.

[20] A. Kos, S. Tomazic, J. Salom, N. Trifunovic, M. Valero, V. Milutinovic, New benchmarking methodology and programming model for big data processing, Int. J. Distrib. Sens. Netw. 1550–1477 (2015) 1–7.

[21] A.V. Aho, J.D. Ullman, The Theory of Parsing, Translation and Compiling, volume 1, Prentice-Hall, New Jersey, 1972.

[22] N. Chomsky, On certain formal properties of grammars, Inf. Control 2 (2) (1959) 137–167.

[23] J.E. Hopcroft, J.D. Ullman, Introduction to Automata Theory, Languages and Computation, Addison-Wesley Publishing, Reading, MA, ISBN: 0-201-02988-X, 1979.

[24] S. Warshall, A theorem on Boolean matrices, J. ACM 9 (1) (1962) 11–12.

[25] Y. Yi, C.Y. Lai, S. Petrov, K. Keutzer, Efficient parallel CKY parsing on GPUs, in: Proceedings of the 12th International Conference on Parsing Technologies, Association for Computational Linguistics, Stroudsburg, PA, USA, 2011, pp. 175–185.

[26] H. Casanova, A. Legrand, Y. Robert, Parallel Algorithms, CRC Press, Boca Raton, FL, 2008.

[27] A.G. Manousopoulou, G. Manis, P. Tsanakas, G. Papakonstantinou, Automatic generation of portable parallel natural language parsers, in: Proceedings of the 9th Conference on Tools with Artificial Intelligence, 1997.

[28] M.P. van Lohuizen, Parallel processing of natural language parsers, in: Proceedings of the 15th Conference of Parallel Computing, 1999, pp. 17–20.

[29] A. Dunlop, N. Bodenstab, B. Roark, Efficient matrix-encoded grammars and low latency parallelization strategies for CYK, in: Proceedings of the 12th International Conference on Parsing Technologies, 2011, pp. 163–174.

[30] NVIDIA, NVIDIA's Next Generation CUDA Compute Architecture: FERMI, NVIDIA. Online: http://www.nvidia.com/content/PDF/fermi_white_papers/NVIDIA FermiComputeArchitectureWhitepaper.pdf, 2009 (accessed 13.08.15).

[31] Maxeler Technologies, MaxCompiler White Paper, Maxeler Technologies. Online: http://www.maxeler.com/media/documents/MaxelerWhitePaperProgramming.pdf, 2011 (accessed 13.08.15).

[32] V. Blagojević, et al., A systematic approach to generation of new ideas for PhD research in computing, Adv. Comput. 104 (2017) 1–31.

ABOUT THE AUTHORS

Dragan Bojić received a PhD degree in Electrical Engineering and Computer Science from the University of Belgrade in 2001. He is an associate professor at the School of Electrical Engineering, University of Belgrade. His research interests include formal languages and parsing, software engineering techniques and tools, and e-learning.

Miroslav Bojović received a PhD in Computer Engineering from the University of Belgrade, in 1988. He is an associate professor at the Faculty of Electrical Engineering, University of Belgrade, where he teaches database management systems. Previously, he was with the Pupin Institute, Belgrade and UCLA, Los Angeles. His research interests include database management systems, distributed information systems, fault tolerant computing, software engineering, and Internet technologies.

AUTHOR INDEX

Note: Page numbers followed by "*f*" indicate figures, and "*t*" indicate tables.

A

Adams, D.A., 99
Agarwal, A., 41–42*t*, 43, 49
Ahn, J.H., 44, 49, 61
Aho, A.V., 162
Ailamaki, A., 39–40, 41–42*t*, 43
Alameldeen, A.R., 41–42*t*, 43
Aling, Y., 161
Allison, D., 43
Amant, R., 82–83, 107
AMD White Paper, 52–53
Amdah, G.M., 105
Angepat, H., 37, 40, 41–42*t*
Annavaram, M., 40, 41–42*t*, 43
Aoki, T., 103, 132
Araya-Polo, M., 133, 152, 152*t*
Argollo, E., 36–40, 41–42*t*, 43–45, 61–62
Arnold, J., 97
Arul, J., 36
Arvind, R.A., 99
Asanovic, K., 37, 40, 41–42*t*, 47, 49
Atienza, D., 44, 49
August, D.I., 40, 41–42*t*, 43
Austin, T., 40, 41–42*t*
Ayguade, E., 60
Ayrignac, R., 35–36

B

Badia, R.M., 35, 49–50, 53, 60, 63
Bagrodia, R.L., 43
Balay, S., 134
Baracskai, Z., 3–4
Batanović, V., 14
Baxter, J., 41–42*t*, 43
Beaucamps, P.-E., 35–36
Beausoleil, R.G., 44
Beckmann, B.M., 41–42*t*, 43
Beckmann, N., 41–42*t*, 43, 49
Belady, C., 75
Bellard, F., 39
Ben-Asher, Y., 88, 101–102
Benini, L., 44, 49

Beveridge, R., 97
Bezanic, N., 116, 117*t*
Biesbrouck, M.V., 39–40
Binkert, N.L., 43–44
Bjelica, M.Z., 16–17
Blagojević, V., 2–21, 36–37, 181
Blem, E., 82–83, 107
Blumofe, R.D., 60
Bodenstab, N., 175
Bodin, F., 49–50, 53, 60, 63
Bohm, A., 97
Bojić, D., 2–21, 76–78, 115–116, 117*t*,
    160–197
Bojović, M., 2–21, 74–119, 160–197
Bondalapati, K., 97
Bordim, J.L., 161, 174, 179*t*, 181
Bouganis, C., 127
Brockman, J.B., 38, 41–42*t*, 43
Brown, J., 134
Bunting, T., 49
Burger, D., 82–83, 107
Buschelman, K., 134
Buyukkurt, B.A., 97, 99–100
Buzen, J., 11

C

Cabezas, J., 152, 152*t*
Calder, B., 39–40
Callahan, T.J., 97
Casacuberta, F., 160
Casanova, H., 169
Case, R.P., 8
Catmull, E., 10
Cela, J.M., 133
Celio, C., 41–42*t*, 43, 49
Chaisemartin, N.M., 35–36
Chamberlain, J., 41–42*t*, 43
Chamberlin, D.D., 99, 101
Chambers, C., 89–90*t*, 97
Chappelier, J.C., 161, 170, 172–173, 179*t*
Chawathe, M., 97
Chen, H., 39, 58–59

Chen, J., 39–40, 41–42*t*, 43
Chen, Y., 39, 58–59
Chidester, M., 41–42*t*, 43
Chiou, D., 37, 40, 41–42*t*
Cho, Y.H., 160
Choi, S.M., 161, 175, 177, 179*t*
Chomsky, N., 163
Christensson, M., 41–42*t*, 43
Chung, E.S., 40, 41–42*t*
Ciressan, C., 161, 170, 172–173, 179*t*
Clapp, R.G., 128–129, 133, 137, 146–148, 150–152, 152*t*
Clark, S., 160
Cocke, J., 161–162
Cohen, A., 49–50, 53, 60, 63
Cohen, D., 89–90*t*, 92, 107
Connors, D., 40, 41–42*t*, 43
Conte, T.M., 39–40
Conway, L., 6
Copestake, A., 160
Cortes, J., 97, 99–100
Couleur, J.F., 8
Couvert, P., 35–36
Crago, N.C., 46, 49
Curran, J.R., 160
Cvetanović, M., 2–21, 74–119

D
Das, S., 43
Dave, N., 40, 41–42*t*
Davis, A., 44, 89–90*t*, 92, 107
De Carli, L., 88, 99–100, 102
De Dinechin, B.D., 35–36
de Massas, P.G., 35–36
DeHon, A., 76
Delcev, S., 19–20
Dellson, A., 88, 100
Dickens, P.M., 43
Dimond, R., 89–90*t*, 102
Diniz, P., 97
Đorđević, J., 2–21
Đukić, T., 108, 117*t*
Dorfler, V., 3–4
Drake, J.B., 139
Draper, B., 97
Drašković, D., 19–20
Droz, P.-Y., 40, 47, 49
Dubois, M., 40, 41–42*t*, 43

Duncan, P., 97
Dunleavy, P., 3–4
Dunlop, A., 175
Duran, A., 60
Durbin, R., 160
Đurđević, Đ., 2–21
Dutt, N., 88, 99–101

E
Eastep, J., 41–42*t*, 43, 49
Eddy, S., 160
Eijkhout, V., 134
Eisenbart, T., 12
Emer, J., 40, 41–42*t*
Ernst, D., 40, 41–42*t*
Eskilson, J., 41–42*t*, 43
Esmaeilzadeh, H., 82–83, 107
Essink, B.K., 76–77
Estan, C., 88, 99–100, 102
Evripidou, P., 49–50, 53, 60, 63

F
Falcón, A., 44–45, 49, 61
Falsafi, B., 39–40, 41–42*t*, 43
Faraboschi, P., 36, 44–45, 49–50, 53, 58–61, 63
Faulkner, W., 3–4
Fay, D., 40, 41–42*t*, 43
Fechner, B., 35–36, 45, 49–50, 53, 60, 63
Feichtinger, C., 103
Felder, R., 3–4
Ferdman, M., 39–40, 41–42*t*, 43
Feynman, R.P., 80, 107
Filipi-Matutinovic, S., 3
Filipovic, N., 108, 117*t*
Fiorentino, M., 44
Flynn, M.J., 6, 44, 75, 89–90*t*, 102, 128–129, 133, 137
Forsgren, D., 41–42*t*, 43
Fortes, J.A.B., 89–90*t*, 97
Fotheringham, J., 10
Fournel, N., 59–60
Franceshet, M., 3
Franco, D., 45, 61
Frank, M.I., 46, 49
Frigo, M., 60
Fu, H., 126–153, 152*t*
Fujimoto, R., 43
Furlan, B., 2–21

G

Gajin, S., 2–21
Gan, L., 126–153
Gangadhar, V., 76, 78
Ganne, B., 35–36
Gannon, D., 89–90t, 93–94, 107
Gao, G., 36, 49–50, 53, 60, 63
Garbade, A., 35–36, 45, 49–50, 53, 60, 63
Gardiner, M., 3–4
Gayathri, R., 49–50, 53, 60, 63
Gaydadjiev, G., 130
George, A., 41–42t, 43
Georgia, K., 88, 100–101
Ghose, K., 41–42t, 43
Gibeling, G., 40, 41–42t, 47, 49
Gifford, D., 6
Giménez, G., 45, 61
Giorgi, R., 35–66, 41–42t, 77–78, 99, 129
Girbal, S., 36, 49–50, 53, 60, 63
Girdlestone, S., 130, 130f
Girimajia, S.S., 103
Glaser, E.L., 8
Gledhil, G.A., 12
Gligor, M., 59–60
Gokhale, M.B., 97
Goldberg, M.D., 132
Gomard, C.K., 7
Goodman, D., 36, 49–50, 53, 60, 63
Gordon, W.J., 11
Gottlieb, S., 134
Granacki, J., 97
Gropp, W., 134
Grove, D., 89–90t, 97
Grtker, T., 88, 101
Gruenwald, C., 41–42t, 43, 49
Guo, Z., 97, 99–100
Guodong, S., 161
Gupta, A., 41–42t, 43
Gupta, R.K., 88, 99–101
Gupta, S., 88, 99–101

H

Habich, J., 103
Hack, J.J., 139
Hadžić, F., 19–20
Hall, M., 97
Hallberg, G., 41–42t, 43

Halstead, R., 89–90t, 99–100
Hamerly, G., 39–40
Hamilton, A., 12
Hammes, J., 97
Hammond, L., 82–83, 107
Han, Y.S., 161, 175, 177, 179t
Hanzich, M., 133, 152, 152t
Harel, D., 7
Hatchnel, A., 3–4
Hauser, J.R., 97
Heendaliya, L., 87–88
Herbelot, A., 160
Herlihy, M., 36
Herrod, S., 41–42t, 43
Hill, M.D., 35–36, 38, 41–42t, 43
Hirsch, M.A., 39–40
Hirson, A.R., 36
Ho Ahn, J., 38, 41–42t, 43
Ho, N., 36
Hodgdon, D., 40, 41–42t, 43
Hoe, J.C., 39–40, 41–42t, 43
Hogberg, J., 41–42t, 43
Holland, J.H., 8
Hopcroft, J.E., 163–167
Hopfield, J.J., 7–8
Horowitz, R., 3–4
Huang, B., 132
Huang, H., 132
Huang, Q., 83, 107
Huang, X., 128, 133, 137, 141–142, 145
Huong, G.N.T., 101
Hurson, A.R., 76–78, 87–91, 116, 117t
Huss-Lederman, S., 43
Hybinette, M., 43

I

Iannucci, R.A., 99
Ibarra, O.H., 161
Ibbett, R.N., 13
Intel Corporation, 9
Intel White Paper, 52–53
Ishida, J., 132
Ito, Y., 161

J

Jacquet, F., 35–36
Jain, R., 97
Jain, S., 160

Jakob, R., 139
James, M.H., 160
Janjusic, T., 37
Jin, H., 39–40, 41–42t
Joerg, C.F., 60
John, F., 8
John, L.K., 39–40, 41–42t
Johnson, D.E., 40, 41–42t
Johnson, D.R., 46, 49
Johnson, K.T., 88–91
Johnson, M., 161, 175, 191
Johnson, M.R., 46, 49
Johnsson, L., 89–90t, 92, 107
Jones, N.D., 7
Jones, S., 35–36
Jouppi, N.P., 38, 41–42t, 43–44
Jovanović, Z., 2–21, 129
Jurafsky, D., 160

K

Kakulapati, G., 41–42t, 43
Kal´e, L.V., 41–42t, 43
Kanaujia, S., 41–42t, 43
Kasami, T., 161–162
Kasture, H., 41–42t, 43, 49
Kaushik, D., 134
Kavi, K.M., 36–37
Kawano, K., 132
Kearns, H., 3–4
Keefe, J., 40, 41–42t
Kelm, J.H., 46, 49
Kentaro, T., 161, 171–172, 179t
Keutzer, K., 167–169, 175, 179t
Khan, B., 36, 49–50, 53, 60, 63
Kim, J., 40, 41–42t
Kim, K.H., 161, 175, 177, 179t
Kim, S.J., 88, 99–100, 102
Kim, S.W., 101
Kimble, W., 49
Kirk, D., 80, 107
Knepley, M., 134
Knuth, D., 38
Kojic, N., 19–20
Kolia, S., 36
Koliaï, S., 49–50, 53, 60, 63
Konstantinovic, Z., 12
Koomey, J.G., 75
Korolija, N., 74–119, 117t, 130
Kos, A., 44, 75, 116–117, 117t, 130, 161

Koschke, R., 12
Köstler, H., 103
Kozyrakis, C., 46, 49
Krafczyk, M., 103
Krasnov, A., 40, 47, 49
Krogh, A., 160
Kuhn, R.H., 89–90t, 95, 107
Kung, H.T., 6, 88–91, 89–90t, 94–95, 107
Kurian, G., 41–42t, 43, 49
Kuszmaul, B.C., 60

L

L. Curfman McInnes, 134
Labarta, J., 60
Lai, C.Y., 167–169, 175, 179t
Lalinowski, M., 97
Lam, M., 89–90t, 92–93, 107
Landwehr, J., 49–50, 53, 60, 63
Lange, K.-D., 75
Larson, E., 40, 41–42t
Larsson, F., 41–42t, 43
Larus, J.R., 43
Lee, B., 36
Lee, H., 161, 175, 177, 179t
Legrand, A., 169
Lehman, P.L., 88–91
Leiserson, C.E., 6, 60, 88–91
Lerner, S., 89–90t, 97
Leung, F., 52–53
Li, F., 36, 49–50, 53, 60, 63
Li, J., 83, 107
Li, L., 132
Li, S., 38, 41–42t, 43
Li, Z., 83, 107
Liao, S., 88, 101
Lin, D., 87–88
Lin, W.T., 89–90t, 94–95, 107
Linn, M.C., 3–4
Litzkow, M., 43
Liu, R., 39, 58–59
Lockwood, J.W., 160
Lu, Y., 132
Lugones, D., 45, 61
Lujàn, M., 36, 49–50, 53, 60, 63
Luk, W., 126–153
Lumetta, S.S., 46, 49
Luob, L., 103
Luque, E., 45, 61

M

Magnusson, P., 41–42*t*, 43
Mahesri, A., 46, 49
Mai, K., 40, 41–42*t*
Man, K.L., 161, 175, 177, 179*t*
Manis, G., 170
Manousopoulou, A.G., 170
Marongiu, A., 44, 49
Marrocu, M., 132
Marshall, K., 3–4
Martin, G., 88, 101
Martin, M.M.K., 41–42*t*, 43
Martinell, L., 60
Martorell, X., 60
Marty, M.R., 35–36, 41–42*t*, 43
Marxen, H., 76–77
Masselos, K., 88, 100–101
Mattson, T., 46
Mauer, C.J., 38
McCulloch, W.S., 7
McLaren, M., 44
McNamara, G.R., 103
Mead, C., 6
Mencer, O., 44, 75, 89–90*t*, 102, 126–153, 130*f*
Mendelson, A., 35–36, 45, 49–50, 53, 60, 63
Menezes, K.N., 39–40
Mesquita, A., 3–4
Mielikainen, J., 132
Milenković, A., 16
Milenković, K., 19–20
Milićev, D., 2–21
Miller, J.E., 41–42*t*, 43, 49
Milutinovic, M., 3, 44
Milutinovic, V.M., 2–21, 44, 75–78, 108, 115–117, 117*t*, 129–130, 161
Mingas, G., 127
Minh, N., 49–50, 53, 60, 63
Miranker, W.L., 89–90*t*, 95–96, 107
Mišić, M., 19–20
Mitchinson, G., 160
Mitra, A., 97, 99–100
Moestedt, A., 41–42*t*, 43
Mohl, S., 88, 100
Moldovan, D.I., 89–90*t*, 97
Monchiero, M., 44, 49, 61
Mondelli, A., 36
Moore, K.E., 41–42*t*, 43
Morin, L., 36, 49–50, 53, 60, 63

Moscola, J., 160
Moss, J.E.B., 36
Mostow, J., 89–90*t*, 92–93, 107
Moure, J.C., 45, 61
Mukherjee, S.S., 43
Muroi, C., 132
Mutlu, O., 35–36

N

Na, Y., 101
Najjar, W.A., 89–90*t*, 97, 99–100
Nakano, K., 161, 174, 179*t*, 181
Navarro, N., 36, 49–50, 53, 60, 63
Neiger, G., 52–53
Newell, G.F., 11
Nicolau, A., 88, 99–101
Nikolaides, M., 99
Nikolić, B., 2–21
Nikolić, P.M., 12
Nowatzki, T., 76, 78
Nurvitadhi, E., 40, 41–42*t*

O

Ogot, M., 3–4
Okudan, G., 3–4
Olukotun, K., 82–83, 107
Omerović, S., 3
Oriato, D., 130, 130*f*, 132
Ortega, D., 44–45, 49, 61
Osborne, W., 133, 147, 150–151

P

Padegs, A., 8
Panesar, K., 43
Paolucci, P., 35
Papakonstantinou, G., 170
Papamichael, M.K., 40, 41–42*t*
Papazian, I.E., 41–42*t*, 43
Parisi-Presicce, F., 89–90*t*, 97
Park, A., 89–90*t*, 99–100
Patejko, T., 49–50, 53, 60, 63
Patel, S.J., 46, 49
Patil, N.A., 37, 40, 41–42*t*
Patt, Y.N., 35–36
Patterson, M., 75
Pavlou, D., 99
Pavlović, M.B., 12
Pell, O., 89–90*t*, 102, 128, 133, 137, 150
Pellauer, M., 40, 41–42*t*

Pellerin, D., 88, 99, 107
Penry, D.A., 40, 41–42t, 43
Perelman, E., 39–40
Petri, C.A., 7
Petrides, P., 99
Pétrot, F., 59–60
Petrov, S., 167–169, 175, 179t
Pinto, C., 44, 49
Pitts, W., 7
Planas, J., 60
Ponomarev, D., 41–42t, 43
Pop, A., 36, 49–50, 53, 60, 63
Popović, I., 116, 117t
Popović, Z., 63, 99
Popović-Božović, J., 116, 117t
Portero, A., 36
Prakash, S., 43
Prete, C.A., 41–42t, 43–44
Prina, G., 41–42t, 43–44
Prodanov, M., 19–20
Prost O'Leary, D., 3–4
Protić, J., 2–21
Punt, M., 2–21
Purić, S., 19–20
Pusceddu, G., 132
Puzović, N., 63

Q

Qureshi, M.K., 35–36

R

R. De la Cruz, 133
Racanière, S., 89–90t, 102
Radivojević, Z., 2–21
Raghav, S., 44, 49
Raghavendra, C.S., 89–90t, 97
Rajman, M., 161, 170, 172–173, 179t
Rakočević, G., 19–20, 75, 129
Raković, D.I., 12
Randall, K.H., 60
Rank, E., 103
Ranković, V., 44, 116, 117t, 130
Reinhardt, S.K., 41–42t, 43
Reinhart, W., 40, 41–42t
Renau, J., 41–42t, 43
Rexach, D., 45, 61
Ricciardi, L., 41–42t, 43–44
Rinker, R., 97
Riss, F., 35–36

Roark, B., 175
Robert, Y., 169
Rodgers, D., 52–53
Rodriguez, J.E., 99
Rosenblum, M., 41–42t, 43
Ross, C., 97
Rotem, N., 88, 101–102
Ruan, H., 128, 133, 137
Rubio, A., 35
Rubio, F., 133
Rüde, U., 103
Ruggiero, M., 44, 49

S

Salom, J., 44, 75, 77–78, 117, 129–130, 161
Sanchez, D., 46, 49
Sanchez, E., 161, 170, 172–173, 179t
Sandberg, G., 88, 100
Sankaralingam, K., 76, 78, 82–83, 88,
    99–100, 102, 107
Santoni, A., 52–53
Santos, A., 75
Sarvestani, S.S., 87–88
Scarpazza, D.P., 133
Schelle, G., 40, 41–42t, 43
Schreiber, R., 44
Schryver, C., 76–77
Schubert, L., 35
Schüller, P., 160
Schultz, A., 40, 41–42t, 47, 49
Schulz, M., 103
Scionti, A., 36, 45, 61
Senk, V., 116, 117t
Sestoft, P., 7
Shai, O., 3–4
Sherwood, T., 39–40
Shimokawabe, T., 132
Shirazi, B., 88–91
Shu, C.W., 134
Shukla, P., 160
Silverman, L., 3–4
Simon, D., 12
Smith, B., 134
Solinas, M., 36
Sorin, D.J., 41–42t, 43
Spector, A., 6
Stanisavljević, Ž., 2–21
Stanojević, I., 116, 117t
Stavrou, K., 99

Stenstrom, P., 75, 129
Stierand, M., 3–4
Stojanović, S., 2–21, 76–78, 115–116, 117t,
  160, 190–191
Stone, J.M., 97
Strand, G., 132
Strong, R.D., 38, 41–42t, 43
Strudel, T., 35–36
Subrahmanian, E., 3–4
Suleman, M.A., 35–36
Sumner, F.H., 13
Sun, J., 132
Sunwoo, D., 37, 40, 41–42t
Šuštran, Ž., 19–20
Swan, S., 88, 101
Swarztrauber, P.N., 139

T

Tadmor, E., 134
Takashi, N., 161, 171–172, 179t
Tartalja, I., 2–21
Taura, K., 161, 171–172, 179t
Teslic, N., 16–17
Tibault, S., 88, 99, 107
Tilbury, S., 132
Tokekar, S., 160
Tölke, J., 103
Tomašević, M., 2–21
Tomažič, S., 3, 44, 75, 116, 117t,
  130, 161
Toselli, A.H., 160
Trancoso, P., 36, 49–50, 53, 60, 63
Trifunovic, N., 44, 75, 77–78, 117,
  129–130, 161
Trobec, R., 75, 129
Tsanakas, P., 170
Tsujii, J., 161, 171–172, 179t
Tubic, S., 19–20
Tullsen, D.M., 38, 41–42t, 43
Tuohy, W., 46, 49

U

Uhlig, R., 52–53
Ullman, J.D., 162–167
Ungerer, T., 35–36, 45, 49–50, 53,
  60, 63
Upadhuay, S.B., 12

V

Valero, M., 36, 44, 49–50, 53, 60, 63, 75,
  129–130, 161
van Lohuizen, M.P., 170
Vantrease, D., 44
Varma, A., 89–90t, 97
Veen, A.H., 76
Velašević, D., 12
Velencei, J., 3–4
Vidal, E., 160
Villareal, J., 97, 99–100
Villarreal, J., 89–90t, 99–100
Vitas, D.M., 19–20
Voros, N.S., 88, 100–101
Vujicic Stankovic, S., 19–20
Vuletić, P., 2–21

W

Wang, L., 132
Wang, X., 132
Wang, Z., 39, 58–59
Warshall, S., 167
Watson, I., 49–50, 53, 60, 63
Wawrzynek, J., 40, 47, 49, 76, 97
Wehn, N., 76–77
Weis, S., 35–36, 45, 49–50, 53,
  60, 63
Weiser, U., 89–90t, 92, 107
Weithoffer, S., 76–77
Wells, R., 40, 41–42t, 43
Wenisch, T.F., 39–40,
  41–42t, 43
Werner, B., 41–42t, 43
Wesner, S., 35
Wilkes, M.V., 10
William, D.J., 88, 100–101
Williamson, D.L., 139
Winkler, A., 89–90t, 95–96, 107
Wisely, M., 87–88
Witchel, E., 41–42t, 43
Wolf, J., 35–36, 63
Wood, D.A., 38, 41–42t, 43
Wu Fudan, X., 39, 58–59
Wu, H., 83, 107
Wunderlich, R.E., 39–40, 41–42t, 43

X

Xiaokang, W., 161
Xu, M., 41–42t, 43

Xu, Y., 132
Xue, W., 128, 132, 141–142, 145

Y

Yang, C., 83, 107, 128, 132, 141–142, 145
Yang, G., 126–153
Yi, Y., 167–169, 175, 179*t*
Yoram, R., 3–4
Younger, D.H., 161–162
Yourst, M., 41–42*t*, 43
Yu, Z., 39–40, 41–42*t*
Yua, H., 103
Yuqiang, S., 161
Yuwan, G., 161

Z

Zanetti, G., 103
Zang, B., 39, 58–59
Zdravković, V., 16–17
Zeigler, H., 97
Zelkowitz, M.V., 36
Zeng, H., 41–42*t*, 43
Zhang, H., 134
Zhang, W., 39, 58–59
Zhang, Y., 128, 145, 160
Zheng, G., 41–42*t*, 43
Zheng, W., 132
Zhou, Y., 60
Zhu, X., 132
Zuckerman, S., 36, 49–50, 53, 60, 63

SUBJECT INDEX

Note: Page numbers followed by "*f*" indicate figures, and "*t*" indicate tables.

A

Adaptation *(A)*, 9
Adaptive switching mechanism, 9
Algebraic transformations, 94–95
Algorithmic offsetting method, 143–144
Amdahl's law, 105, 116
Architectural paradigms, 75

C

Cache memories, 82
Cell-OS, 172
Cellular automata models, 103
COALA (CryptOgraphic Algorithms visuaL simulAtion) system, 17
Cocke–Younger–Kasami (CYK) algorithm
  context-free languages, 162–164
  existing solutions
    distributed memory systems, 171–172
    many-core (GPU) systems, 175–178
    reconfigurable hardware systems, 172–175
    shared memory multicore systems, 170–171
    summary comparison, 178–180, 179*t*
  experimental analysis, 187–190
  extensibility, 170
  Maxeler hardware acceleration system
    address generators, 182–183
    architecture of, 180–181, 180*f*
    GTMEM memory instance, 183
    hardware counters, 182–183
    kernel, 181–182, 182*f*
    MaxJ language, 181
    member functions, 184
  modifications, 166–169
  pair-wise approach, 166–167
  parallelization, 169–170
  performance analysis, 184–186
  pseudocode, 165, 165*f*
  scalability, 170
  unary expansion process, 167

Cohen's method, 92, 93*f*
Collide function, 108, 113
Computational fluid dynamics (CFD), 103
Compute unified device architecture (CUDA) programming model, 80, 82–83, 175–176, 176*f*
Context-free grammar G
  binarization, 163
  elimination, 164
  Jack saw telescopes, 163, 163*f*
  syntactic categories, 162
Control-flow algorithms
  dataflow approaches, 80–88
  dataflow potentials
    analytical analysis of, 105–106
    Lattice–Boltzmann implementation, 103–113
  existing solutions and criticism
    dataflow analysis theory, 97–99
    dataflow programming tools theory, 99–102
    systolic arrays theory, 88–97
  Feynman paradigm, 80–88
  performance evaluation
    dataflow acceleration, 116–117
    LBM, control-flow and dataflow implementation of, 113–115
    validity, threat to, 117–118
  problem statement, 78–80
Control-flow processor, 76
1000-core architectures
  Altix UV, 49
  drawback of SMP, 47
  FPGA disadvantage, 47
  MareNostrum-2, 49
  problem of simulators, 47
  simulation
    setup, 51–60
    testbeds features, 49–50, 50*t*
COREMU, 58–59

COTSon simulator, 36–37
    features
        full-system simulators, 43
        multicore simulators, 40
        parallel simulators, 43
        sequential simulators, 43
        single-core simulators, 40
        user-level simulators, 43
    framework, 45–46, 46f
    functional-directed simulation technique,
        38–39
    sampling techniques, 39–40
    simulation vs. emulation, 37–38
    trade-off, 37
Crossdisciplinarization (C), 8, 15
CUDA. See Compute unified device
        architecture (CUDA)
Cycle-accurate software simulator (CAS), 37

D
Dataflow analysis theory, in compilers
    electronic design automation (EDA)
        tools, 97
    Lerner's method, 97, 98f
    Moldovan and Fortes' method, 97, 98f
    processing elements (PEs), 97
Dataflow approaches and Feynman
        paradigm
    algorithm execution limitations, 85, 85f
    cache memories, 82
    control-flow applications, optimization,
        80–81, 81f
    dataflow computing paradigm, 83, 84f
    fast rate, 82
    field programmable gate arrays (FPGAs),
        83–84
    instruction level parallelism (ILP), 82
    multiprocessor computing paradigm,
        82–83, 83f
    pipelined execution, 84–85
    processing elements (PEs), 86–87, 86f
    single-core computing paradigm, 82, 82f
    spatial computing, 83
    tasks queue
        completed, 86–87, 86f
        input, 86–87, 86f
    transistors size, 82
Dataflow compilers, 78–79

Data flow computing model
    architecture of, 129–130, 129f
    challenges, 128–129
    Euler atmospheric equations
        algorithmic offsetting method, 143–144
        on-chip fast memories, 145
        performance and power efficiency,
            145–146, 146t
        problem description, 140–142
        reduced-precision data, 145
    FPGAs, 129
    global shallow water equations
        algorithm and challenges, 134–136,
            135f
        equations and discretization, 133–134,
            133f
        hybrid domain partition scheme,
            136–137
        mixed precision arithmetic, 137–139
        performance and power efficiency, 140
    Maxeler DFE, 130–131
    reverse time migration
        computational challenges, 147–148
        hardware (de)compression scheme, 151
        multiple-time-step approach, 149
        number representations, 149–151
        performance and power efficiency,
            151–152, 152t
        random boundary, 148
        RTM algorithm, 147
        window buffer, 148–149, 149f
Dataflow engines (DFEs), 105
Dataflow kernel code, 78–79
Dataflow potentials
    analytical analysis of, 105–106
    Lattice–Boltzmann implementation
        in C programming language, 104–105
        for Maxeler dataflow architecture,
            106–113
Dataflow processor
    hardware dataflow architectures, 76
    lower frequency, 76
    power consumption, 76
    principle, 76
    reconfigurable computing (RC), 76–77
Dataflow programming tools theory
    field programmable gate arrays (FPGAs),
        99–102

ImpulseC, 100–101
MaxCompiler, 102, 102*f*
Mitrionics-C, 100
riverside optimizing compiler for
    configurable computing (ROCCC),
    99–100, 100*f*
SoftWare Synthesis, 102
SPARK, 101, 101*f*
StreamsC, 100–101
SystemC, 101
Davis method, 92, 93*f*

E

Electronic design automation (EDA) tools,
    97
Euler equations solver
    algorithmic offsetting method, 143–144
    on-chip fast memories, 145
    performance and power efficiency,
        145–146, 146*t*
    problem description, 140–142
    reduced-precision data, 145
Execution time, 104–105
Extraparameterization *(E)*, 10–11

F

Field programmable gate arrays (FPGAs), 40,
    83–84, 88, 101–102, 129
FPGA design, 172–173, 173*f*
Full-system simulators, 43
Functional-directed simulation technique,
    38–39
Functional simulator, 38
Functional specification, 93–94

G

Gannon's method, 93–94, 95*f*
GEMS, 43
Generalization *(G)*, 6–7
Graphite, 44
Gross–Pitaevskii equation, 116

H

Hardware (de)compression scheme, 151
High-performance computing (HPC)
    data flow computing, 128–131
    geoscience applications
        climate modeling, 132

exploration geophysics, 132–133
    summary, 131–132
Hybrid domain partition scheme, 136–137
Hybridization *(H)*, 9–10

I

Implantation *(I)*, 8, 15
ImpulseC, 100–101
Instruction level parallelism (ILP), 82

J

Java float variable, 108
Johnson's method, 92, 93*f*

K

Kernel code, 108, 109*f*
Kuhn's method, 95
Kung and Lin's method, 94–95, 96*f*

L

Lam and Mostow's method (SYS), 92–93,
    94*f*
Lattice–Boltzmann method (LBM)
    advantages, 103
    cellular automata models, 103
    computational fluid dynamics (CFD), 103
    control-flow and dataflow
        implementation, 113–115
    in C programming language, 104–105,
        104*f*
    execution on CPU *vs.* FPGA, 113–115,
        114*f*
    execution times of CPU *vs.* Maxeler
        implementation, 113, 114*f*
    Kernel code, 108, 109*f*
    manager, 110–113, 112*f*
    for Maxeler dataflow architecture,
        106–113, 109*f*
    potentials, analytical analysis of, 105–106
    power consumptions of CPU *vs.* Maxeler,
        115, 115*f*
    stream-based processing, 110, 111*f*
    stream function, 110, 111*f*
Lerner's method, 97, 98*f*
LInSTSS, 14
Logging instructions, 79–80

M

Massive parallelism, 88–91
MaxCompiler, 102, 102*f*
Maxeler card, 106, 110
Maxeler Data Flow processing system
　　(Maxeler DFE)
　architecture of, 130–131, 130*f*
　Kernels and Manager, 131
　on-board large memory (LMem),
　　130–131
　on-chip fast memory (FMem),
　　130–131
Maxeler DFE, 130–131
Maxeler hardware acceleration system
　address generators, 182–183
　architecture of, 180–181, 180*f*
　GTMEM memory instance, 183
　hardware counters, 182–183
　kernel, 181–182, 182*f*
　MaxJ language, 181
　member functions, 184
MaxJ language, 181
Mendeleyevization (M), 5–6
Miranker and Winkler's method, 95–96, 96*f*
Mitrionics-C, 100
Moldovan and Fortes' method, 97, 98*f*
MPTLsim, 43
Multicore simulators, 40
Multiple-time-step approach, 149
Multiprocessor computing paradigm,
　　82–83, 83*f*

O

Odd–even merge sort algorithm, 116

P

Parallelization, 75
Parallel simulators, 43
Pascal-like language, 92–93
Performance simulator, 38
PEs. *See* Processing elements (PEs)
PhD thesis research in computing
　of Bojan Furlan, 14
　of Boško Nikolić, 16
　characteristics, 3
　classification, 19, 19*t*
　of Đorđe Đurđević, 13

of Dragan Bojić, 12
of Dragan Milićev, 15
of Igor Tartalja, 18
of Jelica Protić, 16
by Jovan Đorđević, 13
of Marija Punt, 16–17
of Miloš Cvetanović, 13
of Milo Tomašević, 18
of Miroslav Bojović, 12
of Pavle Vuletić, 18–19
publication habits, 3
of Saša Stojanović, 17–18
scientific innovations
　Adaptation (A), 9
　Crossdisciplinarization (C), 8
　evolutionary, 4
　Extraparameterization (E), 10–11
　Generalization (G), 6–7
　Hybridization (H), 9–10
　Implantation (I), 8
　Mendeleyevization (M), 5–6
　phases, 4–5
　Revitalization (R), 7
　revolutionary, 4
　Specialization (S), 7
　Transgranularization (T), 10
of Slavko Gajin, 14
of Veljko Milutinović, 15
of Vladimir Blagojević, 12
of Zaharije Radivojević, 17
of Žarko Stanisavljević, 17
of Zoran Jovanović, 14–15
Power consumption, 106
Processing elements (PEs), 75–76, 86–87,
　　86*f*, 97

Q

QEMU (quick emulator), 39

R

Real-time application, 79–80
Reverse time migration (RTM)
　computational challenges, 147–148
　hardware (de)compression scheme, 151
　multiple-time-step approach, 149
　number representations, 149–151
　performance and power efficiency,
　　151–152, 152*t*

random boundary, 148
RTM algorithm, 147
window buffer, 148–149, 149f
Revitalization (R), 7
Riverside optimizing compiler for
configurable computing (ROCCC),
99–100, 100f

S

Sampling technique, 39–40
Sequential simulators, 43
Shallow water equations (SWEs) solver
algorithm and challenges, 134–136, 135f
equations and discretization, 133–134,
133f
hybrid domain partition scheme, 136–137
mixed precision arithmetic, 137–139
performance and power efficiency, 140
SimFlex, 43
Single-core computing paradigm, 82, 82f
Single-core simulators, 40
SoftWare Synthesis, 102
SPARK, 101, 101f
Spatial computing, 83
Specialization (S), 7, 14–15
Stream-based processing, 110, 111f
Stream function, 110, 111f, 113
StreamsC, 100–101
SystemC, 101
Systolic array processor
algebraic transformations, 94–95
Cohen's method, 92, 93f
complex computing problems, 88–91
dataflow computing, 92
Davis method, 92, 93f
functional specification, 93–94
Gannon's method, 93–94, 95f
Johnson's method, 92, 93f
Kuhn's method, 95
Kung and Lin's method, 94–95, 96f
Lam and Mostow's method (SYS), 92–93,
94f
limitation, 92–93

massive parallelism, 88–91
methods, 91, 92f
Miranker and Winkler's method, 95–96,
96f
Pascal-like language, 92–93
processing elements (PEs), 88–91
vector operators, 93–94
Weiser's method, 92, 93f

T

Tasks queue, 86–87, 86f
TERAFLUX evaluation framework
benchmarks, 60–61
challenges, 36
1000-core architectures
Altix UV, 49
drawback of SMP, 47
FPGA disadvantage, 47
MareNostrum-2, 49
problem of simulators, 47
simulation, 49–60
1024-core machine, 63–65
with 32 cores, 62
COTSon simulator, 36–37
fault detection unit, 35–36
thread scheduling unit, 35–36
with two nodes, 62
vision of, 35–36
Transgranularization (T), 10
Translation lookaside buffer (TLB), 8, 76

U

Unary expansion process, 167
User-level simulators, 43

V

Validity threat, 117–118
Vector operators, 93–94
Very large-scale integration (VLSI), 88

W

Web-based simulator, 16
Weiser's method, 92, 93f

CONTENTS OF VOLUMES IN THIS SERIES

Volume 60

Licensing and Certification of Software Professionals
DONALD J. BAGERT
Cognitive Hacking
GEORGE CYBENKO, ANNARITA GIANI, AND PAUL THOMPSON
The Digital Detective: An Introduction to Digital Forensics
WARREN HARRISON
Survivability: Synergizing Security and Reliability
CRISPIN COWAN
Smart Cards
KATHERINE M. SHELFER, CHRIS CORUM, J. DREW PROCACCINO, AND JOSEPH DIDIER
Shotgun Sequence Assembly
MIHAI POP
Advances in Large Vocabulary Continuous Speech Recognition
GEOFFREY ZWEIG AND MICHAEL PICHENY

Volume 61

Evaluating Software Architectures
ROSEANNE TESORIERO TVEDT, PATRICIA COSTA, AND MIKAEL LINDVALL
Efficient Architectural Design of High Performance Microprocessors
LIEVEN EECKHOUT AND KOEN DE BOSSCHERE
Security Issues and Solutions in Distributed Heterogeneous Mobile Database Systems
A. R. HURSON, J. PLOSKONKA, Y. JIAO, AND H. HARIDAS
Disruptive Technologies and Their Affect on Global Telecommunications
STAN MCCLELLAN, STEPHEN LOW, AND WAI-TIAN TAN
Ions, Atoms, and Bits: An Architectural Approach to Quantum Computing
DEAN COPSEY, MARK OSKIN, AND FREDERIC T. CHONG

Volume 62

An Introduction to Agile Methods
DAVID COHEN, MIKAEL LINDVALL, AND PATRICIA COSTA
The Timeboxing Process Model for Iterative Software Development
PANKAJ JALOTE, AVEEJEET PALIT, AND PRIYA KURIEN
A Survey of Empirical Results on Program Slicing
DAVID BINKLEY AND MARK HARMAN
Challenges in Design and Software Infrastructure for Ubiquitous Computing Applications
GURUDUTH BANAVAR AND ABRAHAM BERNSTEIN
Introduction to MBASE (Model-Based (System) Architecting and Software Engineering)
DAVID KLAPPHOLZ AND DANIEL PORT

Software Quality Estimation with Case-Based Reasoning
   TAGHI M. KHOSHGOFTAAR AND NAEEM SELIYA
Data Management Technology for Decision Support Systems
   SURAJIT CHAUDHURI, UMESHWAR DAYAL, AND VENKATESH GANTI

Volume 63

Techniques to Improve Performance Beyond Pipelining: Superpipelining, Superscalar, and VLIW
   JEAN-LUC GAUDIOT, JUNG-YUP KANG, AND WON WOO RO
Networks on Chip (NoC): Interconnects of Next Generation Systems on Chip
   THEOCHARIS THEOCHARIDES, GREGORY M. LINK, NARAYANAN VIJAYKRISHNAN,
   AND MARY JANE IRWIN
Characterizing Resource Allocation Heuristics for Heterogeneous Computing Systems
   SHOUKAT ALI, TRACY D. BRAUN, HOWARD JAY SIEGEL, ANTHONY A. MACIEJEWSKI,
   NOAH BECK, LADISLAU BÖLÖNI, MUTHUCUMARU MAHESWARAN, ALBERT I. REUTHER,
   JAMES P. ROBERTSON, MITCHELL D. THEYS, AND BIN YAO
Power Analysis and Optimization Techniques for Energy Efficient Computer Systems
   WISSAM CHEDID, CHANSU YU, AND BEN LEE
Flexible and Adaptive Services in Pervasive Computing
   BYUNG Y. SUNG, MOHAN KUMAR, AND BEHROOZ SHIRAZI
Search and Retrieval of Compressed Text
   AMAR MUKHERJEE, NAN ZHANG, TAO TAO, RAVI VIJAYA SATYA, AND WEIFENG SUN

Volume 64

Automatic Evaluation of Web Search Services
   ABDUR CHOWDHURY
Web Services
   SANG SHIN
A Protocol Layer Survey of Network Security
   JOHN V. HARRISON AND HAL BERGHEL
E-Service: The Revenue Expansion Path to E-Commerce Profitability
   ROLAND T. RUST, P. K. KANNAN, AND ANUPAMA D. RAMACHANDRAN
Pervasive Computing: A Vision to Realize
   DEBASHIS SAHA
Open Source Software Development: *Structural Tension in the American Experiment*
   COSKUN BAYRAK AND CHAD DAVIS
Disability and Technology: Building Barriers or Creating Opportunities?
   PETER GREGOR, DAVID SLOAN, AND ALAN F. NEWELL

Volume 65

The State of Artificial Intelligence
   ADRIAN A. HOPGOOD
Software Model Checking with SPIN
   GERARD J. HOLZMANN

Early Cognitive Computer Vision
JAN-MARK GEUSEBROEK
Verification and Validation and Artificial Intelligence
TIM MENZIES AND CHARLES PECHEUR
Indexing, Learning and Content-Based Retrieval for Special Purpose Image Databases
MARK J. HUISKES AND ERIC J. PAUWELS
Defect Analysis: Basic Techniques for Management and Learning
DAVID N. CARD
Function Points
CHRISTOPHER J. LOKAN
The Role of Mathematics in Computer Science and Software Engineering Education
PETER B. HENDERSON

Volume 66

Calculating Software Process Improvements Return on Investment
RINI VAN SOLINGEN AND DAVID F. RICO
Quality Problem in Software Measurement Data
PIERRE REBOURS AND TAGHI M. KHOSHGOFTAAR
Requirements Management for Dependable Software Systems
WILLIAM G. BAIL
Mechanics of Managing Software Risk
WILLIAM G. BAIL
The PERFECT Approach to Experience-Based Process Evolution
BRIAN A. NEJMEH AND WILLIAM E. RIDDLE
The Opportunities, Challenges, and Risks of High Performance Computing in
Computational Science and Engineering
DOUGLASS E. POST, RICHARD P. KENDALL, AND ROBERT F. LUCAS

Volume 67

Broadcasting a Means to Disseminate Public Data in a Wireless Environment—Issues
and Solutions
A. R. HURSON, Y. JIAO, AND B. A. SHIRAZI
Programming Models and Synchronization Techniques for Disconnected Business
Applications
AVRAHAM LEFF AND JAMES T. RAYFIELD
Academic Electronic Journals: Past, Present, and Future
ANAT HOVAV AND PAUL GRAY
Web Testing for Reliability Improvement
JEFF TIAN AND LI MA
Wireless Insecurities
MICHAEL STHULTZ, JACOB UECKER, AND HAL BERGHEL
The State of the Art in Digital Forensics
DARIO FORTE

Volume 68

Exposing Phylogenetic Relationships by Genome Rearrangement
    YING CHIH LIN AND CHUAN YI TANG
Models and Methods in Comparative Genomics
    GUILLAUME BOURQUE AND LOUXIN ZHANG
Translocation Distance: Algorithms and Complexity
    LUSHENG WANG
Computational Grand Challenges in Assembling the Tree of Life: Problems
and Solutions
    DAVID A. BADER, USMAN ROSHAN, AND ALEXANDROS STAMATAKIS
Local Structure Comparison of Proteins
    JUN HUAN, JAN PRINS, AND WEI WANG
Peptide Identification via Tandem Mass Spectrometry
    XUE WU, NATHAN EDWARDS, AND CHAU-WEN TSENG

Volume 69

The Architecture of Efficient Multi-Core Processors: A Holistic Approach
    RAKESH KUMAR AND DEAN M. TULLSEN
Designing Computational Clusters for Performance and Power
    KIRK W. CAMERON, RONG GE, AND XIZHOU FENG
Compiler-Assisted Leakage Energy Reduction for Cache Memories
    WEI ZHANG
Mobile Games: Challenges and Opportunities
    PAUL COULTON, WILL BAMFORD, FADI CHEHIMI, REUBEN EDWARDS, PAUL GILBERTSON,
    AND OMER RASHID
Free/Open Source Software Development: Recent Research Results and Methods
    WALT SCACCHI

Volume 70

Designing Networked Handheld Devices to Enhance School Learning
    JEREMY ROSCHELLE, CHARLES PATTON, AND DEBORAH TATAR
Interactive Explanatory and Descriptive Natural-Language Based Dialogue for Intelligent
Information Filtering
    JOHN ATKINSON AND ANITA FERREIRA
A Tour of Language Customization Concepts
    COLIN ATKINSON AND THOMAS KÜHNE
Advances in Business Transformation Technologies
    JUHNYOUNG LEE
Phish Phactors: Offensive and Defensive Strategies
    HAL BERGHEL, JAMES CARPINTER, AND JU-YEON JO
Reflections on System Trustworthiness
    PETER G. NEUMANN

Volume 71

Programming Nanotechnology: Learning from Nature
    BOONSERM KAEWKAMNERDPONG, PETER J. BENTLEY, AND NAVNEET BHALLA
Nanobiotechnology: An Engineers Foray into Biology
    YI ZHAO AND XIN ZHANG
Toward Nanometer-Scale Sensing Systems: Natural and Artificial Noses as Models for
Ultra-Small, Ultra-Dense Sensing Systems
    BRIGITTE M. ROLFE
Simulation of Nanoscale Electronic Systems
    UMBERTO RAVAIOLI
Identifying Nanotechnology in Society
    CHARLES TAHAN
The Convergence of Nanotechnology, Policy, and Ethics
    ERIK FISHER

Volume 72

DARPAs HPCS Program: History, Models, Tools, Languages
    JACK DONGARRA, ROBERT GRAYBILL, WILLIAM HARROD, ROBERT LUCAS,
    EWING LUSK, PIOTR LUSZCZEK, JANICE MCMAHON, ALLAN SNAVELY, JEFFERY VETTER,
    KATHERINE YELICK, SADAF ALAM, ROY CAMPBELL, LAURA CARRINGTON, TZU-YI CHEN,
    OMID KHALILI, JEREMY MEREDITH, AND MUSTAFA TIKIR
Productivity in High-Performance Computing
    THOMAS STERLING AND CHIRAG DEKATE
Performance Prediction and Ranking of Supercomputers
    TZU-YI CHEN, OMID KHALILI, ROY L. CAMPBELL, JR., LAURA CARRINGTON,
    MUSTAFA M. TIKIR, AND ALLAN SNAVELY
Sampled Processor Simulation: A Survey
    LIEVEN EECKHOUT
Distributed Sparse Matrices for Very High Level Languages
    JOHN R. GILBERT, STEVE REINHARDT, AND VIRAL B. SHAH
Bibliographic Snapshots of High-Performance/High-Productivity Computing
    MYRON GINSBERG

Volume 73

History of Computers, Electronic Commerce, and Agile Methods
    DAVID F. RICO, HASAN H. SAYANI, AND RALPH F. FIELD
Testing with Software Designs
    ALIREZA MAHDIAN AND ANNELIESE A. ANDREWS
Balancing Transparency, Efficiency, and Security in Pervasive Systems
    MARK WENSTROM, ELOISA BENTIVEGNA, AND ALI R. HURSON
Computing with RFID: Drivers, Technology and Implications
    GEORGE ROUSSOS
Medical Robotics and Computer-Integrated Interventional Medicine
    RUSSELL H. TAYLOR AND PETER KAZANZIDES

Volume 74

Data Hiding Tactics for Windows and Unix File Systems
 HAL BERGHEL, DAVID HOELZER, AND MICHAEL STHULTZ
Multimedia and Sensor Security
 ANNA HAĆ
Email Spam Filtering
 ENRIQUE PUERTAS SANZ, JOSÉ MARÍA GÓMEZ HIDALGO, AND JOSÉ CARLOS
 CORTIZO PÉREZ
The Use of Simulation Techniques for Hybrid Software Cost Estimation and Risk Analysis
 MICHAEL KLÄS, ADAM TRENDOWICZ, AXEL WICKENKAMP, JÜRGEN MÜNCH,
 NAHOMI KIKUCHI, AND YASUSHI ISHIGAI
An Environment for Conducting Families of Software Engineering Experiments
 LORIN HOCHSTEIN, TAIGA NAKAMURA, FORREST SHULL, NICO ZAZWORKA,
 VICTOR R. BASILI, AND MARVIN V. ZELKOWITZ
Global Software Development: Origins, Practices, and Directions
 JAMES J. CUSICK, ALPANA PRASAD, AND WILLIAM M. TEPFENHART

Volume 75

The UK HPC Integration Market: Commodity-Based Clusters
 CHRISTINE A. KITCHEN AND MARTYN F. GUEST
Elements of High-Performance Reconfigurable Computing
 TOM VANCOURT AND MARTIN C. HERBORDT
Models and Metrics for Energy-Efficient Computing
 PARTHASARATHY RANGANATHAN, SUZANNE RIVOIRE, AND JUSTIN MOORE
The Emerging Landscape of Computer Performance Evaluation
 JOANN M. PAUL, MWAFFAQ OTOOM, MARC SOMERS, SEAN PIEPER,
 AND MICHAEL J. SCHULTE
Advances in Web Testing
 CYNTRICA EATON AND ATIF M. MEMON

Volume 76

Information Sharing and Social Computing: Why, What, and Where?
 ODED NOV
Social Network Sites: Users and Uses
 MIKE THELWALL
Highly Interactive Scalable Online Worlds
 GRAHAM MORGAN
The Future of Social Web Sites: Sharing Data and Trusted Applications with Semantics
 SHEILA KINSELLA, ALEXANDRE PASSANT, JOHN G. BRESLIN, STEFAN DECKER,
 AND AJIT JAOKAR
Semantic Web Services Architecture with Lightweight Descriptions of Services
 TOMAS VITVAR, JACEK KOPECKY, JANA VISKOVA, ADRIANMOCAN, MICK KERRIGAN,
 AND DIETER FENSEL

Issues and Approaches for Web 2.0 Client Access to Enterprise Data
AVRAHAM LEFF AND JAMES T. RAYFIELD
Web Content Filtering
JOSÉ MARÍA GÓMEZ HIDALGO, ENRIQUE PUERTAS SANZ, FRANCISCO CARRERO GARCÍA,
AND MANUEL DE BUENAGA RODRÍGUEZ

Volume 77

Photo Fakery and Forensics
HANY FARID
Advances in Computer Displays
JASON LEIGH, ANDREW JOHNSON, AND LUC RENAMBOT
Playing with All Senses: Human–Computer Interface Devices for Games
JÖRN LOVISCACH
A Status Report on the P Versus NP Question
ERIC ALLENDER
Dynamically Typed Languages
LAURENCE TRATT
Factors Influencing Software Development Productivity—State-of-the-Art and
Industrial Experiences
ADAM TRENDOWICZ AND JÜRGEN MÜNCH
Evaluating the Modifiability of Software Architectural Designs
M. OMOLADE SALIU, GÜNTHER RUHE, MIKAEL LINDVALL,
AND CHRISTOPHER ACKERMANN
The Common Law and Its Impact on the Internet
ROBERT AALBERTS, DAVID HAMES, PERCY POON, AND PAUL D. THISTLE

Volume 78

Search Engine Optimization—Black and White Hat Approaches
ROSS A. MALAGA
Web Searching and Browsing: A Multilingual Perspective
WINGYAN CHUNG
Features for Content-Based Audio Retrieval
DALIBOR MITROVIĆ, MATTHIAS ZEPPELZAUER, AND CHRISTIAN BREITENEDER
Multimedia Services over Wireless Metropolitan Area Networks
KOSTAS PENTIKOUSIS, JARNO PINOLA, ESA PIRI, PEDRO NEVES, AND SUSANA SARGENTO
An Overview of Web Effort Estimation
EMILIA MENDES
Communication Media Selection for Remote Interaction of *Ad Hoc* Groups
FABIO CALEFATO AND FILIPPO LANUBILE

Volume 79

Applications in Data-Intensive Computing
ANUJ R. SHAH, JOSHUA N. ADKINS, DOUGLAS J. BAXTER, WILLIAM R. CANNON,
DANIEL G. CHAVARRIA-MIRANDA, SUTANAY CHOUDHURY, IAN GORTON,

DEBORAH K. GRACIO, TODD D. HALTER, NAVDEEP D. JAITLY, JOHN R. JOHNSON, RICHARD T. KOUZES, MATTHEW C. MACDUFF, ANDRES MARQUEZ, MATTHEW E. MONROE, CHRISTOPHER S. OEHMEN, WILLIAM A. PIKE, CHAD SCHERRER, ORESTE VILLA, BOBBIE-JO WEBB-ROBERTSON, PAUL D. WHITNEY, AND NINO ZULJEVIC
Pitfalls and Issues of Manycore Programming
    AMI MAROWKA
Illusion of Wireless Security
    ALFRED W. LOO
Brain–Computer Interfaces for the Operation of Robotic and Prosthetic Devices
    DENNIS J. MCFARLAND AND JONATHAN R. WOLPAW
The Tools Perspective on Software Reverse Engineering: Requirements, Construction, and Evaluation
    HOLGER M. KIENLE AND HAUSI A. MÜLLER

Volume 80

Agile Software Development Methodologies and Practices
    LAURIE WILLIAMS
A Picture from the Model-Based Testing Area: Concepts, Techniques, and Challenges
    ARILO C. DIAS-NETO AND GUILHERME H. TRAVASSOS
Advances in Automated Model-Based System Testing of Software Applications with a GUI Front-End
    ATIF M. MEMON AND BAO N. NGUYEN
Empirical Knowledge Discovery by Triangulation in Computer Science
    RAVI I. SINGH AND JAMES MILLER
StarLight: Next-Generation Communication Services, Exchanges, and Global Facilities
    JOE MAMBRETTI, TOM DEFANTI, AND MAXINE D. BROWN
Parameters Effecting 2D Barcode Scanning Reliability
    AMIT GROVER, PAUL BRAECKEL, KEVIN LINDGREN, HAL BERGHEL, AND DENNIS COBB
Advances in Video-Based Human Activity Analysis: Challenges and Approaches
    PAVAN TURAGA, RAMA CHELLAPPA, AND ASHOK VEERARAGHAVAN

Volume 81

VoIP Security: Vulnerabilities, Exploits, and Defenses
    XINYUAN WANG AND RUISHAN ZHANG
Phone-to-Phone Configuration for Internet Telephony
    YIU-WING LEUNG
SLAM for Pedestrians and Ultrasonic Landmarks in Emergency Response Scenarios
    CARL FISCHER, KAVITHA MUTHUKRISHNAN, AND MIKE HAZAS
Feeling Bluetooth: From a Security Perspective
    PAUL BRAECKEL
Digital Feudalism: Enclosures and Erasures from Digital Rights Management to the Digital Divide
    SASCHA D. MEINRATH, JAMES W. LOSEY, AND VICTOR W. PICKARD
Online Advertising
    AVI GOLDFARB AND CATHERINE TUCKER

Volume 82

The Hows and Whys of Information Markets
AREEJ YASSIN AND ALAN R. HEVNER
Measuring and Monitoring Technical Debt
CAROLYN SEAMAN AND YUEPU GUO
A Taxonomy and Survey of Energy-Efficient Data Centers and Cloud Computing
Systems
ANTON BELOGLAZOV, RAJKUMAR BUYYA, YOUNG CHOON LEE, AND ALBERT ZOMAYA
Applications of Mobile Agents in Wireless Networks and Mobile Computing
SERGIO GONZÁLEZ-VALENZUELA, MIN CHEN, AND VICTOR C.M. LEUNG
Virtual Graphics for Broadcast Production
GRAHAM THOMAS
Advanced Applications of Virtual Reality
JÜRGEN P. SCHULZE, HAN SUK KIM, PHILIP WEBER, ANDREW PRUDHOMME,
ROGER E. BOHN, MAURIZIO SERACINI, AND THOMAS A. DEFANTI

Volume 83

The State of the Art in Identity Theft
AMIT GROVER, HAL BERGHEL, AND DENNIS COBB
An Overview of Steganography
GARY C. KESSLER AND CHET HOSMER
CAPTCHAs: An Artificial Intelligence Application to Web Security
JOSÉ MARÍA GÓMEZ HIDALGO AND GONZALO ALVAREZ
Advances in Video-Based Biometrics
RAMA CHELLAPPA AND PAVAN TURAGA
Action Research Can Swing the Balance in Experimental Software Engineering
PAULO SÉRGIO MEDEIROS DOS SANTOS AND GUILHERME HORTA TRAVASSOS
Functional and Nonfunctional Design Verification for Embedded Software Systems
ARNAB RAY, CHRISTOPHER ACKERMANN, RANCE CLEAVELAND, CHARLES SHELTON,
AND CHRIS MARTIN

Volume 84

Combining Performance and Availability Analysis in Practice
KISHOR TRIVEDI, ERMESON ANDRADE, AND FUMIO MACHIDA
Modeling, Analysis, and Testing of System Vulnerabilities
FEVZI BELLI, MUTLU BEYAZIT, ADITYA P. MATHUR, AND NIMAL NISSANKE
Software Design and Verification for Safety-Relevant Computer-Based Systems
FRANCESCA SAGLIETTI
System Dependability: Characterization and Benchmarking
YVES CROUZET AND KARAMA KANOUN
Pragmatic Directions in Engineering Secure Dependable Systems
M. FARRUKH KHAN AND RAYMOND A. PAUL

Volume 85

Software Organizations and Test Process Development
  Jussi Kasurinen
Model-Based GUI Testing: Case Smartphone Camera and Messaging Development
  Rupesh Dev, Antti Jääskeläinen, and Mika Katara
Model Transformation Specification and Design
  K. Lano and S. Kolahdouz-Rahimi
Advances on Improving Automation in Developer Testing
  Xusheng Xiao, Suresh Thummalapenta, and Tao Xie
Automated Interoperability Testing of Healthcare Information Systems
  Diana Elena Vega
Event-Oriented, Model-Based GUI Testing and Reliability Assessment—Approach
and Case Study
  Fevzi Belli, Mutlu Beyazit, and Nevin Güler
Deployable Capture/Replay Supported by Internal Messages
  Steffen Herbold, Uwe Bünting, Jens Grabowski, and Stephan Waack

Volume 86

Model-Based Testing: Achievements and Future Challenges
  Michael Mlynarski, Baris Güldali, Gregor Engels, And Stephan Weißleder
Cloud Computing Uncovered: A Research Landscape
  Mohammad Hamdaqa and Ladan Tahvildari
Advances in User-Session-Based Testing of Web Applications
  Sreedevi Sampath
Machine Learning and Event-Based Software Testing: Classifiers for Identifying Infeasible
GUI Event Sequences
  Robert Gove and Jorge Faytong
A Framework for Detecting and Diagnosing Configuration Faults in Web Applications
  Cyntrica Eaton
Trends in Model-based GUI Testing
  Stephan Arlt, Simon Pahl, Cristiano Bertolini, and Martin Schäf
Regression Testing in Software Product Line Engineering
  Per Runeson and Emelie Engström

Volume 87

Introduction and Preface
  Sahra Sedigh and Ali Hurson
Techniques to Measure, Model, and Manage Power
  Bhavishya Goel, Sally A. McKee, and Magnus Själander
Quantifying IT Energy Efficiency
  Florian Niedermeier, Gergő Lovász, and Hermann de Meer
State of the Art on Technology and Practices for Improving the Energy Efficiency
of Data Storage
  Marcos Dias de Assunção and Laurent Lefèvre

Optical Interconnects for Green Computers and Data Centers
    SHINJI TSUJI AND TAKASHI TAKEMOTO
Energy Harvesting for Sustainable Smart Spaces
    NGA DANG, ELAHEH BOZORGZADEH, AND NALINI VENKATASUBRAMANIAN

Volume 88

Energy-Aware High Performance Computing—A Survey
    MICHAEL KNOBLOCH
Micro-Fluidic Cooling for Stacked 3D-ICs: Fundamentals, Modeling and Design
    BING SHI AND ANKUR SRIVASTAVA
Sustainable DVFS-Enabled Multi-Core Architectures with On-Chip Wireless Links
    JACOB MURRAY, TENG LU, PARTHA PANDE, AND BEHROOZ SHIRAZI
Smart Grid Considerations: Energy Efficiency vs. Security
    ANDREAS BERL, MICHAEL NIEDERMEIER, AND HERMANN DE MEER
Energy Efficiency Optimization of Application Software
    KAY GROSSKOP AND JOOST VISSER

Volume 89

Testing Android Mobile Applications: Challenges, Strategies, and Approaches
    DOMENICO AMALFITANO, ANNA RITA FASOLINO, PORFIRIO TRAMONTANA,
    AND BRYAN ROBBINS
Regression Testing of Evolving Programs
    MARCEL BÖHME, ABHIK ROYCHOUDHURY, AND BRUNO C.D.S. OLIVEIRA
Model Inference and Testing
    MUHAMMAD NAEEM IRFAN, CATHERINE ORIAT, AND ROLAND GROZ
Testing of Configurable Systems
    XIAO QU
Test Cost-Effectiveness and Defect Density: A Case Study on the Android Platform
    VAHID GAROUSI, RILEY KOTCHOREK, AND MICHAEL SMITH

Volume 90

Advances in Real-World Sensor Network System
    DEBRAJ DE, WEN-ZHAN SONG, MINGSEN XU, LEI SHI, AND SONG TAN
Novel System Architectures for Semantic-Based Integration of Sensor Networks
    ZORAN BABOVIC AND VELJKO MILUTINOVIC
Mobility in Wireless Sensor Networks
    SRIRAM CHELLAPPAN AND NEELANJANA DUTTA
A Classification of Data Mining Algorithms for Wireless Sensor Networks, and Classification
Extension to Concept Modeling in System of Wireless Sensor Networks Based on Natural
Language Processing
    STAŠA VUJIČIĆ STANKOVIĆ, NEMANJA KOJIĆ, GORAN RAKOČEVIĆ, DUŠKO VITAS,
    AND VELJKO MILUTINOVIĆ

Multihoming: A Comprehensive Review
  BRUNO SOUSA, KOSTAS PENTIKOUSIS, AND MARILIA CURADO
Efficient Data Analytics Over Cloud
  RAJEEV GUPTA, HIMANSHU GUPTA, AND MUKESH MOHANIA

Volume 91

Reverse-Engineering Software Behavior
  NEIL WALKINSHAW
Understanding Application Contentiousness and Sensitivity on Modern Multicores
  JASON MARS AND LINGJIA TANG
An Outlook of High Performance Computing Infrastructures for Scientific Computing
  AMJAD ALI AND KHALID SAIFULLAH SYED
Model-Driven Engineering of Reliable Fault-Tolerant Systems—A State-of-the-Art Survey
  VIDAR SLÅTTEN, PETER HERRMANN, AND FRANK ALEXANDER KRAEMER

Volume 92

Register-Level Communication in Speculative Chip Multiprocessors
  MILAN B. RADULOVIĆ, MILO V. TOMAŠEVIĆ, AND VELJKO M. MILUTINOVIĆ
Survey on System I/O Hardware Transactions and Impact on Latency, Throughput, and
Other Factors
  STEEN LARSEN AND BEN LEE
Hardware and Application Profiling Tools
  TOMISLAV JANJUSIC AND KRISHNA KAVI
Model Transformation Using Multiobjective Optimization
  MOHAMED WIEM MKAOUER AND MAROUANE KESSENTINI
Manual Parallelization Versus State-of-the-Art Parallelization Techniques: The SPEC
CPU2006 as a Case Study
  ALEKSANDAR VITOROVIĆ, MILO V. TOMAŠEVIĆ, AND VELJKO M. MILUTINOVIĆ

Volume 93

Recent Advances in Web Testing
  PAOLO TONELLA, FILIPPO RICCA, AND ALESSANDRO MARCHETTO
Exploiting Hardware Monitoring in Software Engineering
  KRISTEN R. WALCOTT-JUSTICE
Advances in Model-Driven Security
  LEVI LÚCIO, QIN ZHANG, PHU H. NGUYEN, MOUSSA AMRANI, JACQUES KLEIN,
  HANS VANGHELUWE, AND YVES LE TRAON
Adapting Multi-Criteria Decision Analysis for Assessing the Quality of Software Products.
Current Approaches and Future Perspectives
  ADAM TRENDOWICZ AND SYLWIA KOPCZYŃSKA
Change-Effects Analysis for Evolving Software
  RAUL SANTELICES, YIJI ZHANG, HAIPENG CAI, AND SIYUAN JIANG

Volume 94

Comparison of Security Models: Attack Graphs Versus Petri Nets
    STEVEN C. WHITE AND SAHRA SEDIGH SARVESTANI
A Survey on Zero-Knowledge Proofs
    LI FENG AND BRUCE MCMILLIN
Similarity of Private Keyword Search over Encrypted Document Collection
    YOUSEF ELMEHDWI, WEI JIANG, AND ALIREZA HURSON
Multiobjective Optimization for Software Refactoring and Evolution
    ALI OUNI, MAROUANE KESSENTINI, AND HOUARI SAHRAOUI

Volume 95

Automated Test Oracles: A Survey
    MAURO PEZZÈ AND CHENG ZHANG
Automated Extraction of GUI Models for Testing
    PEKKA AHO, TEEMU KANSTRÉN, TOMI RÄTY, AND JUHA RÖNING
Automated Test Oracles: State of the Art, Taxonomies, and Trends
    RAFAEL A.P. OLIVEIRA, UPULEE KANEWALA, AND PAULO A. NARDI
Anti-Pattern Detection: Methods, Challenges, and Open Issues
    FABIO PALOMBA, ANDREA DE LUCIA, GABRIELE BAVOTA, AND ROCCO OLIVETO
Classifying Problems into Complexity Classes
    WILLIAM GASARCH

Volume 96

An Overview of Selected Heterogeneous and Reconfigurable Architectures
    SAŠA STOJANOVIĆ, DRAGAN BOJIĆ, AND MIROSLAV BOJOVIĆ
Concurrency, Synchronization, and Speculation—The Dataflow Way
    KRISHNA KAVI, CHARLES SHELOR, AND DOMENICO PACE
Dataflow Computing in Extreme Performance Conditions
    DIEGO ORIATO, STEPHEN GIRDLESTONE, AND OSKAR MENCER
Sorting Networks on Maxeler Dataflow Supercomputing Systems
    ANTON KOS, VUKAŠIN RANKOVIĆ, AND SAŠO TOMAŽIČ
Dual Data Cache Systems: Architecture and Analysis
    ZIVOJIN SUSTRAN, GORAN RAKOCEVIC, AND VELJKO MILUTINOVIC

Volume 97

Comparing Reuse Strategies in Different Development Environments
    JULIA VARNELL-SARJEANT AND ANNELIESE AMSCHLER ANDREWS
Advances in Behavior Modeling
    ELLA ROUBTSOVA
Overview of Computational Approaches for Inference of MicroRNA-Mediated and Gene
Regulatory Networks
    BLAGOJ RISTEVSKI

Proving Programs Terminate Using Well-Founded Orderings, Ramsey's Theorem, and Matrices
    WILLIAM GASARCH
Advances in Testing JavaScript-Based Web Applications
    ALI MESBAH

Volume 98

An Overview of Architecture-Level Power- and Energy-Efficient Design Techniques
    IVAN RATKOVIĆ, NIKOLA BEŽANIĆ, OSMAN S. ÜNSAL, ADRIAN CRISTAL, AND
    VELJKO MILUTINOVIĆ
A Survey of Research on Data Corruption in Cyber–Physical Critical Infrastructure Systems
    MARK WOODARD, SAHRA SEDIGH SARVESTANI, AND ALI R. HURSON
A Research Overview of Tool-Supported Model-based Testing of Requirements-based Designs
    RALUCA MARINESCU, CRISTINA SECELEANU, HÈLÉNE LE GUEN, AND PAUL PETTERSSON
Preference Incorporation in Evolutionary Multiobjective Optimization: A Survey of the State-of-the-Art
    SLIM BECHIKH, MAROUANE KESSENTINI, LAMJED BEN SAID, AND KHALED GHÉDIRA

Volume 99

Combinatorial Testing: Theory and Practice
    D. RICHARD KUHN, RENEE BRYCE, FENG DUAN, LALEH SH. GHANDEHARI, YU LEI,
    AND RAGHU N. KACKER
Constraint-Based Testing: An Emerging Trend in Software Testing
    ARNAUD GOTLIEB
Automated Fault Localization: Advances and Challenges
    WES MASRI
Recent Advances in Automatic Black-Box Testing
    LEONARDO MARIANI, MAURO PEZZÈ, AND DANIELE ZUDDAS
Inroads in Testing Access Control
    TEJEDDINE MOUELHI, DONIA EL KATEB, AND YVES LE TRAON

Volume 100

Power Management in Data Centers: Cost, Sustainability, and Demand Response
    THANT ZIN OO, NGUYEN H. TRAN, CHOONG SEON HONG, SHAOLEI REN,
    AND GANG QUAN
Energy-Efficient Big Data Analytics in Datacenters
    FARHAD MEHDIPOUR, HAMID NOORI, AND BAHMAN JAVADI
Energy-Efficient and SLA-Based Resource Management in Cloud Data Centers
    ALTINO M. SAMPAIO AND JORGE G. BARBOSA
Achieving Energy Efficiency in Datacenters by Virtual Machine Sizing, Replication, and Placement
    HADI GOUDARZI AND MASSOUD PEDRAM
Communication-Awareness for Energy-Efficiency in Datacenters
    SEYED MORTEZA NABAVINEJAD AND MAZIAR GOUDARZI

Volume 101

Security Testing: A Survey
MICHAEL FELDERER, MATTHIAS BÜCHLER, MARTIN JOHNS, ACHIM D. BRUCKER, RUTH BREU, AND ALEXANDER PRETSCHNER
Recent Advances in Model-Based Testing
MARK UTTING, BRUNO LEGEARD, FABRICE BOUQUET, ELIZABETA FOURNERET, FABIEN PEUREUX, AND ALEXANDRE VERNOTTE
On Testing Embedded Software
ABHIJEET BANERJEE, SUDIPTA CHATTOPADHYAY, AND ABHIK ROYCHOUDHURY
Advances in Web Application Testing, 2010–2014
SREEDEVI SAMPATH AND SARA SPRENKLE
Approaches and Tools for Automated End-to-End Web Testing
MAURIZIO LEOTTA, DIEGO CLERISSI, FILIPPO RICCA, AND PAOLO TONELLA

Volume 102

Advances in Software Engineering and Software Assurance
DAN SHOEMAKER, CAROL WOODY, AND NANCY R. MEAD
Privacy Challenges and Goals in mHealth Systems
FARZANA RAHMAN, IVOR D. ADDO AND SHEIKH IQBAL AHAMED, JI-JIANG YANG AND QING WANG
A Survey of Data Cleansing Techniques for Cyber-Physical Critical Infrastructure Systems
MARK WOODARD, MICHAEL WISELY AND SAHRA SEDIGH SARVESTANI
Indexing and Querying Techniques for Moving Objects in Both Euclidean Space and Road Network
LASANTHI HEENDALIYA, MICHAEL WISELY, DAN LIN, SAHRA SEDIGH SARVESTANI AND ALI HURSON

Volume 103

How Elasticity Property Plays an Important Role in the Cloud: A Survey
M.A.N. BIKAS, A. ALOURANI, AND M. GRECHANIK
Input-Sensitive Profiling: A Survey
A. ALOURANI, M.A.N. BIKAS, AND M. GRECHANIK
Recent Advances in Regression Testing Techniques
H. DO
Coverage-Based Software Testing: Beyond Basic Test Requirements
W. MASRI AND F.A. ZARAKET

Printed in the United States
By Bookmasters